Praise for *Edith: The Rogue Rockefeller McCormick*

"This is a fascinating, well-researched book about the life of John D. Rockefeller's most intelligent, creative and misunderstood child."   —Ann McCauley, *Story Circle*

"Meticulously researched and featuring a number of black/white historical photos, *Edith: The Rogue Rockefeller McCormick* is an inherently fascinating life story of a remarkable woman who lived a wealthy yet unconventional life."
                    —James A. Cox, *Midwest Book Review*

"A research tour de force that reads like a novel. . . . This book is so involving, I even enjoyed consulting the footnotes."
                    —J. Wynn Rousuck, Theater Critic,
                    Midday, WYPR Radio, Baltimore

"*Edith: The Rogue Rockefeller McCormick* is an exceptional book about an exceptional woman. . . . This is a remarkable work that honors Edith's many legacies and highlights a history that might otherwise have been lost."
                    —Valerie Biel, author of the *Circle of Nine* series

"In this well-researched and nuanced biography, Ross recounts how Edith's determination, boldness, and sheer will defied her patriarchal family. Her belief in a socially responsible life led to significant contributions in medicine, philosophy, psychology, and the civic life of Chicago. The arc of her life reveals startling shifts certain to surprise and engage the reader."
                    —Clarice Stasz, author of *The Vanderbilt Women:
                    Dynasty of Wealth, Glamour, and Tragedy*

Edith

Edith

THE ROGUE
ROCKEFELLER MCCORMICK

ANDREA FRIEDERICI ROSS

Southern Illinois University Press
Carbondale

Edith Rockefeller McCormick

Southern Illinois University Press
www.siupress.com

24 23 22 21   4 3 2 1

Use of Edith Rockefeller McCormick's monogram as a design element throughout the book is courtesy of the Rockefeller Archive Center.

Frontispiece: photographic portrait of Edith Rockefeller McCormick. Courtesy Chicago History Museum, ICHi-176315. Edith's signature courtesy of the author.

Cover illustration: Edith strolls Michigan Avenue on a rainy day in 1930; the Drake Hotel looms in the background. Two years later, she would die in the hotel. DN-0091741, *Chicago Sun-Times/Chicago Daily News* collection, Chicago History Museum (cropped).

ISBN 978-0-8093-3862-7

The Library of Congress has catalogued the hardcover edition as follows:
Names: Ross, Andrea Friederici, 1965– author.
Title: Edith : The Rogue Rockefeller McCormick / Andrea Friederici Ross.
Other titles: Rogue Rockefeller McCormick
Description: First edition. | Carbondale : Southern Illinois University Press, [2020] | Includes bibliographical references and index.
Identifiers: LCCN 2019049343 (print) | LCCN 2019049344 (ebook) | ISBN 9780809337903 (cloth) | ISBN 9780809337910 (ebook)
Subjects: LCSH: McCormick, Edith Rockefeller, 1872–1932. | Art patrons—United States—Biography. | McCormick, Harold F. (Harold Fowler), 1872–1941. | Socialites—Illinois—Chicago—Biography. | Philanthropists—United States—Biography. | McCormick family—Art patronage. | Rockefeller family. | Chicago (Ill.)—Social life and customs—20th century.
Classification: LCC N5220.M27 R67 2020 (print) | LCC N5220.M27 (ebook) | DDC 707.5092 [B]—dc23
LC record available at https://lccn.loc.gov/2019049343
LC ebook record available at https://lccn.loc.gov/2019049344

To those who blaze their own trail.

Nevertheless.

With head erect and eyes wide open, we take the next step forward, ready to grasp the new values and to feel the understanding love of the laws of universal life.

—*Edith Rockefeller McCormick*

CONTENTS

Galleries of illustrations beginning on pages 61 and 157

PREFACE

What is it about Edith? I've been working on this project for a decade, searching for traces of an eccentric woman who lived a century ago. Digging in archives, making trips to far-flung places, scouring old newspapers and magazines, trying to read between the lines of personal correspondence . . . I have been obsessed. Why?

Her former chauffeur claimed she'd hypnotized him. I know the feeling. There's just something about this woman. She baffles, she frustrates, she fascinates.

I first learned about Edith when I wrote a history book about Brookfield Zoo. That book begins, "An unusual woman made Brookfield Zoo possible." Since then, she's tickled the back of my mind, silently standing watch as I made my way through daily life, until one day, my children grown enough to be able to manage without me for longer stretches, Edith came roaring to the fore, a spot she simply refused to cede.

At first, I thought Edith was just a colorful character: extravagant, unusual, quirky. Surrounded by these powerful families and famous people, it was a perfect story to tell. But somewhere along the line, she captured my heart. Yes, she was difficult. Yes, she made some terrible decisions. But she tried so damn hard! All her life, over and over, she pushed forward, trying to enact change, trying to make a positive difference in the world. She never gave up. So I decided to champion her story, to try to tell it fully and honestly.

The unfairness boggles me. Had Edith been male, her life trajectory would have been entirely different from the get-go. With her intellect, she could have made a formidable contribution at Standard Oil, International Harvester, or any one of the philanthropic organizations for which her families were known. But, merely because she was a woman, she was set aside, told over and over again she couldn't join the game. During my research, I came across a copy of the promisingly titled book *A Rockefeller Family Portrait*. Eager to discover more tidbits about Edith's childhood, I was to be disappointed, for the 1958 publication makes no single mention of Edith by name, referring to her only in phrases such as "Junior and his three sisters" or "Rockefeller women worried about Junior."[1] Edith had never been anyone's main focus.

And the injustice continues today: despite her efforts and accomplishments, she hasn't gotten the credit she deserves. Chicago should know this patron saint, this enigmatic woman who helped elevate the city from stockyards and industry to one rife with cultural and artistic organizations. A hospital, a zoo, the opera, real estate: she provided so much! Even the family's copious front-page scandals have been forgotten, though I doubt she'd appreciate those being dragged back out into the sunlight.

Reconstructing her life hasn't been easy. Though both the Rockefeller and McCormick families left behind meticulous archives, down to the monthly receipts for coal and the mundane annual birthday telegrams, Edith's papers are largely missing. I thought at first it was a question of gender, but, no, her sister-in-law Anita McCormick Blaine's collection contains hundreds of boxes, and her mother-in-law's even more.

It was Edith. She'd gone missing. Her papers were scattered to the wind, likely destroyed. Why? By whom? And upon whose request? It seems her voice was deliberately erased. Were the exterminators protecting her or their own precious reputations?

So my quest began as a puzzle, searching for pieces of Edith's life wherever I could find them. A letter here, a boxful there, some articles over here. I went to dozens of archives, historical societies, universities, libraries. There was a lot of misinformation. Newspapers often got the story wrong, leading to false conclusions about her in books or magazines. Feeling I'd already somewhat misrepresented Edith in my zoo history book, I didn't want to do it again. I was trying to set the record straight, not convolute it further.

I'll admit there was obstinacy involved. Once embarked on a task, I am determined to see it through to the end. When all common sense says to walk away, I am just getting started. Like a dog with a bone, no one could wrest this idea from my head until it was complete, no marrow left.

Sometimes it felt as if the Fates were against me, throwing up obstacles just for sport. A trip to New York to meet with great-nephew Steven Rockefeller nearly proved disastrous when the connecting flight out of Philadelphia was canceled. But I barreled through the airport, got myself a rental car, and raced to Sleepy Hollow, New York, arriving with just minutes to spare. My reward was a fascinating two-hour discussion and a personal tour of the family mansion. Unforgettable.

Another time I mistakenly got off at the wrong train stop one night in Zurich, on my way to meet Edith's great-granddaughter and others at the Jung Institute. A quick scramble resulted in my teenage daughter and me sitting in the back seat of a complete stranger's car, rushing to beat the train. Not something I'd ordinarily consider, but it was Switzerland—how dangerous could it be? It was not lost on me that this was the same route Edith's chauffeur had taken frequently, racing alongside the train to help her overcome her travel phobias. It seemed fitting; I'd been chasing her ghost all day.

Edith was at the height of Chicago society during a time of tremendous change for women. During her lifetime, upper-class women went from focusing on household management and planning cotillions to winning the right to vote and venturing into the workplace. Her gradual awareness of the boundaries imposed upon her is a case study in women's rights. Raised to believe her job was to elevate her husband to his highest possible station and to prepare her children for their futures, Edith spent the first half of her life sublimating her own desires. She was well into adulthood before she turned her attention to herself, and then only out of sheer panic. The efforts of the suffrage movement and the passing of the Nineteenth Amendment threw her transition into full gear. That she established a large realty business as her father's disapproving voice rang in her ear speaks volumes about her determination. Jaw set, eyes flashing, she ran headlong into complete disaster.

So, in part, this is a history lesson, a perfect example of how women's roles have changed. (And a quick note about organization: chapters are chronological, but the years at the head are merely guideposts, with some material fitting better thematically in neighboring chapters.) Each generation takes up where the last left off, moving us slowly down the evolutionary line toward greater fulfillment, productivity, and success. And while I shudder at Edith's early beliefs about her role, I cannot judge, for she was a product of her time. She was used to being a second-class citizen: no vote, no voice.

It does make me wonder about my own evolution. How are women's issues developing in this generation? How will things be different from beginning to end of my own life? And let there be no mistake, this is a watershed moment, with the #MeToo movement and the women's marches challenging why women must still fight for equal respect.

Larger picture aside, I suspect one reason I couldn't let Edith's story go is that it mirrored my own (minus the jewels, the collections, the millions). Cast in the role of mother and wife, my husband making his mark in the world while I took the back seat, it was time to allow myself to take the wheel. In fighting to get Edith's story properly recorded, it was also a chance to hone my own voice: to be heard.

I am roughly the same age Edith was when she returned from Zurich. With my children off to college and beyond and my marriage now dissolving, I find myself similarly alone. I take courage from Edith's example: starting new ventures, developing new routines, always looking forward with curiosity and anticipation. One of the lessons for women of my generation is to put ourselves first, and I'm working on that. My vote, my voice, indeed.

I admire that, at the end of her life, faced with disasters on all sides—familial, financial, medical, social—Edith somehow managed to remain optimistic. On yet another gray Chicago day, I try to adopt her belief: "How can one rise in the morning, bored with life, tired of routine and putting on his clothes, say, 'Well, it's another cold day and we'll have to go at it again?' How can one say that when each day is a brand-new day, never lived before? How does he know what the day will bring? It is filled with possibilities, it is filled with magic. It is a brand-new day."[2]

It is, Edith. It's a brand-new day. Let's see where this one takes us.

Rockefeller Family Tree

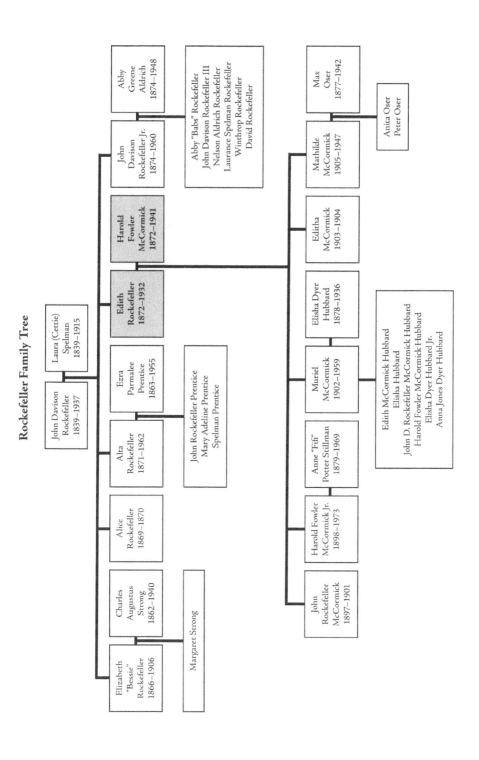

McCormick Family Tree

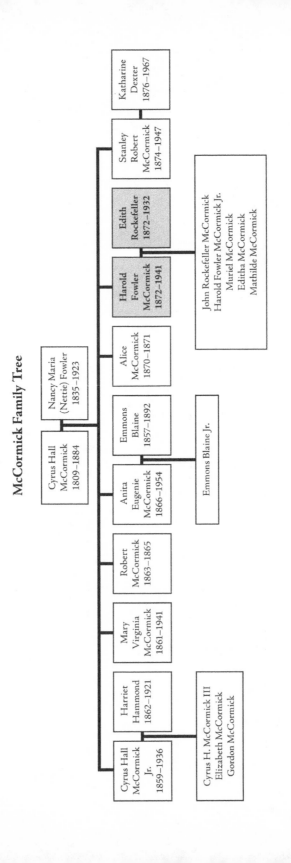

Edith

GROWING UP ROCKEFELLER

1872-88

*T*here were no great celebrations upon Edith's birth.

Sure, the doctor overseeing the delivery in their upstairs bedroom on Euclid Avenue in Cleveland on August 31, 1872, would have offered Laura "Cettie" Spelman Rockefeller and John Davison Rockefeller sincere congratulations. Edith was their fourth daughter. Baby Alice had died of scarlet fever as an infant; the other two girls, Elizabeth (Bessie) and Alta, were healthy and strong.

But another daughter was not what Senior had desired. His wishes would be fulfilled two years later when John D. Rockefeller Jr. was born. That day would feature office toasts, backslaps, and hearty celebrations. Years later, Mother Cettie recalled, "How glad all were that the baby was a boy—for there had been four girls . . ."[1] It is said Senior "literally danced" about the office.[2] Once Junior came aboard, there were no more pregnancies. There was no need. The longed-for son had arrived.

This is not to say that Edith wasn't loved. She was. The Rockefeller family was a close one, tight-knit for a reason. The year of Edith's birth would be marked in the history books by the Cleveland Massacre, the year her father, at the helm of Standard Oil, claimed control of twenty-two of twenty-six competing oil companies in Cleveland—quite ruthlessly, some would maintain. It was the year in which John D. Rockefeller began keeping a revolver by his bed for safety.[3] The Rockefellers drew together in part to keep the public at arm's length, for they were hated.

But as a small child, Edith had no idea. Her childhood in Cleveland was fairly idyllic. A few years after Edith's birth, the family purchased a large property in Forest Hill, an estate that grew to seven hundred acres. Originally intended as a hotel, it was an ideal retreat including two artificial lakes, hiking trails through woods and ravines, bridle paths and a racetrack for horses, and tennis courts. The children could ride bicycles and horses, sled, swim, and explore to their hearts' content, without ever encountering another human being.

There were scant reasons to leave the property, with church being the chief exception. Church also provided one of the few opportunities for play with children beyond siblings or cousins (Uncle William lived nearby with his family). Their closest friends were the children of Minister Strong.[4] There were precious few opportunities for bad influences.

Governesses and tutors were brought to the house to instruct the children, including accomplished musicians who shaped the foursome into a formidable quartet, with Junior on violin, Bessie on viola, Edith on the cello, and Alta at the piano. They could earn five cents an hour for practicing, and Edith would spend many hours at a stretch with her arms encircling her cello—easily her favorite chore. Music would be a lifelong passion for Edith.

Other chores for which the children could earn pennies included raking leaves, pulling weeds, sharpening pencils, killing flies, and similar mundane tasks. They earned five cents for attending Sunday school.[5] While Senior was making millions in scandalous new ways, his children dutifully earned and saved cents. Spending was heartily discouraged, except as donations to the church plate. Giving to others was the priority before spending for self.

Once Junior was old enough, Senior appointed him the family accountant, responsible for overseeing his older sisters' ledgers, where they were required to account for every single penny. Junior would continue this role well into adulthood. And, yes, even then, pennies counted. Junior reported that, "because I was the only boy in the family," he played a key go-between role: "Although I was the youngest, my parents turned to me for advice on many questions, including my sisters, particularly their love affairs . . ."[6]

Growing up Rockefeller wasn't butlers and ball gowns. Rather, it was a constant tug-of-war between wealth and denial. Despite the family's incredible wealth and their expansive estate, they lived fairly frugally. The children all wore hand-me-downs, including Junior, who was sometimes attired in his older sisters' outgrown dresses. Even Cettie's dresses were patched numerous times. Senior was fond of preaching, "Willful waste makes woeful want."[7] Only Senior knew the full extent of their wealth: this was not information he shared, even with his wife. Cettie would never really understand the magnitude of their estate. Even if Senior had divulged this information, in Cettie's defense, it was virtually incomprehensible at the time.

It was a household under very tight, very deliberate rein.

Every minute of their day was carefully scheduled: prayer, study, chores, music, play. For, while work was the focus, Senior and Cettie recognized that daily play was critical to mental well-being. It was to be wholesome activity, however; there would be no card playing or dancing or other activities Senior and Cettie deemed frivolous.[8]

Surprisingly, one of the children's favorite playmates was Senior. Though the public saw John D. Rockefeller as a brutal capitalist, savage in his business dealings and largely humorless, the children knew a different side of him. It was frequently Senior who instigated the games, with Junior reporting their father participated in rounds of blindman's bluff "with all the zest of a child."[9] Or he might tie a white handkerchief to his back so they could chase him on a nighttime bicycle race through the wooded trails.[10] At dinner, his eyes twinkling, he might suddenly balance a porcelain plate on his nose, much to Cettie's dismay.[11] He was adept at telling mesmerizing tall tales or suddenly bursting into song, though it was most likely to be a hymn.

Caution was a keyword in the family, with nothing ever taken for granted. When they went ice-skating on the pond, each child was issued a long board to tuck under their arms for safety should the ice break. Swimming required large hats as protection from the sun.[12]

More than anything, the Rockefeller clan worshipped together. As Baptists, their days began with family prayer before breakfast, with latecomers charged five cents. In an ironic twist, it was Senior who most frequently had to pony up.[13] The children learned the value not only of a cent but also of being punctual. Later in life, all would maintain a strict and unforgiving adherence to punctuality, down to the minute. It all mattered: every cent, every minute. Visiting ministers were their most frequent dinner guests, and the day ended with more prayer.

Cettie and Senior were united in their beliefs that service to God was of paramount importance. The Rockefeller family was the first to arrive at church on Sundays, where Senior would toll the large bell to welcome others. Both parents taught Sunday school and were very active church members. When the collection plate passed, the children were expected to deposit a good percentage of their hard-earned pennies. Senior made modest donations, with none of the children suspecting that behind the scenes he was writing much larger checks, accounting for nearly half the church's entire income. And when the service was over, Senior, as volunteer janitor, promptly went around extinguishing all the gaslights, mindful of saving every possible penny.[14] Perhaps he used religion as a way to cleanse his sins.

Sundays also brought Cettie's "Home Talks," in which she would discuss a passage from the Bible, followed by summoning each child before her individually to discuss their digressions and determine how they could improve. Her favorite phrase was "Is it right, is it duty?"[15]

Edith always seemed to have more to confess than her siblings. Not that Bessie, Alta, and Junior didn't occasionally misbehave, but Edith had a rebellious streak her siblings lacked. Whereas her sisters and particularly Junior accepted the rules as a given, Edith went beyond and questioned why, frequently pushing to test her real boundaries.

"Why can't I have a second piece of cheese?" There was no shortage of cheese in the house; one piece a day seemed a meaningless rule. But when she dared to break this arbitrary rule and sneak a second piece, it resulted in Alta tattling to Senior, who would solemnly proclaim that "Edith was greedy" on numerous occasions the rest of the day.[16] Restraint and economy were the constant ideals.

"Why must we share one tricycle?" Initially they were consigned to one tricycle so they would learn to share; later the bicycle races commenced.[17] They were not to have their wishes granted too easily. Cettie was once overheard telling a neighbor, "I am so glad my son has told me what he wants for Christmas, so now it can be denied him."[18]

Perhaps the biggest "why" Edith dared was "Why does the minister know better than anyone else?" For pious Senior, this was the ultimate rebellion. Shortly before her death, Edith recalled, "When I was a child I was sent to the Baptist Sunday School, in Cleveland. . . . Even in those days my questionings began but because of my youth (or so I thought) I was silenced. I bore with my doubts, hoping that maturity might make my vision clearer or perhaps give me an opportunity to confront the church with my convictions and endeavor to reach a reconciliation."[19] In the years to come, religious differences would starkly divide Edith and her father in a way not experienced by her siblings.

Though the children knew no other environment, to visitors the house seemed solemn and gloomy. Rare moments of jollity and noise occurred when Grandfather William "Bill" Avery Rockefeller appeared. A traveling salesman, he would swagger in unannounced, sporting a colorful vest, floppy hat, and a glittering diamond button in his shirtfront, with five-dollar gold pieces in his pocket for the grandchildren.[20] The next few days would be filled with laughter, bawdy humor, fiddle music, and tales of the road. On one such visit, Bill taught the children to shoot, hanging a target on a large oak and instructing them how to manipulate a rifle. When Edith hit the bull's-eye, her grandfather did a jig of happiness and shouted, "Bet you she hits it eight times out of ten!"[21]

Whereas Junior described his grandfather as a most lovable person, a great storyteller, and very entertaining,[22] the relationship between Senior and his father was frosty. The children wouldn't learn why until adulthood. In the meantime, they delighted in his impromptu visits and were saddened on the days when they awoke to discover he had mysteriously disappeared again, his joyful energy gone. He was a breath of fresh air in an otherwise stale household.

Standard Oil business demanded more and more that Senior be in New York. For nearly ten years, the family assumed winter residence in hotels there—first the Windsor, then the Buckingham.[23] When Edith was in her teens, the family finally moved to a four-story brownstone on West Fifty-Fourth Street in New York City, returning to Cleveland for summers or vacation. And here in Manhattan the world closed in, Edith's parents no longer able to keep the news and public at bay. By now, all four children were old enough to read the papers and letters, and the nation did not seem to be fond of the Rockefeller success.

Growing up as part of the nation's wealthiest family seems desirable. But if one's father is the most hated man in America, the day's newspaper is likely to have a cartoon lampooning him as an octopus or anaconda or to feature headlines maligning his business practices. The daily mail brought hundreds of letters of request, many detailing terribly sad circumstances and pleas for financial assistance. The children once endeavored to tally up the number of letters received in a month: a whopping fifty thousand.[24]

Occasionally, people took to camping out on the doorstep or tailing Senior to and from work in order to plead their case. Despite the fact that they stayed away from society events and tried to keep a low profile, it was hard to hide that Rockefeller surname.

As the children gradually became aware of their unusual position in society, Senior drew them into the action, asking them to read the letters of request and selecting ones that were most worthy. It was part of their education. Mixed in with the mail, however, would be angry letters of disappointment and even death threats. By 1884, all four children were also learning about investments, purchasing Standard Oil stocks through their father's account and keeping track of their growth. As burgeoning family accountant, Junior assiduously oversaw all their progress.[25]

The outside world became a scary place to Edith and to the other three children. Best to draw together, to keep their distance from others. This was a learned behavior Edith would find impossible to shake in later years. Danger lurked around every corner. The public wanted, needed, demanded.

Rockefeller biographer Ron Chernow concluded, "Junior developed an upside-down worldview in which the righteous Rockefeller household was always under attack by a godless, uncomprehending world."[26] In *The Rockefeller Century*, the authors surmised that "a childhood . . . perpetually concerned with introspective soul-searching and striving to perfect one's conduct, left Junior with both a lifetime creed and an initial fear of normal social contact."[27] Safety could be found only within—in the home, in the family, in a piece of music, in the pages of a book.

Edith was a natural student. She was quoted as saying that reading was "more important to me than eating. . . . I must feed my mind more than my body."[28] She was able to process and remember facts with remarkable accuracy. In particular, she was drawn to language and soon was reading great works of literature in their native languages. Linguistics was not a field her father considered of great value, but for Edith, it was like breathing.

Edith later recalled, "As a little girl every hour of my day was scheduled and efficiently occupied. In my primary school days I had tutors in each subject that I was to study. I quickly began with foreign languages. I seemed to feel that spoken and written languages of different peoples offered gateways to the mind that made other studies not only less difficult but gave to me easier access to the path of education which I was seeking to pursue. And so it was that before I was ten years of age I was proficient in three languages and gradually, and with most carefully considered outline of study, I was to become fluent in all the modern languages and an earnest student of ancient tongues."[29]

Rockefeller historian Clarice Stasz stated, "Edith was the most like her father in disposition, if not in interests. She was the most intelligent of the four children, a natural scholar, at ease with abstract thought. She absorbed languages easily. . . . On the other hand, she was certainly the one passionate member of the family, as expressed by long hours with legs wrapped about the resonating buzz of her cello."[30]

Living nearby, having also moved to New York, were Uncle William and his wife Almira, with Edith's cousins Emma, William, Percy, and Ethel. Though he was Senior's brother and business partner, William was cut from a different cloth. For every ounce of Senior's thriftiness, William matched it with extravagance. The cousins were fond of each other and often spent time together, but their lives were very different. While Edith and her siblings were studying, practicing music, and attending prayer meetings and temperance gatherings, her cousins were out in society, attending parties and costume balls. In later years, Junior stated, "We children didn't have what those children had and we used to notice the difference. They had a gay kind of social life, with many parties which we used to wish we could have."[31]

It was a somber life but a safe one. While Edith may have envied her cousins' elegant dresses or social ease, she found solace in her studies. This childhood stew of fear, piety, frugality, and envy was a potent mix and would leave permanent marks on Edith.

As Edith approached adulthood, her path forward was still unclear. Junior's, on the other hand, was well marked, as Senior began grooming his only son for a role in the family business. Had Edith been born several decades later or to a different strata of society, her life surely would have been remarkably different, as wryly noted by Dr. S. M. Melamed, a scholar assessing her library after her death: "She possessed all the qualities of a great intellectual. Her thirst for knowledge, her devotion to philosophical truth, her evaluation of the creative personality, her sweeping historical concepts and her great . . . learning made her the outstanding feminine intellectual of her generation in America. Because she was very careful in the selection of her parents she undoubtedly missed a great academic career."[32]

THE PRINCE OF
MCCORMICK REAPER

1888–95

*I*n 1888, when Edith was a hormone-filled sixteen years of age, a happy-go-lucky blue-eyed boy with a penchant for whistling entered her life.

Once the Rockefeller children were in their teens, Cettie and Senior selected private schools in New York for them to attend. But frequent headaches and nervous issues caused Junior to have too many absences, so Senior established his own school. Together with Uncle William, who enrolled his son Percy, they hired instructor John Browning and recruited several like-minded (wealthy, similarly religious) young men to join them in lessons at the house on West Fifty-Fourth Street. This small enterprise would grow into the Browning School, which still operates as a college preparatory school in New York City.

Among the group of twenty-five handpicked young male scholars deemed worthy of admittance were brothers Harold and Stanley McCormick. The youngest children of "Reaper King" Cyrus McCormick and his wife, Nettie Fowler McCormick, their childhood, in Chicago, was not unlike Edith's. Gilbert Harrison, biographer of their sister Anita McCormick Blaine, wrote, "After early morning family prayers in the library, there was Sunday school, and after supper came evening services. Play was prohibited. One would have said it was not a playful house on any day, and the young McCormicks' circle of acquaintances was narrowly circumscribed. They were never permitted to associate either with the children of Chicago's more worldly upper class or with the lower orders."[1]

Like the Rockefeller household, the McCormick home was not a place of frivolity or joy. Emphasis was on piety, community service, and hard work. Harold was born in 1872, one year after the Great Chicago Fire devastated the McCormick Reaper Works; Stanley came along two years later. Damage from the fire cost the family $1.5 million in losses. The family rebuilt, largely on the insistence of Mother Nettie, herself a force of nature. Nettie continued that fighting spirit when Cyrus died in 1884, forcing her—twenty-six years younger than her husband—to single-handedly oversee not only the McCormick name and philanthropies but also the raising of their children. Suffering from nearly complete hearing loss, Nettie compensated by using an ear trumpet. All communication with her needed to be yelled into the device. She was chubby-cheeked and short in stature, but behind her sweet, matronly look lay a will of steel. History would mark Nettie as one of Chicago's greatest philanthropists.

Two McCormick children, Robert and Alice, had died of scarlet fever, leaving five behind to carry on the family—Cyrus Jr., Mary Virginia, Anita, Harold, and Stanley. Nettie was an inconsistent mother, vacillating between overprotective hovering and complete distraction. When she was focused on her children, she smothered them with constant attention, panicking at the smallest sniffle, packing them in multiple layers of clothing whenever they left the house, and preaching about the world's manifold dangers. When she had other matters to attend to, she seemed to forget entirely about her children, leaving the mothering to household staff and her daughter Anita, six years Harold's senior.[2]

Shortly after Father Cyrus's death, the oldest daughter, Mary Virginia, began to exhibit severe signs of mental illness. She would play the piano for hours until her fingers bled, had bouts of hysterical sobbing or prayer, would climb out of top-floor windows to roam the rooftop at night, or run around the neighborhood in the middle of the night ringing doorbells.[3] The family did their best to hide her condition but ultimately, following a diagnosis of dementia praecox (now schizophrenia), had her committed to a mental institution.

Mother Nettie was bereft and loath to accept Mary Virginia's diagnosis. As she had done when infants Robert and Alice died, she viewed the tragedy as God's punishment for her own sins. She would redouble her efforts to serve the church and the community without ever coming up for air. For the rest of her life, Nettie agonized over poor Mary Virginia's care; when there was bad news from her health-care team, Nettie could be heard in the middle of the night, praying for long stretches, then dissolving into weeping and wailing.[4]

Like the Rockefellers, the McCormick family had known its share of public hatred, peaking in 1886 when a bomb exploded near the McCormick plant, where workers were striking for better conditions. The resulting Haymarket Riot would leave approximately a dozen dead and many others injured. Some historians claim the event was the single most important episode in labor history. It was a trial by fire for young Cyrus Jr., who had been thrust into his role at the head of the company after his father's death. At ages fourteen and twelve, respectively, Harold and Stanley would have been old enough to be aware of the public sentiment against their family, despite Nettie's best efforts to shield them.

Being wealthy had many perks, but public admiration was not one of them.

By the time Harold and Stanley appeared on the doorstep for Junior's elite school, their brother Cyrus was already running the reaper works, Anita was soon to marry, and Mary Virginia was locked away. Harold, as Anita's favorite, had been shielded from Nettie's hovering and emerged from his childhood relatively unscathed. But Stanley, the baby of the family, overprotected and coddled, would turn out to have a difficult road ahead.

Harold may not have been the star student in Junior's private little enclave, preferring entertainment over scholarship. He held the family record for slipper spankings from his mother and was quoted as saying, "They had to run and find me in the morning and catch me for school."[5] He acknowledged his failings readily; even in a letter to Santa at the age of seven he admitted, "I think I could be a better boy than I am. I will try to be."[6] But Harold and Stanley became regulars around the Rockefeller household, and that would pay dividends down the road.

There is no indication that Senior ever considered starting a private girls' school for his daughters, despite their own nervous maladies and frequent absences. Edith and Alta were both enrolled at the Rye Female Seminary (with a motto that appealed to Cettie and Senior: "Not for Self but for Service"),[7] and Bessie, the oldest daughter, was in college at Vassar. After Vassar, in 1889, Bessie married her childhood sweetheart, Charles Augustus Strong, the son of their childhood minister.[8]

The pressures upon the Rockefeller children were not insignificant, and the entire family suffered from nervous disorders. At the time of her marriage Bessie was already showing signs of mental instability, Edith and Alta were both diagnosed with neurasthenia (exhaustion of the central nervous system, a common malady for young women at that time), and Junior struggled with debilitating headaches and weakness. Even Senior and Cettie exhibited nervous disorders. Life in the House of Rockefeller was not without its stressors.

By the time she hit twenty, Edith was on a round-robin tour of the East Coast's best rest cures and sanatoriums, including frequent visits to Laurel-in-the-Pines in Lakewood, New Jersey, where she took in the good, pure air by practicing driving a carriage. She also undertook a four-month stay at the famous Philadelphia clinic of Dr. Silas Weir Mitchell, who diagnosed her with anorexia and stated she had overexerted herself with her studies.[9] The treatment, common among wealthy young women, involved complete rest: no reading, no sewing, no conversations with anyone besides Mitchell. Edith's daily interactions with Mitchell, called "moral medication," were her first step toward psychotherapy.[10] Immediately after checking out of Mitchell's clinic, she returned to Laurel-in-the-Pines.

It is possible that these nervous maladies curtailed Edith's education, for, unlike Bessie, Edith and Alta were not given the opportunity to attend college, despite Edith's obvious intellectual ability. The path for her brother was very different; Junior was sent off to Brown University in preparation for a career in Standard Oil. Edith and Junior, who had been very close, kept up a furious correspondence. One of her letters ran to seventeen pages. She affectionately called him Lou, while he referred to her as Rhody.[11] But while they were like-minded and intimate as children, their later experiences and ethics would carry them down very different paths.

What was the role for a daughter of John D. Rockefeller and for other upper-class young ladies at that time? To marry well. To entice a fitting suitor, unite two powerful families, and then to bear children, preferably male. Though Edith briefly considered missionary work in Japan—she would always have a fascination with the Far East—the pressures to take the traditional path overrode her intellectual curiosity. After all, Cettie's favorite maxim was "To be a good wife and mother is the highest and hardest privilege of woman."[12] Edith, dutiful daughter, would embrace this paradigm without hesitation. In an article she wrote in the early 1900s, she opined, "It is a question of what is best for the husband, then what is best for the home, then what is best for the children, and, lastly, what is best for the mother."[13]

While her intellect and inheritance must have made Edith a tantalizing prospect for young suitors, her emotional fragility would warrant a careful selection of husband. Fortunately, an appropriate choice was virtually underfoot: young Harold McCormick, just recently graduated from Princeton University. Harold had been the classic bon vivant in college, playing football and tennis and always carousing with a pretty girl on his arm, while brother Stanley, an assiduous student, carried his older brother "through on his hip."[14]

Regardless, Harold ticked all the right boxes. He was from a prominent, wealthy family—albeit Presbyterian, not Baptist—was the right age, and was equally driven toward community service. Exhibiting a carefree attitude the rest of his family utterly lacked, Harold's mischievous nature paired well with Edith's rebellion. While Harold couldn't match Edith intellectually, that seemed immaterial. In later years, Junior would state he always thought of Harold in "terms of happiness and generosity. He was one of the kindest people I ever knew."[15]

Another plus for Harold: having already witnessed his sister Mary Virginia descend into full-blown schizophrenia, nervous conditions were not new to him. In fact, one of the lingering effects of his childhood would be a serious dose of hypochondria. Harold nearly always traveled with an assortment of pills in his pocket and a pair of galoshes, just in case. Throughout his life, he dutifully sent his mother copies of his doctor reports.

Edith and Alta, both in their twenties, had just returned from a long Mediterranean tour, including stops in Egypt, France, and Spain,[16] when Harold proposed in May 1895. An excited Edith wrote to her future mother-in-law, Nettie, "I cannot refrain from writing you this morning to tell you of this great happiness that has come to me, although Father has not given his answer yet and none of the family know of it but Alta. . . . You do not know, dear Mrs. McCormick, how much I feel the honor that Harold has conferred upon me in asking me to share his life and how utterly unworthy I feel. . . . I hope that I may be so moulded—so lifted out of myself into a higher sphere—that I may be a true helpmate to the man to whom I have plighted my troth and that I may do honor to the name that is sacred to you and cherished by me."[17]

Nettie, needless to say, was delighted at the prospect of uniting the two families, telegramming Edith, "Such good news. You have been like a daughter to me. Now you will be so forever."[18]

It is telling of the time that, while Edith strove to be a worthy "helpmate," Harold, when making his case to Senior, promised that he was capable of caring for Edith.[19] This would come back to haunt him in later years. Harold wrote to his sister Anita expressing his joy: "I never imagined such happiness would fall to my lot. Anita, may I always do toward Edith such that she will always be happy, and may I acquit myself honorably of my great responsibility!"[20] Senior, aware that Harold was known to enjoy both alcohol and tobacco, had some concerns but approved the match after thoughtful consideration.

Time magazine would state, "As near to royalty as it is possible to come in the U.S. was Edith Rockefeller when, in 1895, she married that most handsome and eligible of contemporary Princetonians, Harold McCormick. . . . She was a demure little blonde, with a high forehead, grey eyes and a mass of ringlets under her hat. She swam, skated, rode a horse and bicycle, but preferred to read and study."[21]

The press took delight in the story: Prince of McCormick Reaper to Marry Princess of Standard Oil![22] Greatest Catch of the Year! Two Great Fortunes to Be Joined! Journalists estimated Edith's worth at $35 million.[23] It would be the wedding—or merger—of the decade. Senior made a statement to reporters: "Harold Fowler McCormick has known the family and Miss Edith for a good many years and the engagement is not the result of a sudden acquaintance. Both the young people understand each other thoroughly. . . . We are pleased and I believe my daughter is happy."[24]

For Edith, marriage must have represented liberation from tight parental constraints. No more cheese rules, no more forced marches to the Baptist church. Most of all, with their combined funds, Edith and Harold would finally be free to spend, something that had been denied her thus far. There would be no more counting pennies.

Senior insisted the wedding be held at their small Fifth Avenue Baptist Church in New York City. While not ideal for a large ceremony, Edith accommodated his wish by having a special podium built for the occasion and by arranging for the removal of several rows of pews. The open space would be filled by tremendous quantities of palm trees, ferns, orchids, chrysanthemums, and roses.[25] In a year that had seen several lavish, over-the-top society weddings, Edith was determined hers would be the most tasteful.

But fate intervened in grand fashion. Harold came down with pleurisy shortly before the event, and his doctors warned it might turn into pneumonia if he ventured out. Therefore, on the eve of the wedding, telegrams were hurriedly sent out informing the twelve hundred invited guests that the ceremony would be a private affair at Harold's Buckingham Hotel bedside. The New York Times helped spread the word with a headline that read "No Ceremony in Church . . . Illness Causes Change of Plans."[26] The reception would take place afterward, as originally planned, at the Rockefeller mansion on West Fifty-Fourth Street.

Neither did Mother Nature cooperate. November 26, 1895, dawned gloomy, and shortly before the noon service, the skies opened up with a deluge the likes of which New York City hadn't seen in years. It was dark as night at midday, with thunder and lightning, and the streets turned into muddy rivers.[27]

Just before the ceremony began, Senior, looking very serious, asked Edith if he might have a word with her in private. They stepped off to the side, where he solemnly said, "Daughter, you have been educated and prepared for your position in life according to the very highest standards and with the most careful consideration of the responsibilities of the career that lies before you, and I must say that I consider you well equipped to assume your new social position. However, I have brought you here to make a request that lies very close to my heart and a request that has been very carefully considered."

Edith, heart pounding, replied, "Yes, Father, but why be so serious . . . what is this request that stirs you so much?"

"It is this, daughter. I want you to promise never to serve a drink of liquor in your home. Promise me that and you will never regret it."

Having already signed while just a teenager a pledge abstaining from alcohol, tobacco, and profanity, and relieved Senior hadn't a greater concern (one that might imperil the wedding), Edith let out a burst of laughter and agreed, "Of course, Father."[28] Whether it was because of the pleurisy or just plain relief, she failed to consider Harold's opinion on the matter.

Leading up to that day, Senior had tried, and failed, to get Harold to take a similar vow. Harold's written response to his future father-in-law's repeated requests had been surprisingly defiant: "While I believe we hold the same general views as to the ruin wrought in the world by strong drink, and as to individual responsibility with regard to it, I am convinced that for me, a life pledge is not for the best."[29]

Edith would keep her promise to Senior, but not without ramifications.

At the stroke of noon, the family assembled in the hotel suite, with a flushed Harold leaning hard on best man Stanley's shoulder, his eyes feverish and a bead of sweat along his brow. Edith wore an ivory satin gown with a long, round train and delicate lace trim at the sleeves and bodice. Harold had given her a diamond tiara, which was used to hold the veil (Bessie's—something old, something new) in place. Around her neck was the gift from her parents, a string of pearls worth $15,000, more than the entire price of Bessie's wedding.[30]

Half of the bridesmaids wore pink, the other half mauve; their hats featured towering plumes; and they carried sable muffs instead of bouquets. Alta, Edith's older and yet unmarried sister, was maid of honor. Harold's groomsmen looked dapper in their black frock coats, gray trousers, and shiny top hats.[31]

Vows were exchanged, the deal was sealed, and only the reception remained. Nettie later described it: "At the appointed time all, except Harold, went to the bride's home, where she, with her father by her side, under the canopy of flowers, received hundreds who came to offer their congratulations. This, too, was a beautiful scene, and Edith was most courageous, feeling keenly not having Harold at her side yet feeling there was nothing else right to do but to receive the guests:—and she stood there calm, and sweet, and dignified until all the guests had been received."[32] Once everyone had been greeted, Edith donned her going-away dress and hightailed it back to the Buckingham, leaving the party in full gear. When she returned to the hotel, both the weather and Harold's fever had broken.

The wedding over, though not remotely as Edith had planned, Edith and Harold were husband and wife, certain great things lay ahead.

TRICKLE-DOWN EDITH

1896–99

*A*fter an extended honeymoon in Italy, married life got off to a rural start for Edith and Harold with two years in Council Bluffs, Iowa, where Harold learned the nitty-gritty of farm equipment sales at McCormick Reaper. He wrote to sister Anita that he was "making pretensions at being a thorough business man" and that Edith was "well and happy."[1] They continued the impressive shopping begun on their honeymoon, assembling a household: one carriage, one bedroom set, one monogrammed handkerchief at a time. Sometime later, Edith would refer to these years as the happiest of her life.[2] Then the newlyweds moved to Chicago so Harold could take an executive role with the business, joining older brother Cyrus Jr.

While most of Chicago's elite lived in the south shore area, Harold's relatives had claimed the near north side, such that it was informally called McCormickville. Harold and Edith purchased (it was falsely rumored it may have been a wedding gift from one of their parents) a forty-one-room Romanesque mansion at 88 Bellevue Place. It was within throwing distance of mother-in-law Nettie's house (where Stanley also resided), sister-in-law Anita's home, brother-in-law Cyrus's mansion, and a cadre of McCormick cousins.[3] They would eventually change the address to 1000 Lake Shore Drive, a far more illustrious address for the same plot of land.

Edith dubbed the house the Bastion. It was her fortress, her safe place in the world, and took up nearly the entire city block between Oak Street and Bellevue Place. Bordered by a massive ornamental iron fence originally built for the 1893 World's Fair, it felt impregnable.[4] She nicknamed the wooded gardens surrounding her home the "Bosque."

Designed by Solon Beman in 1888, the Bastion was of rough gray cut stone with numerous turrets and chimneys. The first floor held an assortment of parlors, a paneled library, a large dining room, a breakfast room, an observatory, and several open porches, in addition to the necessary service rooms. The second floor had four bedrooms, a sitting room, and dressing rooms. The third floor was for staff bedrooms, and the attic was storage space. The look was dark and ornate, with heavily patterned wallpapers, low-hanging chandeliers, multiple fireplaces, and elaborate hand-carved railings and pillars in every room.[5]

The staff grew quickly to a full contingent of seventeen employees: stewards, secretaries, footmen, charwomen, cooks, chauffeurs, sewing women. Edith believed that a house must be run as a business.[6] She maintained that her staff's service in life was to tend to her, whereas Edith's role in the bargain was to make it possible for them to serve her efficiently. Toward that end, Edith spoke only to her secretary, Gertrude Hellenthal, or the head steward, Fred Baxter, trusting them to deliver assignments down the line. In later years, servants recalled, "She was easy to work for, never complained, never asked us to do anything extra. . . . She never spoke to us, we never spoke to her. She didn't hear us if we did."[7]

Running the household was quite the business. There was a printed schedule for every day, with every minute carefully planned, a habit all the Rockefeller children had learned early in life. Edith's routine was to rise at the same time every morning, dress, have a small breakfast, read several newspapers, work with her secretary on correspondence, and then begin her day of multiple meetings and social engagements.

Meals were regimented as well. Monday meant filet mignon with mushrooms. No leftovers were ever served; staff members were generous in doling out scraps to hungry tramps who asked for handouts.[8] A printing press in the basement churned out daily gold menu cards for each meal in French.[9]

And the serious spending began. Harold and Edith acquired some of the furnishings, hundreds of library books, and other household items from the estate of General Joseph Torrence, the former owner of the house.[10] The neighborhood was full of elaborately decorated mansions, but a Rockefeller-McCormick home would need to be a showpiece, and Harold and Edith were up to that task.

Edith became a top client of several antique dealers and enjoyed perusing the catalogs that arrived regularly. Fifteenth-century laces, Gothic tapestries, bronze Buddhas, French candelabras, English silver, a Steinway grand piano: Edith's taste was eclectic, mixing time periods and styles without pause. But she had a particular fondness for Napoleon and bid generously on anything with verifiable ties to him. Edith managed to obtain a dinner service Napoleon had gifted to his sister Pauline Bonaparte upon her marriage to Camillo Borghese: sixteen hundred pieces of gilded silver (it was very complete, including such specific items as cake baskets, bonbon dishes, and mustard spoons).[11] Chicago's upper crust would know they had been at a dinner party of merit when Edith chose to use that set.

Particularly lucky guests were invited to sit in some of Napoleon's royal chairs, bearing his initials. A long gold box Napoleon had given to Empress Marie Louise, engraved with her initials, became a personal favorite of Edith's.[12] Her bedroom was all in Louis XVI style, from the oversized bed with a rose taffeta canopy to the gilded dressing table and mirrors and an elegant carved writing table.[13] The Bastion was quickly becoming a palace.

Harold and Edith were assembling not just a household but a collection. These were items that rightfully belonged in museums, and ultimately this would be Edith's aim. That goal would be mostly dashed, but for the time being, Edith basked in the presence of her treasures.

Edith's view of her spending was trickle-down economics at its finest: "A person with even the simplest knowledge of economics must know that by so doing the woman of wealth is only doing her duty. When I buy lovely, fragile laces I give employment to delicate, frail little hands that might find no other means of self-support. My linens are made by the thriftiest folk, but folk who but for me and others who can afford to buy expensive materials would find no market for their labor. The diamond fields of Africa, where thousands find employment and thousands more have made fabulous fortunes would be as so much worthless dirt if men and women . . . were not willing to spend their money to purchase them."[14]

The money flowed fast and furiously. At the time of the wedding, the newspapers surmised the union would make Edith the richest woman in the country. But the truth is that neither Harold nor Edith had any idea how to manage money, and they soon found themselves running short. Most of their fortune was caught up in stocks; cash flow was an issue.

It would have been with considerable shame that Harold penned this note to Senior: "I acknowledge with deep gratitude your check for $50,000—a very, very large sum for you to give me. I know why you give it to me and, in a sense, how indefensible my position is which calls for such loving consideration on your part. . . . I will put the check in just the channels that you desire—'to reduce my indebtedness.' You would not countenance what we have done, I am sure, in permitting ourselves to get where we are."[15] Those large checks from Father were a yearly event: Edith received her annual allowance of $17,000, and Harold always feigned surprise at his large gifts, sometimes $25,000, other times $50,000. Harold, with his ebullience, had managed to find a way into Father's heart. Whereas brother-in-law Parmalee Prentice, married to Alta in 1901, always addressed Senior as "Mr. Rockefeller," it had taken Harold a mere six months to win the right to call him "Father." Having joined Junior's school as a teenager, Harold held a special place in the family.

However, the rift between trickle-down Edith and penny-pincher Senior had begun.

Life as a city's grande dame comes with responsibilities—many responsibilities, none of which Edith particularly enjoyed. While Harold went off to work each morning at McCormick Reaper Works—soon to merge, with the help of Senior's backing, with other farm implement companies and become International Harvester—and spent his evenings in board meetings for local clubs, Edith had her own schedule. Her life was a merry-go-round of social engagements: clubs like the Fortnightly, the Antiquarians, the Lovers of Italy; fundraising efforts for local hospitals and charities; lectures and musical events (which Edith often hosted); and planning for cotillions and masquerade balls. In between, she had luncheons, teas, and dinners; huge amounts of correspondence; and a host of dress fittings.

One doesn't sit atop the social ladder without a considerable wardrobe. Dresses of the time were floor-length and full with puffy shoulders and huge amounts of ornamentation. Edith ordered her dresses from New York and Europe, and if she found a style she particularly liked, she ordered one in every color. Her staff kept a catalog of her dresses on hand and fetched the appropriate one from the upper floor of the mansion for each occasion. She possessed four fur coats: an ermine cape, a sable, and two chinchillas. Her favorite was a chinchilla wrap sporting a silver fox collar, with over one hundred skins carefully stitched together.[16] Edith owned over two hundred hats. Merely deciding what to wear for each occasion was time-consuming. A typical day required three different outfits.

As hemlines began to creep upward, Edith was among the first to bare her ankles—considered quite rakish. She also introduced the ankle bracelet to Chicago, a five-strand gold anklet, the *Chicago Daily Tribune* suggesting it was a new fashion for the world: "Mrs. McCormick bears the reputation of leading Chicago in presenting new styles, but an attempt to lead the world is so far as known a new venture."[17] Edith was additionally fond of wearing long diamond pendant earrings that dangled down her neck.[18] Harold was also known to be a snappy dresser with the trendiest collars and suits and a proliferation of monograms on his handkerchiefs and cuffs.[19] A newspaper article adjudged that Harold "has a fancy for fine raiment, but is not a dude."[20]

A champion collector, Edith could not be outdone in the jewelry category. On the middle finger of her right hand she always wore a ring with a 5½-carat square-cut diamond and button-shaped Oriental pearl.[21] Her rope of perfectly matched pearls, with some as wide as three-quarters of an inch, was later valued at $2 million.[22] Some believed it was the "finest string of pearls in the world" at the time.[23] She owned several of the Russian crown jewels assembled into a spectacular necklace: 23 large pearls, 21 large diamonds, and 100 lesser diamonds.[24] Her Cartier emerald necklace had 10 incandescent green jewels originally belonging to Catherine the Great spaced between 1,657 diamonds.[25] Had there been a jewelry competition, she would have won hands-down.

Friend Arthur Meeker wrote, "She knew the weight of every stone, its history, and what she'd paid for it. There were the Catherine of Russia emeralds for state occasions, and a kind of glittering stomacher, which—when asked by my mother where she'd got it—she announced, surprisingly, had been made up out of some diamonds she'd found 'round the house.'"[26] For the price tag of $350,000, Chicago craftsman Frank Boyden created a square-cut necklace (perhaps that "stomacher") for Edith that was deemed "one of the most important pieces of jewelry ever created in the United States."[27]

Edith felt it her duty to elevate Chicago to a more refined city, to be known for more than the stench of its stockyards and no-nonsense industry. Despite its rough-and-tumble reputation, a great amount of wealth was centered in Chicago. In one effort to raise Chicago's image, Edith championed a regular society promenade. Every Tuesday and Thursday afternoon, the leaders of society, dressed in the latest styles and millinery, touting feather fans and parasols, would parade up Michigan Avenue, ending in Lincoln Park, where they enjoyed a pavilion tea. But Chicago's fickle weather put a damper on the festivities, which dropped to once a week, then changed to more of an automobile parade, and ultimately ceased altogether.[28]

In many ways, Edith was a duck out of water. A lone Rockefeller in Chicago. An intellectual amid a sea of socialites. Though she tried to fit in, she was perceived as having an imperial complex, giving the appearance of being above it all.[29] The truth is, Edith would have preferred an intellectual debate over small talk any day. Harold was little help, as his last name and gregarious nature granted him acceptance in any Chicago gathering. Try as he may, he couldn't understand Edith's discomfort.

Historian Clarice Stasz described Edith's climb up Chicago's social ladder: "She was rather plain, with an odd figure, and too temperamental for many people. Nonetheless, Edith would establish her position in society on the basis of her intelligence, taste, and energy, as expressed in stylish house and entertainments, and especially in her contributions to the cultural life of the city."[30]

Having succeeded in marrying well, the next expectation was that Edith would bear children. She and Harold had been delighted to welcome their first child, John Davison Rockefeller McCormick (Jack), while in Iowa in February 1897, and a second boy, Harold Fowler McCormick Jr. (first called Hal; later the name Fowler stuck) in late 1898.

Upon firstborn Jack's birth, Harold had written to sister Anita exclaiming that "we have received our little boy and we would have been very much pleased had it been a daughter—at least we tell each other so."[31] Mother-in-law Nettie, visiting the little family in Iowa, wrote with excitement to Edith's mother, Cettie, "What a joyful time we had when they had reached the decision to name him John Rockefeller McCormick—so happy they were in doing it—so devoted to him for whom they named this boy."[32]

On the topic of male offspring, Junior once told a group of Princeton fathers that "just about the best thing a man could do . . . was to give society a fine son."[33]

At least on the question of producing an heir, Edith was living up to her familial responsibilities. Two sons! An heir and a spare.

That is, until tragedy struck.

THE SHOW MUST GO ON

1900–1904

*E*dith's role as mother, as the calendar page turned from the 1800s to the 1900s, was different from what we might expect today. As a gold-star member of the upper crust, she would not have been deeply involved in the day-to-day aspects of parenting. That task fell to nurses and governesses, highly qualified and thoroughly vetted. Edith's role was to oversee the staff handling her children's development and occasionally make an appearance.

Edith later penned an article for a popular woman's magazine, *The Delineator*, titled "What My Children Mean to Me": "Perhaps we have not cared for children as young girls—books, music, art, have filled our minds and established our longings. But when we waken to the realization that the baby in our arms is our own, that we have the right, the privilege, the honor, to be called mother, we find that something new is within us, a love so different from any that we have experienced before—a pride, a jealous care, a great overwhelming joy. All this we could not know before, and how wonderful it is! A little soul loaned to us to love and to care for. What great confidence God has put in our love and our wisdom to make us such a gift! Life now has a new aspect."[1]

In golden-haired firstborn Jack and happy little Fowler, Edith at last had done something of which Senior could approve. She had created two worthy male heirs, certain to take their rightful places in the pantheon of either Standard Oil or International Harvester. She had finally done something right, and she certainly gave the appearance of relishing her role as dutiful mother.

Toward the end of 1900, Edith, suffering from a cold that wouldn't go away, packed up the two boys for a visit in the country air with Cettie and Senior at their vacation home in Pocantico Hills, outside Tarrytown, New York. It was a favorite family retreat, set on three thousand acres of rolling hills. Aside from the Bastion, it was one of the few places where Edith felt completely safe from the dangers of the outside world.

This sense of security was demolished when both boys, three-year-old Jack and two-year-old Fowler, came down with scarlet fever. The family was no stranger to the disease: Edith had lost a baby sister to scarlet fever, and two of Harold's infant siblings had died from it.

Senior did everything he could, having a separate staircase constructed connecting the boys' sick room to an enclosed porch so the brothers could benefit from the sunshine without endangering other members of the household; hiring first-rate nurses; muffling the doorbell; offering $500,000 to any doctor who could cure them.[2] The family and the physicians were even debating the merits of performing a tracheotomy when it became clear that Jack would not survive. Their herculean efforts may have saved Fowler's life, for he made a full recovery. But golden Jack died January 2, 1901. One of the three doctors in attendance confessed, "I am ashamed that I could do nothing. A case like this makes me feel as if I wanted to lay aside the profession."[3]

The family was shattered. Growing up in the Rockefeller household, under constant bombardment from the public and press, family members had developed a hard outer shell. They were accustomed to death threats, fear, hatred. They were used to holding their heads high, keeping a stiff upper lip, hiding raw emotion. But this . . . this was different.

Senior wept, one of the few times Edith saw him shed a tear: his first grandson, his namesake gone. Harold could barely function and later would refer to the event as his "crushing sorrow."[4] Many months later he would check into the psychiatric clinic at the Burghölzli Hospital in Zurich, Switzerland, still reeling from grief. This would be Harold and Edith's first encounter with a psychiatric discipline that would eventually play a great role in Edith's life.

Edith withdrew. Uncomfortable with emotion by nature, this painful loss shocked her further back into her shell. Loving was not safe. Loving led to pain. Loving brought danger into her carefully created cocoon. Her letters to her exceedingly devout mother-in-law, Nettie, in which she mentions family members already passed, indicate she was looking to religion for solace, a tone that would be absent in her writings in years to come: "Trusting that our all-loving Father will guide our steps through this dark way where we must needs stumble and fall were it not for His strong arm encircling us. The darling is preparing the 'mansion above' for us all, in the presence of the loving Saviour, and surrounded by our dear ones who have gone before—Papa, Emmons, Robert, Alice."[5]

Jack's death spurred the development of two major health institutions: Senior followed through on a promise to donate $1 million to endow a medical research organization, the Rockefeller Institute for Medical Research,[6] and Edith and Harold founded the John R. McCormick Memorial Institute for Infectious Diseases and provided the underwriting for the *Journal of Infectious Diseases*.[7] Their institute supported research that would ultimately lead to isolating the bacterium that causes scarlet fever and creating a vaccine to prevent it. Little Jack's abbreviated life would have purpose. But they didn't know that yet.

Grandmother Nettie summed up Jack's personality: "His mind was so poised that he was every way charming to converse with. For two hours he would do the things we were doing, whether looking at pictures or reading the story, without once running away. How I loved that golden hair; that spirited little figure, springing over his toy wagons with a leap and bound,—that obedient little spirit—which, even if crying, would cry so softly, as if disciplined to hold himself in. . . . Young as he was, he always left an impression of great strength of character."[8]

Life went on, but Edith and Harold struggled to keep up. Later that month, in a subdued affair, the family gathered as Edith's sister Alta married E. Parmalee Prentice, a Chicago attorney. The wedding had already been postponed once due to Jack and Fowler's illness. Their presence was mandatory, as Harold had introduced the couple.[9] Furthermore, Alta had been resentful following the great fanfare over younger sister Edith's high-profile match. This was in part because as a teenager, Alta had fallen in love with their Cleveland minister, a forty-seven-year-old widower. When he dared to consider marrying Alta, Senior swiftly saw to it that the minister was reassigned to a parish in the Midwest.[10] Alta's love life had been lackluster, to say the least.

Alta would be overshadowed again, by a different sibling, when in October, Junior married Abby Aldrich, daughter of esteemed senator Nelson Aldrich from Rhode Island. But Harold and Edith were in Switzerland and missed the grand event.[11]

The turn of the century ushered in a horrible time. A hurricane devastated Galveston. President McKinley was assassinated and a very young Theodore Roosevelt was appointed president, promising to break up the large trusts, the "malefactors of great wealth." Standard Oil was at the top of his list. The Iroquois Theater fire in Chicago killed over six hundred people. Sadness hung over the country.

And then there was the Tarbell series in *McClure's Magazine*. From 1902 to 1904, journalist Ida Tarbell authored a series of nineteen articles about John D. Rockefeller, beginning with a history of Standard Oil, interviewing many of the people he had wronged along the way, and then branching out to include the family. Her final installment was a scathing two-part character study about Senior, in which Tarbell portrayed him as money-mad, crafty, cruel, and repulsive.

Worse, perhaps, was the information about Edith's paternal grandfather that she had likely never heard: "He was a dare-devil with horses . . . he had all the vices . . . a famous trickster . . . irregular and wild . . . mystery surrounding him . . . favorite with the young women . . ."[12] The children had always been told he was a traveling salesman.

Tarbell had done considerable digging and had learned that, among other things, William Avery Rockefeller was a flimflam man (his techniques included posting public signs such as "Here for One Day Only. All cases of cancer cured unless too far gone and they can be greatly benefited"),[13] a horse thief, a suspected rapist, and a bigamist. Tarbell's discovery of a second wife and an $8,000 finder's fee offered by Joseph Pulitzer set off a nationwide search for "Big Bill."[14] While none was successful, it was an embarrassment and source of stress for the entire family. It appeared that Bill was everything that sanctimonious Senior had railed against, which would explain why Senior always kept his father at arm's length. How much had Senior known?

The public scrutiny brought about by the Tarbell series exacerbated nervous conditions for many family members. Cettie suffered a stroke that required years of recovery; Senior had terrible bronchial problems and alopecia that resulted in the loss of all of his hair and eyebrows; Junior experienced a nervous collapse that caused him to take a six-month leave from Standard Oil and convalesce in France (he would eventually step back entirely to focus on philanthropy);[15] Alta complained of shattered nerves; and, worst of all, eldest sister Bessie underwent a mysterious attack (perhaps a stroke) from which she would never fully recover.[16]

Was Edith the daughter of a pious church elder or a manipulative monster? Was her grandfather a lovable free spirit or a rapist? The assumptions of her childhood collided with the facts presented in adulthood. Already wary of interacting with the public, already terrified of the dangers that lay beyond her front door, Edith struggled to find the strength to venture forth.

In this stressful environment, Edith attempted to heal from Jack's death. In 1902, she gave birth to her first daughter, Muriel, and a second girl named Editha followed in 1903. But these were not to be easy children. Muriel was a firebrand with a trigger-quick temper, and Editha suffered from respiratory problems from birth and was not expected to live long. Harold and Edith, preferring to keep their misery quiet, decided to forgo birth announcements and installed Editha in a private home outside of the city where she could be given twenty-four-hour care. Then they waited for her to die. And waited. And waited.

As leading figures in Chicago's social circles, Edith and Harold were expected to host several large parties each year. In 1904 they waited as long as they could, until just before the end of the social season in June (when most wealthy families departed for Europe or wooded retreats in better climates than Chicago), before hosting their fête champêtre. The papers would later claim it was the most costly and elaborate party Chicago had ever seen, complete with five thousand electrical lights and Tiffany lamps strung throughout Edith's Bosque, thirty truckloads of imported flowers and trees, an arbor vitae maze thirty-seven feet long by twenty-eight feet wide, vaudeville dancers, sword jugglers, and a percussion tent. Dinner was served at midnight.[17]

Throughout the evening, as the 420 guests, attired in eighteenth-century costumes and white wigs, danced, ate, and laughed, a car idled at the Bastion, ready for action at any moment. This was for Edith and Harold, should baby Editha take a turn for the worse. Their secret hung between them that horrendously festive night. Though they were both draped all in white—from Edith's lace hat, pearls, and gown to Harold's waistcoat and kid gloves—their moods were dark. And as they kicked off the dancing to Johnny Hand and His Orchestra, the parents masked their worries with pasted smiles and forced gaiety.

Baby Editha made it through that long night but passed a few days later.[18]

Time and time again throughout her life, Edith would choose to uphold her societal role rather than address her own needs, beginning with attending her own wedding reception alone, due to Harold's pleurisy; participating in Alta's wedding just weeks after baby Jack's death; and, particularly, hosting this huge garden party as Editha lay dying. Public appearances seemed paramount to Harold and Edith, even at the expense of their own well-being. The show must go on.

One wonders what proper Senior thought of the fête champêtre. Entertaining had not been a priority in the household of Edith's childhood, unless visiting ministers were considered entertainment. Dancing was forbidden. And because of the promise she'd made Senior at that comedy-of-errors wedding, the outdoor party was dry, but not really by the wishes of its hosts. (Because it was an unseasonably chilly evening with a brutal wind coming off the lake, guests kept slipping off to neighboring homes for hot toddies.)[19] Furthermore, Standard Oil was the nation's top supplier of kerosene, yet Edith had chosen to outfit her Bosque with electrical lights. And then there was Editha: Senior would have known of the state of his granddaughter's health, and he surely would not have approved of the timing of the large entertainment his daughter and son-in-law were hosting.

In the aftermath of it all, Edith would need to consider not only how she had offended Senior but also a larger question: Would people discover that she had partied, clad in white with her $2 million string of pearls, as her child lay suffering?

In *The Delineator* article that Edith wrote a few years after Editha's death, she effused, "The child who today lies in our arms entirely helpless and dependent is going to grow and to develop. We must then bestir ourselves. Are we going to be prepared to meet each phase of development wisely and capably? Is the unfolding of the spirit going to be met by an intelligent, loving mind ready to grasp, to guide, to advise? And if this is so, how wonderful each moment of every day is! Is this not the fullness of living?"[20]

It was a lovely sentiment, beautiful words. The trouble was, having lost two babies, Edith was retreating into herself, afraid to reach out again, afraid to care, to love, to commit. Mothering was not her strength.

A month later, she was pregnant again.

DANGERS

1905-10

*M*cCormicks were master secret-keepers. When sister Mary Virginia suffered a mental breakdown after the death of their father in 1884, brothers Harold and Stanley, though just boys, knew to keep it quiet. The family closed ranks and kept Mary Virginia near and the secret contained to the best of their ability until she finally had to be institutionalized.

Now it seemed a second McCormick sibling was succumbing to madness. This one hit even closer to home: Harold's younger brother, Stanley, so close in age they'd been raised virtually as twins. Again, efforts were made to prevent word getting out. Family reputation was paramount.

Brilliant straight-arrow Stanley graduated cum laude from Princeton and began law school at Northwestern University in preparation for his career at International Harvester. Really, he had no choice; this was what was expected of the McCormick boys. The trouble was, he was poorly suited to that role. He had always been a contemplative, sensitive soul, and what he really wanted was to become an artist. Mother Nettie made it clear that wasn't a viable option.[1]

Stanley had married Katharine Dexter in 1904. It was an illustrious match: Katharine was intelligent, strong, and highly ethical. She was the second female graduate of the Massachusetts Institute of Technology and the first to graduate with a degree in biology. Her great-grandfather Samuel Dexter had served in the cabinets of both John Adams and Thomas Jefferson and had the grim honor of reading George Washington's eulogy before the Senate. The Dexters were from a distinguished line and were a perfect match for the McCormicks.

But shortly after the never-consummated wedding, Stanley's mental well-being collapsed. He suffered tremendous mood swings and became increasingly agitated. Katharine began to fear for her own safety after Stanley became physically violent several times. As her new husband slipped rapidly away from reality, Katharine struggled with what to do. But the incidents multiplied: he attacked his dentist, a German teacher, and an elevator operator and became catatonic on a dance floor.[2] Katharine had no choice; she had him forcibly moved to a Boston mental hospital. When Harold came to visit him, Stanley greeted him with, "Jack London! I'm glad to see you!" He fought with doctors, conversed with imaginary people, had bouts of delusional yelling ("To Windsor! To Windsor!"), and imagined a dog looking back at him when he looked in a mirror.[3]

Like his sister Mary Virginia, Stanley was diagnosed with dementia praecox, in his case with severe sexual side effects. He had manic-depressive episodes, flip-flopping between months of catatonia, during which he needed to be tube-fed, to instances of intense physical outbreaks, when he attacked his nurses (first female, later all male, for safety reasons), often with sexual intent. Numerous doctors were consulted, and they attributed his breakdown to several factors: gastrointestinal abnormalities, an oedipal complex, homosexual tendencies, and heredity, among others.[4] Hearing heredity on the list surely gave Harold pause.

Family members had less scientific theories. Some speculated that the pressures of becoming a Harvester man drove Stanley to a breaking point. Another theory stemmed back to molestation at the hands of a governess when he was quite young. Some relatives blamed overprotective Nettie, believing she "warped Stanley sexually. She was the ultimate castrating and domineering mother."[5] Mother Nettie had preached that sex was only for the purpose of reproduction; therefore, when teen Stanley awoke on occasion to find himself masturbating, he was deeply ashamed and believed himself to be a sexual deviant. In college, he fashioned a harness for his hands so he couldn't please himself in his sleep.[6] Stanley himself told the doctors he believed his breakdown was caused by anxiety over performing sexually with his new wife.[7]

Only Katharine, the ink still drying on her MIT biology diploma, believed there were chemical deficiencies involved. She would push the doctors for endocrine testing year after year but was repeatedly ignored. Doctors and family members alike seemed inclined to lay much of the blame at Katharine's feet: surely this domineering young woman had scared dear Stanley senseless. A decades-long fight over Stanley's well-being would ensue, with Katharine determined to break Nettie's ironclad hold on her youngest son. (Nettie had even insisted on tagging along for the honeymoon.) But doctors would prohibit Katharine from visiting her husband, claiming it was too upsetting to him. She went twenty years without being allowed to be in his presence and would sometimes watch him through binoculars from behind a bush in the garden.[8] The McCormick family urged Katharine to divorce Stanley, believing it would help his recovery. But Katharine refused, certain that back in Nettie's clutches, Stanley wouldn't have a chance.

Once it was apparent Stanley would not be recovering quickly, he was locked in an eight-thousand-square-foot McCormick mansion, Riven Rock, located on eighty-seven acres in Santa Barbara, California. Ironically, Stanley had helped design the house, originally intended for Mary Virginia (who had since been moved to a facility in Asheville, North Carolina). Just prior to his breakdown, the McCormicks—Stanley included—had discussed selling the property.[9] But Stanley would live out the rest of his life behind Riven Rock's barred windows. On the plus side, there was a nine-hole golf course, a movie theater, an orchard, and even overhead sprinklers installed outside to simulate rain (which doctors theorized might calm Stanley).[10] On the downside, the furniture was bolted down, all doctors and nurses were male, and there was no leaving. It was a gilded cage costing the family $400,000 annually. The staff required to run Riven Rock neared fifty, including doctors and researchers to oversee a primate research facility the McCormicks built to gain insight into human sexual urges. Overseen by noted scientist Dr. Gilbert Hamilton, it may have been the first of its kind in the world.[11]

The crises kept coming. And all too close for comfort.

Merely one year after Stanley's breakdown, the Rockefeller side of the family experienced their own tragedy. Edith's oldest sister, Bessie, died in France at age forty, shortly after suffering a paralytic stroke. She had not been well for many years; there was speculation she'd had a stroke a few years earlier, resulting in permanent mental damage. Bessie's form of insanity stemmed from a fear of impoverishment.[12] She hoarded pennies, refused to order food for the household, and obsessed about expenses. Occasionally she reverted into a childlike babble. Her husband, childhood sweetheart Charles Strong, was a brilliant philosopher and psychologist forced to witness his wife's gradual decline.

Madness seemed always to be just around the corner for Harold and Edith. It was a constant shadow in their lives. Would one of them be next? Which one? Or would their children inherit some genetic deficiency?

It is difficult now to understand the pressures this generation of Rockefellers and McCormicks were under. Both sides had fathers who had quite literally changed the face of business. Cyrus McCormick was dubbed the "Father of Modern Agriculture" for how his reaper had revolutionized farming. And John D. Rockefeller had single-handedly changed how business was conducted in the United States. The strain may have overwhelmed their children.

And what of Harold and Edith? Were the "Prince of McCormick Reaper" and the "Princess of Standard Oil" living up to their potential? Could they find a way to make a major contribution to society, or would they be destined to merely inhabit their fathers' shadows?

Meanwhile, the carousel of benefits, dinners, concerts, horse shows, garden parties, fashion shows, fundraisers, cotillions, and lectures went round and round. Edith was barely hanging on. Trying to be model wife and mother in this maelstrom was wearing.

Their last child, daughter Mathilde, was born in 1905. Edith had been ill for most of the pregnancy, complaining of fatigue, abdominal and back pain, fever, and frequent urination. The birth itself was difficult, with the mother too exhausted to push, and required forceps.[13] Baby Mathilde was weak, and doctors predicted she might live only a few years.[14] On the advice of their family physician, Harold and Edith left their older daughter, Muriel, with a nurse in Lakewood, New Jersey, for the winter. The doctor warned that her throat was in an "unhealthful condition" and that being in a big city in the winter would not be beneficial to her.[15]

One can only imagine how Harold and Edith felt at this point, having already lost two children. Self-preservation probably dictated they keep an emotional distance from all of their children. Under the watchful eye of nurses and governesses, baby Mathilde improved, but she would need respiratory therapy and "strengthening" for many years to come. Edith herself was eventually diagnosed with tuberculosis of the kidney, the symptoms having masqueraded as pregnancy side effects. It would take her a full two years to nominally recover, including several stints at rest homes and consultations with a panoply of doctors, including prominent neurologist Bernard Sachs.[16]

Harold reported to Senior, "Edith is doing well, although very slowly. There is a constant temptation to over do, and this we are struggling against. We took our first drive yesterday and remained out about 3/4 of an hour. We have a plan for an automobile tour in Germany and France if the doctors permit, but of course, that is the first consideration."[17]

They took that European automobile tour, leaving all three children with Edith's parents as they motored around for several months. But while they were gone, little Muriel developed appendicitis and underwent a sudden operation.[18] When they returned in early 1906, Edith was more fragile than ever, and Harold later declared he'd been "the most foolish fellow" for insisting upon the vacation.[19] Edith spent several months convalescing in Lakewood before returning to Chicago.[20]

How did they manage? Deaths, breakdowns, public scandals, illness, and so terribly much pressure.

Rockefeller historian Ron Chernow characterized their marriage: "It was, in many ways, a classic mismatch: Harold was free and expansive, while Edith was aloof, imperial and cerebral.... [After the death of two of their children] Edith became more rigid, a stickler for a frosty sort of protocol, even forcing her children to make appointments to see her. Once a brilliant society hostess, Edith became increasingly immured in their mansion at 1000 Lake Shore Drive, incapacitated by a terrifying agoraphobia."[21]

They pushed on. Hard.

Harold was up to his eyeballs in work, clubs, and hobbies. He served as trustee for the McCormick Theological Seminary, the University of Chicago, the Art Institute, the Chicago Symphony Orchestra, the First National Bank, and the Chicago Exchange Building. He participated in the Princeton Club, the Commercial Club, the Merchants' Club, the University Club, the Chicago Club, and the Saddle and Cycle Club. In between, he played competitive tennis at the national level, found time for polo, and enjoyed automobile outings.[22]

Harold was also a leader in the burgeoning sport of aeronautics. A true McCormick, he loved to tinker with plans, dreaming up new designs for airplanes (including a Mary Poppins–like umbrella plane and a strange contraption affectionately nicknamed the Mustard Plaster), underwriting prototypes, and spending free weekends at the airfield. In 1911, he was on the planning team for a nine-day International Aviation Meet that took place in Chicago, a huge effort that provided hundreds of thousands of Chicagoans their first look at an airplane. The event was Harold's idea and underwritten primarily by Harold's money.[23] There were two aviator deaths during the meet, but that didn't dampen Harold's enthusiasm for the sport.

It is notable that Harold managed to convince all members of his family, including what must have been a very nervous Nettie, to take to the air on one of their summer trips to Europe, cabling home to his brother Cyrus Jr., "Congratulations for Anita Mother Edith children self and nineteen trunks just had splendid airplane voyage of 75 feet accurately measured by pedometer."[24]

Edith's schedule was similarly busy, with a major item being the design of a summer house. Harold and Edith and the children, and often Nettie, frequently traveled to Europe in the summer months and also spent long stretches at Paul Smith's Hotel in the Adirondacks, a fashionable yet rustic summer camp for the upper crust drawing U.S. presidents, celebrities, and the elite. But every self-respecting member of the A-list had a summer home, so Edith and Harold got to work on designing theirs. Cyrus Jr. had given them some three hundred acres of land in Lake Forest, twenty miles north of Chicago, close to his own Walden estate. It was a heavily wooded property overlooking Lake Michigan.

Edith began auditioning architects. She began with James Gamble Rogers, a distant relative who had worked with McCormick Reaper in the past and would ultimately become campus architect for Northwestern University. The McCormicks requested a house with "pure Italian lines," powerful yet peaceful.[25] Yet Rogers's plan did not hit the mark. Too Gothic,[26] Edith declared.

Next up, Frank Lloyd Wright. Harold liked the horizontal style of this prominent Chicago architect and invited him to draw up plans. But Edith didn't like the idea. Wright would recall the experience later on:

Harold McCormick was a rich young man at that time driving the great American Roadster over the prairies. He used to come out to Oak Park and take me out for a ride. . . . And I made the plans which you have seen for his house. . . . We finally made an appointment at the old McCormick homestead there on the north side in the garden. And the relatives of the McCormicks were there, we all were there, Harold was waiting for Mrs. Edith Rockefeller to appear. She didn't appear. We waited and Harold began to get red in the face, angry, walking up and down, chewing his lip, mustache. Finally the gate opened at the head of the garden and here with a measured stately tread came this figure with a great wide hat . . . by the way I had to make a place for 250 hats in this house. And standing up on it were flowers on stems—when she walked they waved to and fro. When I caught a glimpse of that, I knew it was a lost cause.

Well, Harold didn't have that sense of it. He kept trying to get her to see the house. She came with her parasol and sat down with her back to the plans that were on the table and wouldn't look at them. She would not turn around. And Harold said, "But you see, Edith, won't you at least look?" "Oh, I know," she said, "it is perfectly lovely for the mountains but hardly the thing for Lake Forest."[27]

Too mountain-y, Edith declared.

The third architect was Charles Adams Platt, who was also a gifted landscape designer. He came up with a design that resembled an Italian villa, with a stucco exterior and a flat, hipped roof. Architectural historians believe this must have been a considerable blow to Wright and the Chicago School of architecture: "It has been suggested that it was Mrs. McCormick who refused it, saying that her mode of life simply could not be suited by a Prairie House. In any case it was she who suddenly went to New York in August, 1908, and placed the commission for the house which she eventually occupied in the hands of a master of traditional architecture, Charles Augustus [sic] Platt, who gave her a handsome Italian villa that is as knowing a piece of archeology as can be seen in the Middle West. That it was erected upon the ruins of the Chicago School was, for him, unimportant."[28]

Just right, Edith declared.

It took four years and nearly $5 million, but when it was finished, it was a showpiece. Bursting with white columns, vaulted ceilings, arched transom windows, courtyards, and fountains, they dubbed it Villa Turicum (an ancient Celtic word for "settlement on water" as well as the Latin name for Zurich). It boasted forty-four rooms, including thirteen identical master bedrooms,[29] fifteen bathrooms, and fourteen servant rooms. There were twenty-eight rooms for gardeners, twenty-nine for visiting chauffeurs, and a garage for twenty-one cars.[30] The property included an entrance mall, polo grounds, a lakeside pool with cascading terraces, stables, a bowling green, formal gardens, fountains, statues, and a teahouse. There was a bathhouse on the beach providing changing rooms for the pool and an elevator connecting it to the main house. Visitors who chose to use the stairs to the beach rather than the elevator were rewarded: the dual staircase had a waterfall running between and highlighted elaborate sculptures, basins, and planters at each landing.[31]

Architectural journals ran features on Villa Turicum; garden magazines marveled at the grounds. *American Landscape Architect* magazine regarded it as the "finest example in America of the Italian treatment in landscape design" and suggested, "One can almost imagine, upon a blue-skied June day, that a villa from the Italian lake region had been bodily transplanted to Illinois."[32] Edith oversaw it all, shoving aside her anxieties, fears, and maternal responsibilities. She encouraged Senior to consider Platt for renovations to his house at Pocantico, but nothing came of it.[33]

The McCormicks would eventually discover one major drawback to Villa Turicum, one that would prevent Edith from spending any real time there: it was located immediately north of an army training base where, several times each week, shelling practice occurred.[34] Loud artillery booms were not exactly conducive to the quiet, restorative time they had planned for their summer home. Villa Turicum social events would be carefully scheduled not to coincide with shelling practice.

A local poet, Frances Shaw, wrote a poem about Villa Turicum titled "The Garden of No-Delight," capturing the lonely, wasted beauty.

> A pale and wasted moonlight falls
> On lawns of velvet green;
> Twelve stately fountains trickle down
> To pools that lie unseen.
> These fountain pools still wait unstirred—
> No image falls therein;
> Their mirrors, like a witless soul,
> Know neither joy nor sin.[35]

And the money kept pouring out. Now that the Bastion was filled with treasures, they had Villa Turicum to fill, as well as considerable staffs for both houses. And, unfortunately for Edith, the tradition begun in childhood of Junior as family accountant continued, with Edith having to submit her income and expenses to her brother every year for an annual audit.[36] The ensuing letters from Junior invariably pontificated about their overspending.

In addition to their own expenses, Harold and Edith received requests from individuals and organizations daily for financial assistance. Edith gave with judicious thought, supporting those institutions where she felt she could do the most good. She was careful never to pledge her father's assistance in any causes. In February 1909, she was invited to a luncheon at mother-in-law Nettie's at which the current president of Princeton—Woodrow Wilson, a longtime McCormick friend—was outlining his "Quad Plan," which would do away with elite clubs and reorganize the university into separate quads or colleges. "Dear Mr. Wilson," Edith wrote to him after the luncheon, "I was most interested in what you said about the problems and difficulties at Princeton, but we never overstep the rule, now of a number of years' standing, to present no appeals to my father. I would be glad to write to my brother or to Mr. Gates, [Senior's primary business and philanthropic adviser] if that would be of help to you. We enjoyed so much your visit, and I hope that we may have the pleasure of meeting before so very long again. Sincerely, Edith Rockefeller McCormick."[37]

In 1907, Senior and his brother William came to Chicago for an antitrust trial against Standard Oil brought by the government. President Roosevelt was on a mission to break up the business monopolies, and few were more dominant than Standard Oil. Over twenty times the size of its nearest competitor, Standard Oil supplied nearly 90 percent of the domestic kerosene business. The Tarbell series in *McClure's* had pointed out just how ruthlessly Standard Oil had brought down the smaller oil companies, attaching names and destroyed families to the narrative to drive the story home. Anti-Rockefeller resentment once again ran high.

As the family gathered at the Bastion, Edith, uncharacteristically, volunteered to speak with the newspapermen gathered outside her front door. She delivered her words with her usual deliberate, carefully enunciated manner: "My father is a much persecuted man. It seems the more remarkable, inasmuch as he is not an enemy to anyone in the world. He is one of the most genial, great hearted men in this whole world. He lives in the clouds with his God rather than with worldly things. It is his greatest pleasure to promote happiness among those with whom he comes in contact."[38]

The next morning twenty detectives, armed with clubs, stood on the sidewalk outside the Bastion's gates, ready to escort Senior and William to the courthouse. The rowdy onlookers overwhelmed the detectives and even ripped buttons off of Senior's coat. The court ruled in favor of the government and served the maximum penalty: $29,240,000, by far the largest fine in American corporate history. Senior's personal portion would run around $8 million.[39]

Another danger that lurked constantly was kidnapping—of all the children, but Fowler in particular, as the lone male heir of these two American dynasties. The *New York Times* covered a visit Harold and Edith's family made to Cleveland in 1906, indicating security had been doubled at Forest Hill: "The boy plays in the grounds, but is attended by a maid, while two men are always within calling distance."[40]

Yes, Harold and Edith were pushing on. Hard, indeed. But it would take a toll. As it turned out, neither was immune to the pressure. Behind all the entertaining, planning, and community involvement, the cracks were getting deeper. Pretty soon they would form a chasm.

It seemed the world was rife with ideas, progress, change. The Panama Canal was under construction. Frederick Cook and Robert Peary raced to the North Pole, Roald Amundsen reached the South Pole, and archeologists discovered the ancient city of Machu Picchu. Sigmund Freud published his theory of sexuality and Albert Einstein was working on his theory of relativity. More specific to Chicago, Upton Sinclair penned his shocking *The Jungle*, and Daniel Burnham unveiled his *Plan of Chicago*.

And all eyes turned skyward as Halley's Comet blazed across the night sky—not unlike Edith, a bright flash determined to attract attention but ultimately burn out.

GRAND CAUSES

1909–11

Not yet welcome in the workforce, women in society had their causes. While the husbands were at work or sitting on boards or relaxing at their clubs, the wives were pursuing their pet projects.

For Edith's beleaguered sister-in-law Katharine Dexter McCormick, her interests were many. Because of Stanley's condition, she was a champion for medical causes, supporting endocrine research and mental illness issues. While her disastrous marriage brought her almost crushing disappointment and pain, she was financially free and able to spend her time as she liked. Katharine became a vocal leader in the woman suffrage movement, working alongside Carrie Chapman Catt and other indomitable women to finally pass the Nineteenth Amendment in 1920. She would serve as vice president for the League of Women Voters. And, in a curious twist of fate, she worked with Margaret Sanger to help make birth control more accessible (even smuggling thousands of diaphragms in her personal trunks from Europe by having them sewn into the hems of her clothing) and funded most of the research necessary for the birth control pill[1]—a strange epitaph for a woman who was never able to consummate her marriage or bear the children she longed to have. As Katharine was forever at odds with Nettie, Anita, and Harold regarding the proper care for Stanley, Edith kept her at arm's length. Katharine may have further alienated herself from the family when she served on the Women's Committee of the Council of Defense alongside Rockefeller enemy Ida Tarbell.[2]

For another sister-in-law, Anita McCormick Blaine, the cause was education. Several years older than Harold and Stanley, she had been almost a second mother to them, stepping in for an overwhelmed and preoccupied Nettie. In 1889 she married Emmons Blaine, son of the distinguished James Gillespie Blaine (senator, Speaker of the House, secretary of state, and presidential hopeful). When Emmons died suddenly in 1892, Anita was left to raise their son, Emmons Jr., alone. (A three-year-old Emmons had been one of two pages at Edith and Harold's wedding.)[3] With his education in her hands, she became passionately interested in the school system of Chicago and quickly disheartened. She began her own school, under the guidance of noted educators John Dewey and Francis Parker. Like Katharine, Anita was a strong, determined woman. It took eleven secretaries to keep up with her.[4]

At the juncture of these two issues, it is interesting to note that, before 1913, in Illinois, women were permitted to vote only in school elections. (In 1913, this would expand to include presidential electors and local offices but not other major seats. Women had to use separate ballots and ballot boxes.) It is unknown whether Edith exercised her right during these elections. Sister-in-law Anita ran her private school and Edith herself began a private Montessori school, based on a brand-new educational philosophy, for Mathilde and Muriel, all conducted in French and run out of a ballroom in Nettie's house.

Edith's passion was the arts, much to the dismay of Senior and Junior, who had always favored religion, education, and medicine. And in typical Edith style, she did it in high fashion, helping to found the Chicago Grand Opera Company with an annual infusion of cash and with Harold as president. Forty-nine other wealthy Chicagoans ponied up $5,000 each in order to get the organization started. The demise of a New York group, the Manhattan Opera Company, allowed them to quickly purchase entire sets, props, and costumes, and they jump-started their first season.[5] Years later, when writing about the history of opera in Chicago, Harold gave Edith due credit: "My wife, Mrs. Rockefeller McCormick, began to talk to me about the need of Chicago having its own opera company and of her deep interest in this subject, and she had talked with Oscar Hammerstein both in Chicago and New York."[6]

In a speech to Chicago businessmen, Edith explained, "It is only the cities which have reached a certain cultural height which have opera. From my point of view . . . opera is a proof of culture and therefore not to be considered as a luxury, but to be recognized as a biological necessity, for human development is measured by culture. Where there is no culture there is no actual development."[7] In its first season, 1910–11, the opera company presented twenty-one different operas, most performed only two or three times, a breakneck schedule that provided Chicago with a glimpse of many masterpieces.[8]

Opera historian Ronald Davis suggested the McCormicks ran the opera in a nearly regal manner: "Their domination was almost complete, but in return they underwrote an increasing portion of the company's annual deficit. The opera produced was sumptuous and well rehearsed, for money was scarcely an object. Operas were often given once, then never heard of again. . . . The McCormicks probably gave Chicago the best opera the city has ever seen, supporting it in a manner reminiscent of the royal courts of Eighteenth-century Europe."[9]

An opera evening began with a preconcert dinner at the Bastion, often with the music director Cleofonte Campanini or singers joining Harold and Edith's table. Guests numbered between twenty and forty, and these dinners took place sometimes as often as three times a week during opera season. The Bonaparte dinner service was put to good use on many of these occasions. Dinner began promptly and the courses were served in quick succession, with two footmen standing behind each guest, ready for action.

Edith had a bejeweled alarm clock at her place setting, and when the bell tinkled the plates were summarily removed, whether the diner was finished or not. Guests had to be diligent, for the intervals between courses were brief.

Friend Arthur Meeker described one of these preconcert dinners: "I suavely managed by holding onto my plate with the left hand when I felt that time was about to be called, meanwhile scraping up the final fragments with my right; this worked very well as long as there was nothing that had to be carved. . . . I remember well that, at a luncheon given for Maurice Ravel, my neighbor—a young soprano on tour with the composer—grasped her *caille rotie aux raisins* with both hands, exclaiming firmly: 'Oh no, you don't!'"[10]

He went on to describe the concert scene inside the Auditorium Theater: "Mrs. McCormick sat rigidly in the middle of the front row of her box, scarcely moving, and never allowing herself to relax: at no point did her back touch the chair; her arms in their long white gloves remained rigid, too, with her hands lying quietly in her lap. She really paid attention to the music, and she knew, as few of her friends did, whether it was good or not; her taste was admirable, her experience immense. In the entr'actes she stayed where she was, receiving those who presented themselves with the naive dignity of royalty. This wasn't putting on airs; she just didn't know how else to behave."[11]

Edith presided in the opera. People came to see her, unfailingly stationed in box 5, almost as much as the production itself. The morning papers invariably carried detailed descriptions of her gown and jewelry. The evening would end with a post-concert reception for the artists and special guests, hosted by Edith and Harold, at the Congress Hotel or other nearby venue. From beginning to end, an opera evening entailed at least six hours of commitment.

The maiden season of the Chicago Grand Opera Company was nearly derailed by a controversial production that caused staid Chicago to gasp. Diva Mary Garden reigned in the title role of *Salome*, Richard Strauss's new opera; the music was uninhibited, raw, sensual. The famous "Dance of the Seven Veils," in which a scantily clad Salome dances seductively with a dismembered head, was perfect for outrageous Mary, who performed it with gusto. A media firestorm erupted, with the chief of police complaining that Mary had wallowed around like a cat in a bed of catnip and the *Chicago Tribune* reporting that the audience had been "oppressed and horrified."[12]

After sitting through the first and second performances, Edith made the apparently unilateral decision to cancel the remaining two *Salome* evenings. When Mary Garden questioned Edith on this decision, she responded, "Last night, at the performance, I said to myself, 'Edith, your vibrations are all wrong.'"[13] End of discussion. End of *Salome*. Edith's decision would stand. Diva or no diva, it was clear who ran the show. Many years later, the *New York Times* explained, "One of the characteristics of her 'imperial complex' was her refusal to be drawn into either defense or explanation of any action, regardless of public opinion."[14]

Harold and Edith supported struggling composers and underwrote Charles Henry Meltzer's translations of over two dozen operas into English.[15] Ermanno Wolf-Ferrari's *The Jewels of the Madonna* and *The Secret of Suzanne*, both underwritten by the McCormicks, would become Chicago favorites. Chamber concerts were frequent happenings at the Bastion, including world-famous pianist Jan Paderewski, who went on to become

prime minister of Poland.[16] The McCormicks were also among a hand-
ful of guarantors who backed the purchase price for the site of Orchestra
Hall, to be home to the still new Chicago Orchestra under the baton of
Theodore Thomas.[17]

While the composers Edith underwrote (Wolf-Ferrari, Philipp Jarnach,
Otto Luening) were all male, she did serve as one of the founding members,
alongside Jane Addams and sister-in-law Harriet McCormick, of the Three
Arts Club, a home and club designed for young women studying music,
painting, and drama.[18]

Chicago theater got a boost from Edith's support as well. She served
as the first president of the Chicago Theater Society, donating $10,000 a
year to the organization, purchasing twenty-five seats for each performance
to be utilized by theater students, and helping select the ten plays for each
season. Of the ten slots, three were earmarked for new American plays in
order to stimulate young playwrights.[19]

The concerts and causes multiplied, the calendar was full to bursting,
the children were growing, and the cash was flowing.

Nearly each summer included several months with the entire family
(children, Nettie, governesses, maids, a doctor) motoring around Europe—
Germany, Austria, Hungary, France—and Russia. One such trip resulted
in new full-body portraits for both Edith and Harold by noted painter
Friedrich August von Kaulbach, at $15,000 each, as well as for Nettie.[20]
Von Kaulbach's father had been the court painter for King George V.
Edith wears a lace-trimmed silk gown, her favorite ostrich wrap, a diamond
necklace, and a jeweled tiara in hers. Edith tried to convince Senior to have
von Kaulbach paint portraits of him and Cettie, but the price escalated
to $25,000 each, and he opted for artist John Singer Sargent instead.[21] It
should also be noted that years earlier, while in Rome on their honeymoon,
Edith sat for several sessions with famed sculptor Moses Ezekiel, but he
abandoned her bust mid-production due to a family emergency.[22]

On a 1909 trip, Harold and Edith acquired three Tournai tapestries:
the 11' x 19' *Verdure with Animals* dating back to 1550 and two 8' x 8' pieces
titled *The Boar and Bear Hunt* from 1420. All were historically significant.
There is no record of their purchase price. In later years, Edith would commission an art historian to compile a detailed record of these works.[23] The
McCormicks displayed them in Villa Turicum.

Travels weren't just for recreation. Harold also used them to recruit the world's most prominent doctors in nervous disorders. He traveled to Munich to convince noted professor Emil Kraepelin to serve as resident doctor for Stanley, following up on a letter of introduction from McCormick family doctor Henry Favill asking, "Can you come to America to pass judgment upon a case of manic depression insanity which is expected to recover? Every facility afforded for effective treatment."[24] In another instance, he cabled Anita about a young man prone to epileptic fits who had been cured with brain surgery, wondering if it might be effective for Stanley.[25] Harold suffered considerable guilt and anxiety over his younger brother: "Poor dear Stanley, what a load he has struggled under and how little I have helped him. I feel as if I had done nothing but as if I saw it all at the time and allowed him to slip away from us."[26] As penance, Harold searched—in vain—for effective treatments.

And the money kept flowing out: $30,000 for portraits, $5 million for Villa Turicum, $2 million for pearls, $150,000 on airplane development,[27] $10,000 for the theater, generous donations to the opera and the infectious diseases institute, payroll for the full staffs at both the Bastion and Villa Turicum, and countless purchases of furniture, jewelry, and artwork.

It was too much. Even for the Rockefellers and the McCormicks, it was too much. Senior disapproved. Junior disapproved. Edith and Harold wheedled for financial help, for more stocks, for more cash. It was a slippery slope, and they were headed down.

TRYING TO STAY SANE

1911–13

*T*he mad pace couldn't continue. Edith's panic attacks began in 1911. Ironically, the first one took place at the opera, one of Edith's favorite places. Heart pounding, sweaty, dizzy, she alerted Harold, who quietly escorted her home. They chalked the first episode up to illness, but several months later it happened again, this time at a private dinner at brother-in-law Cyrus's house in Lake Forest. Apologies were made, a quick exit managed, and then concerns set in. A doctor was summoned: Edith needed rest.

It came in the wake of witnessing the deaths at the 1911 International Aviation Meet.

It came in the wake of a minor automobile accident involving fourteen-year-old son Fowler as passenger. He was fine, but there were too many cars, too many possibilities for disaster.[1]

It came in the wake of a train catastrophe. Harold had been on board the Twentieth Century Unlimited when a broken rail tossed five train cars into the Hudson River. While Harold had not been hurt, twenty-five people were injured.[2] All forms of transportation were treacherous.

It came in the wake of a fire at the Bastion that fairly destroyed the top three floors. The family had been in Europe at the time and remained out of the country, buying replacement furniture and artwork, until the repairs were complete.[3] No place was safe, not even her Bastion.

It came in the wake of everything: two dead children, tuberculosis of the kidney, mentally ill siblings, public disapproval, endless social engagements and financial obligations. Danger was everywhere. Everything threatened risk: planes, trains, cars, fire, children, love.

Edith was down for the count. Year after year of stress had finally taken its toll. Insanity was a real threat: it had already claimed Stanley, Bessie, and Mary Virginia.

Like all the Rockefellers, Edith was no stranger to nervous maladies, having visited more than her share of rest cures and sanatoriums over the years. In this case, frustrated by the lack of lasting results at these august institutions, she simply took to her own bed. Her nights were haunted with such bad dreams that she would walk the rooms of the Bastion at night and sleep during the day.[4] She spent most of her time in her Bosque, her private garden. Taking air was crucial for the constitution.

Harold and Edith had planned a grand cotillion at Villa Turicum for early September 1911. Always loath to cancel a good party, they kept it on the books, and soon the decorators, cooks, and household staff were in full swing. However, this time, unlike all the others—her wedding, Alta's wedding, their 1904 fête champêtre—Edith couldn't do it. Despite weeks of forced rest, of peace and quiet, her nerves were still frayed. She could not be in such a crowd, with so many people. The day before the cotillion, Harold and Edith canceled. This cancellation speaks volumes about their level of concern.

Edith, more than anything, feared breaking down in public. Brother-in-law Stanley had suffered a major episode in the middle of a dance floor. The McCormicks knew any such event would be front-page news across the country. Instead, the *Daily Tribune* reported, "Mrs. Harold F. McCormick, her nerves unstrung, has left Chicago precipitously in search of rest. Mrs. McCormick on Monday recalled invitations for a dinner dance planned for last night. She left Monday evening for Tarrytown, N.Y., where she will be the guest of her parents, Mr. and Mrs. John D. Rockefeller, until late in October. 'Mrs. McCormick has been going about a great deal this summer,' Harold F. McCormick said last night at his town residence. 'She is simply tired and has gone away to rest up. There is nothing serious about her condition.' . . . Mrs. McCormick has not been strong for the last two years. With a manner which indicates entire lack of nerves, Mrs. McCormick in reality has been a sufferer from great nervousness for some time."[5]

While Harold announced to the papers that Edith had departed for Pocantico, in fact she remained holed up at the Bastion. It is quite possible she was simply unable to travel. In any case, only family and the household staff knew she was there. Villa Turicum, with its idyllic setting and lavish space, was not an option due to the neighboring naval base's bombastic shelling practice.[6]

Harold wrote to Senior, "Edith is now taking a rest at 1000 Lake Shore Drive isolating herself from everybody and spending from 5 to 8 hours a day out in the air and I think this will do her more good than anything else at the present time if she will just keep it up long enough."[7]

She had every intention of remaining isolated longer, of continuing her healing, but Edith couldn't resist the opera season. When the 1911–12 season began in November, she was once again in box 5—terrified of another panic attack but present nonetheless.

Other obligations were knocking too. City planner Daniel Burnham was working with Edith on a lakefront beautification plan for Lake Forest that involved offshore manmade islands, pleasure piers, harbors, and beaches.[8] Edith explained to the mayor of Lake Forest that the plan involved driving piles in the lake at various points, around which sand would accumulate and create islands.[9] Despite her need for rest, Edith would not have been inclined to deny Daniel Burnham.

In July 1912 the Aero Club honored Harold at a gala event for four hundred people, thanking him for his efforts with the Aviation Meet.[10] Edith and Harold had to attend. Once people knew she was back in circulation, it was harder to decline invitations, and soon Edith was back to her untenable schedule.

Perhaps getting away was the answer? Some time away from the demands of Chicago, of Harold's work and Edith's social commitments. Making no small plans, Edith and Harold decided on a world tour: a full year of travel with the three children, mother-in-law Nettie, governesses and tutors, maids, and the family doctor. Europe, then Russia and the Far East, a leisurely journey filled with beautiful sights, fresh air, and plenty of time. Edith had a particular interest in Japan, and the couple had tried numerous times, including back in 1897 while still in Iowa, to make that part of their travel plans, but there never seemed to be enough time to make it worthwhile.[11]

But even as they planned, it became clear that Harold couldn't be away from his multitude of responsibilities (International Harvester, Stanley, Mary Virginia, the Grand Opera Company, Jack's memorial institute, all his boards) for that long, so they scaled back. They settled on just a few months of motoring in England and some time on the Continent. They'd leave in the summer and be back in time for the opera season in November.

Planning for the journey involved so many logistics: schedules, reservations, trunks, gowns, paperwork. Somehow, miraculously, the entourage managed to get to New York City on July 3, scheduled to sail for Europe on July 5. But that never happened.

Edith couldn't do it. She could not even begin to think about boarding that ship. She couldn't fathom spending two weeks trapped on a vessel surrounded by the black depths. The *Titanic* had gone down just three months earlier. Risks. Everywhere.

The crossing was canceled; the tour was scrapped. The children went to stay with Senior, Nettie went to vacation with Harold's sister Anita in the Adirondacks, and Harold took Edith to Dr. Andrew Foord's private sanatorium outside of Ellenville, New York.[12]

Harold wrote to Senior: "Well, here we are after cancelling at the last moment our sailings. I really believe this is the great place for Edith. The Doctor—a splendid man told me confidentially that if Edith would give him her interest, heart, and cooperation, that he could cure her in 10 weeks. But if she fights and opposes the treatment would be of much much less effect if any at all would be realized. The difficulty Edith has to contend with is the giving up of herself entirely to the treatment. . . . This has always been her difficulty."[13]

While Harold and Senior urged Edith to submit herself entirely to Dr. Foord's treatment, she had other ideas. Harold's cousin Medill McCormick, who suffered from alcoholism and depression, had recommended Dr. Carl Jung to Harold.[14] Jung worked at the Burghölzli Hospital in Zurich, where Harold had been seen years earlier. Jung had recently broken off with Dr. Sigmund Freud, developing a new field that he called "synthetic psychology," which involved personality analysis, dream interpretation, and other, more mystical elements. Edith felt this was worth a try. Fortunately, Dr. Jung was in New York for a conference at Fordham University and agreed to meet Edith at Pocantico, where they spent several days talking.

Jung wrote to a physician colleague, Dr. Smith Ely Jelliffe, about Edith years later: "You mention Mrs. McCormick. . . . She was such a case of latent sch[izophrenia] and was very much on the edge when I treated her. She dreamt right in the beginning of her analysis of a tree struck by lightning and split in half. ('Bruchlinie!') This is, what one calls a 'bad' symbol. Another case, that suffers now from hallucinations and ideas of perseveration, formerly produced pictures with 'Bruchlinien,' breaking lines."[15]

It is interesting to note that brother-in-law Stanley McCormick's barred mansion, Riven Rock, was given its name because of a large boulder that had been divided in half by a large oak, perhaps a perfect (and fitting) example of *Bruchlinie*.[16] Jelliffe was also one of the many prominent doctors who consulted on Stanley's case. By now, the McCormick siblings were amateur experts on nervous disorders.

Jung met Senior; this did not go well. Senior was not a fan of the "talking cure" and, given his own father's career choice as charlatan, was immediately suspicious. The relationship would never improve.[17]

There was plenty of work for Jung. Harold urged Anita to come to New York to meet Jung and discuss Stanley;[18] Nettie begged Jung to travel to California for an in-person assessment.[19] Everyone was desperate for answers. Harold and Jung got along well, the beginnings of what would be a lasting friendship.

Jung agreed to work with Edith, although he confided to Harold that Edith was "the toughest problem he ever had to deal with."[20] While Edith offered to buy him a house in America and provide him with a steady stream of clients, he insisted on returning to Switzerland.[21] This, then, was a problem. In order to work with Jung, the only person she felt might be able to help her, Edith would need to travel to Zurich. That seemed an impossibility.

For the time being, fortified enough by her retreat, Edith and family returned to Chicago to prepare for what lay ahead. From November through February, the social dance card was full. The McCormicks hosted opera dinners and postconcert receptions and attended nearly every one of the sixty nights of opera. In addition, they had their usual complement of club meetings and charity events, and Edith even hosted a series of dance lessons at the Bastion to teach ladies how to dance rags and the Argentine tango.[22] She attended a lecture by explorer Roald Amundsen[23] and hosted a discussion at the Bastion on the "History of Manhood Suffrage."[24]

It is notable that Edith was taking her first steps to support the woman suffrage movement, also attending a conference on the topic at Orchestra Hall. She was clearly not at the forefront of this cause, as the newspapers noted: "Practically all of her north side friends had joined the . . . suffrage organization before Mrs. McCormick was converted. Her friends urged her to join. Mr. McCormick proclaimed his allegiance to the women's cause before she made up her mind."[25]

At this point, Edith's views on gender roles seem to have been thoroughly traditional, her mother's maxims still ringing in her ears. While sister-in-law Katharine was traveling around the country to rally support for woman suffrage and meeting with the president to advocate for the vote, Edith was stuck in an older framework. In 1911, she warned women against putting themselves first: "I have noticed that when the wife assumes the responsibility of leading, her husband almost invariably ceases to develop and becomes dwarfed in his nature; whereas, on the other hand, when the husband keeps the head and leads in carrying out his profession, the wife has every opportunity of self-improvement and self-development, thereby rising step by step with her husband and being prepared for any position for which his success calls."[26]

While she did finally jump on the bandwagon, it was only after having received her husband's blessing. Edith and Harold also provided use of the Bastion for a gala garden dance for the Chicago Equal Suffrage Association, including heavy-hitters Anna Howard Shaw and Carrie Chapman Catt, an event she missed while abroad with Jung.[27]

Edith would have been far more passionate about attending the opening of the Durand Hospital of the John R. McCormick Memorial Institute for Infectious Diseases that winter, in February 1913, as it was an outgrowth of their tribute to baby Jack. When begun in late 1901, the institute— intended to provide free care for poor patients suffering from scarlet fever, diphtheria, measles, mumps, and whooping cough and also support critical research into those diseases—rented space in the Presbyterian Hospital as a temporary measure until the institute could build a hospital of its own. However, finding a suitable location proved difficult, as residents in targeted neighborhoods protested vehemently against its construction, arguing the risk of contagion was too high.[28] The University of Chicago was interested in doing a joint venture, but Edith refused, fearing loss of control if it was taken under the wing of an existing institution.[29]

Frustrating lost years went by, but now, at last, there was a physical location at the corner of Wood and Flournoy Streets, a two-story building large enough to house sixty beds. A large laboratory building was to follow the next year. Edith was very hands-on in the design of the space. It is notable that the superintendent was a woman: a registered nurse by the name of

Charlotte Johnson.[30] The register of staff members lists a resident physician by the name of Dr. George F. Dick, who—along with his wife, Gladys—would go on to isolate the bacterium for scarlet fever a decade later.[31]

In what was truly a grand facade, Harold and Edith attended the annual Arabian Nights Ball in January 1913, a costume fundraiser representing the royal families of India, Egypt, and Turkey. Edith, about to submit herself to months of treatment for what Jung considered borderline schizophrenia, regaled the crowd as the queen of Sheba, accompanied by six ladies-in-waiting. The *Chicago Daily Tribune* reported she wore "a gown such as might have shamed the simplicity of any costume the real queen ever wore. It was of accordion plaited white chiffon reaching to the ankles and there finished with a fringe of gold. A broad girdle of jewels hung nearly down the front of the gown. From the shoulders swept a mantle of cloth of gold encrusted with jewels of various shades. In her hand she carried a wonderful peacock fan and on her head was a helmet . . . and she was draped in ropes and ropes of jewels, with snakes and bracelets of various designs clasping her arm."[32]

When time came to push off to New York to prepare for their crossing, they did it in style by hosting a gala Italian garden dance for four hundred in the gold ballroom at the Congress Hotel as their farewell. It was a reprise of their fête champêtre years earlier, only indoors, with the ballroom transformed into a garden with hundreds of arbor vitae trees, plants, and flowers. Canvases painted to look like the sky were hung from the ceiling and draped on the walls. Guests dined on imported grapes, Puerto Rican melons, and other out-of-season fruits. The evening began at 11 P.M., and when the dancing commenced after dinner, Edith was ready to show off her new moves.[33] All in all, a remarkable show of planning and execution by someone deemed on the verge of a breakdown.

While Harold participated in a tennis tournament in New York, Edith worked with Dr. Maria Moltzer, an associate of Dr. Jung's, who had been dispatched to the States to coach Edith through the necessary travel. But after several weeks of fruitless therapy, Edith insisted only Jung could do the job. Moltzer returned to Switzerland, practically crisscrossing with Jung as he sailed to New York to fetch his wealthy client.[34]

After three weeks of daily analysis, on April 1, 1913, almost exactly a year after the *Titanic* disaster, Carl Jung managed to coerce Edith onto the steamer *Kronprinzessin Cecilie*. Their sailing party included Fowler and his tutor, Muriel and her guardian, and Edith's trusted maid Emmy. At the very last moment, Harold was called back to Chicago after his tennis tournament, due to a government prosecution of International Harvester.

The plan was for Harold and Mathilde to travel to Switzerland in May.

The plan was for all to return in the fall.

The plan was for a quick recovery.

But things didn't exactly go as planned.

Edith wouldn't touch American soil for many years. Nor would she ever see her mother or father again.

A NEW FATHER FIGURE

1913–14

*O*nce Edith was safely installed in a suite in the stately Hotel Baur au Lac in Zurich, her madly spinning world slowed to a manageable pace. Freed of her social obligations and the duties of two households, she was suddenly responsible only for her own well-being. Here there were no traditional roles to play, no heavy expectations, no demands.

It was time to decompress. There were daily sessions with Dr. Jung to discuss her state of mind, her childhood, and her fears. These took place at his home in Küsnacht, a suburb four miles outside of Zurich. Edith hired a chauffeur to drive her there every morning, wait during her hourlong session, then follow along slowly behind her as she walked home. She was adamant in her belief that the exercise and routine were a vital part of her recovery.

Her driver, Emile Ammann, recalled how important it was for Edith to adhere to that routine, describing one day when they were caught in an unexpected downpour. Edith had forgotten her umbrella, yet she rebuked his suggestion that she might get in the car, creating a bizarre scene that caused passersby to stop and stare: "The torrential rain gradually became a complete deluge. The puddles on the streets swelled to streams and lakes. Still, Mrs. Rockefeller continued her stoic walk . . . and I drove after her at a snail's pace. From the seat of my car, I could watch her precious hat slowly dissolve. Her dripping dress clung to her body like a bathing suit after a water baptism. How Madame began to tremble and freeze, but with such equanimity she strode, as though water was her life-giving element. Was she crazy? Or was I?"[1]

Carl Jung had recently separated philosophically from Sigmund Freud and was still relatively unknown. In the years Edith worked with him, he would publish his revolutionary ideas about archetypes, collective unconscious, personality types such as introverts and extroverts, and the psychological complex. While he tamed Edith's demons, she reciprocated by becoming his leading patroness.

Whether Carl Jung was as useful for Edith as she was for him is questionable. Jung biographer Richard Noll, in *Aryan Christ*, states, "Without her, he might never have succeeded. With her, he became known to the entire world. Yet despite her own celebrity, few know of the fateful collaboration of the Rockefeller psychoanalyst and C. G. Jung."[2]

Her first few months with him were full of dream analysis, mandala drawing, and discussion. Attempting to overturn her imperial complex, he had her scrub the floor in her hotel bathroom.[3] As she flew under the radar, Edith's first few months were refreshingly clear of requests from other people: requests for her time, her attention, her money.

As for her children, the oldest, Fowler, was off touring Italy and Germany—including a flight on the zeppelin—with his tutor and a friend before returning to the States to attend Groton School. Middle child Muriel had her own suite at the Baur au Lac and was tended by her governess, Miss Beley. She remained headstrong, volatile. And the youngest, Mathilde, was still in Illinois, playing hostess for her father's events at Villa Turicum.[4] And it was quite the party.

Harold was a pleasure seeker. Unburdened from his worries of Edith, and finally free to live according to his own (considerably less stringent) rules, he was having the summer of his life. He had installed an aviator friend, Charles Witmer, at Villa Turicum and was hosting flying parties over Lake Michigan on virtually every day that weather allowed. His Curtis flying boat, named *Edith*, was the only privately owned airboat in the country and was quite the lure. Chicago's party crowd showed up in force, clad in bathing suits and cork coats, in case of disaster. Host extraordinaire Harold manned the motorboat that shadowed the aircraft.[5] Society columnist "Mme. X." shared her experience in great detail, concluding, "The writer candidly confesses that her first flight in the 'Edith' was the supreme experience in a not uneventful life. . . . Henceforth the only perfect joy, one that transcends all others, is flying."[6] The newspapers also indicated that the three women included in Harold's flights were the first women ever to fly in an airboat.[7] A few years later, Fowler and Witmer would collaborate with the Army Air Corps to film the first aerial footage of Chicago.[8]

The newspapers were full of Harold's adventures: he'd been aero-commuting, using the airboat to fly from Lake Forest to Chicago each day; Harold was captain of the country club polo team; Harold and his chauffeur had been sideswiped by a train when his car stalled on the tracks;[9] Harold went overboard twice in one day in his motorboat while trying to rescue capsized boaters;[10] unexpected guests were appearing at Villa Turicum at all hours requesting rides in the airboat.

Harold, with his cheerful whistle and friendly smile, was as gregarious as Edith was introverted. While they were perfectly matched in terms of societal standing, civic engagement, and outlandish spending, they were polar opposites in personality and desires. Carl Jung was helping Edith understand her own nature, and she was beginning to realize that her needs were not being met. Gradually she began to leave behind the moral imperatives imposed by her parents and society and cultivate her own set of beliefs.

Having come to recognize that intellectual pursuits were a source of pleasure, Edith began taking classes in a wide variety of subjects: biology, history, music, astronomy, and various languages. Professors from the local university came to her hotel suite to give private lessons.[11] She took all instruction, and her therapy, in German, in which she had become quite fluent. And slowly, Edith began to thrive. She was at the heart of a new type of thought and believed that Jung's ideals of individuation—that every person had a critical role to play in society and must fully utilize their conscious and unconscious self to accomplish this—could be truly life-changing for people. She immersed herself in Kant and adopted Nietzsche's notion of abandoning Christianity in favor of developing a personal sense of morality toward the realization of an Übermensch, or superman.

Noll suggests, "Jung's magical world must have been tremendously attractive to Edith at that time. She had suffered the loss of two children and had withdrawn emotionally from her husband and from her surviving children. She needed help and found it in Zurich. She came alive for the first time. Her former life, her former country, could not compare with the opportunity to participate in the salvation of the world and the birthing of a new god."[12]

Ron Chernow describes Edith as "a dreamer caught up in the cultlike atmosphere of Jung's practice. Yet in the Rockefeller family, she was a pioneer, the first to peer into the mysteries of human nature and confront social inhibitions and moral restraints that had long been held sacrosanct by the family."[13]

When Harold and Mathilde finally made the crossing in September, Edith was firm that she would not be returning in November.[14] She had found a place to belong. They enrolled Mathilde in the Sanatorium Schweizerhof in Davos, a mountain retreat several hours away to "brace up" her respiratory issues; Fowler returned to the States to attend Groton; and Muriel was assigned to a day school in Zurich. Though Harold had to travel back and forth between Chicago and Zurich, Edith and the two girls were going to stay in Switzerland.

At the end of 1913 Harold tried to reassure an unimpressed Senior, "In a word, Edith is becoming very real, and true to herself, and is seeking and I am sure will succeed, to find her path. . . . At any rate, she is in absolutely safe and trustworthy hands, for no finer man ever breathed than Dr. Jung. He has an intense admiration for Edith and yet recognizes that she is the toughest problem he ever had to deal with. At first he was doubtful of success and questioned what he would find. Now he sees a wonderful personality to engage his thought and his very best and most conscientious efforts. He sees it is much worthwhile!"[15]

Shortly after Harold penned this letter, Jung abruptly ended his sessions with Edith. In fact, he ceased treating patients entirely while he undertook his own "descent into the underworld," a series of experiments in which he tried to actively explore his own unconscious.[16] Edith continued the assignments he had given her: dream analysis, journaling, drawing, reading, studying. Part of her treatment concerned her travel fears, now full blown into phobia. Jung had assigned her ever-longer train journeys, suggesting that she have her chauffeur Ammann follow the train in the limousine in case she needed a quick exit and return home.

Ammann gave this entertaining rendition of the experience: "Mrs. Rockefeller approached me and said, 'I must learn to ride on the train. Tomorrow, take me to the train station. I will take the 9:00 A.M. train towards Rapperswill. Stay on the platform until the train departs. But then drive the car as fast as possible. Make sure you meet the train at each station, for I shall not be able to go far.' Said and done. I drove her to the station and watched from a distance as she boarded the train. Everything went according to plan. At the first whistle, however, the train door opened. From the compartment of her car bolted—no, flew—Mrs. Rockefeller. The station master had just enough time to catch her in his arms. 'Ammann,' she gasped, 'Ammann, I won't be traveling today. But maybe . . . tomorrow.' This scene repeated itself in the days to follow.'"[17]

As Edith progressed in her ability to travel, Ammann would indeed race alongside the train, so as to meet her at the next stop. Edith's short-term goal was to be able to travel to the city of Parma, Italy, where her friend, conductor Cleofonte Campanini, was the chief organizer and financial guarantor of a festival to honor composer Giuseppe Verdi. Loath to deny Maestro Campanini any wish, Edith and Harold had been among the principal contributors to an imposing monument honoring the composer.[18]

Verdi's hometown had decided to celebrate the centenary of his birth with the creation of a triumphal arch. On top of the massive arch was a chariot drawn by four lions and driven by the allegorical figure of Glory. The base of the arch expanded into two arms forming a semicircle encompassing seventeen smaller arches housing twenty-eight statues of key figures from Verdi's operas. The pillars were inscribed with lyrics from Verdi's choruses. Standing before the main archway was a rectangular granite prism with bronze bas-reliefs representing the composer, in a classical robe, accompanied by the figures of Poetry, Melody, and Music.[19] Designed by architect Lamberto Cusani and incorporating the beautiful sculptures of Ettore Ximenes, when finished in 1919, after utilizing 250 workers in the process, the monument would be considered one of Italy's greatest architectural works.[20]

Along with a large contribution toward the monument, the McCormicks had given additional money to establish the Edith McCormick Prize, worth $4,000, for the best new opera. To thank them for their generosity, Parma appointed Harold an honorary citizen, though Harold was the first to admit the contributions had been Edith's idea.[21]

Parma hosted what was almost a miniature World's Fair for the centennial, with aviation displays, agricultural exhibits, motoring tournaments, donkey and ostrich rides, fireworks, and open-air movies. It was right up Harold's alley—and thus a pity neither McCormick was able to attend. Harold was still in Chicago, and Edith, in tremendous frustration, found herself unable to get on the train.[22] To fail in her attempt to be with Campanini on this festive occasion must have deeply pained her.

When she did manage to overcome her fears, a week late, the organizers in Parma staged a second ground-breaking for her. In his book about Campanini, Gaspare Nello Vetro describes Edith's arrival in a private train car, accompanied by Muriel and a physician: "The station was paved with Italian and American flags, a squad of traffic policemen in uniform made the honors and, to welcome the host, together with the Campanini spouses, there was the mayor Mariotti and municipal authorities. Between two wings of a cheering crowd, they accompanied the lady to the Croce Bianca hotel."[23] Aside from this adoration, they presented Edith with a proclamation on parchment, framed in silver, and it is said she accepted these honors with perfect Italian and presented the workmen with a crisp one hundred dollars to share.[24]

But the trip came at great cost. The dangers of travel and the foreignness of new places overwhelmed Edith's sensitivities. She would not leave Switzerland again for a very long time.

Zurich was a good place to be. While tensions were mounting in Germany, France, Russia, and Austro-Hungary, Switzerland sat quietly amid its mountains and neutrality. Edith had no desire to venture out.

Back in the States, the Rockefeller name was again under attack. Frustrated by a nine-month standoff by coal miners striking for better pay and conditions, the Colorado National Guard set fire to a tent city in Ludlow. Tragically, the fire resulted in the death of two dozen people, including eleven children. Junior owned Colorado Fuel and Iron, one of the companies involved. Dubbed the Ludlow Massacre, the event was another opportunity to portray the Rockefellers as greedy barons.[25] The wealthy had become targets, with financier J. P. Morgan even being attacked in his home.

Yes, Switzerland was a good place to be.

In June 1914, Edith sent her father birthday greetings: "Dear Father, This little word I am sending to you for your birthday with much love. I know and have felt deeply what this last year has meant to you. We all have our hard problems to face—this is living. And I feel that you will rise above the things which are difficult for us all now, and realize that we must all fulfill our greater Destiny. The Great Divine guiding Spirit cannot do things wrong. And when we feel them wrong it is because we ourselves are not in tune. You have a trust which has always been near and strong, and I know that with each coming new day it grows brighter and stronger. I love you and I am happy in your continued health and vigor."[26]

The letters from home were frequent and demanding. They came not only from Senior but from mothers Cettie and Nettie, Fowler, Junior, Alta, even Cyrus. Come home now! The situation is dangerous; come back now! You must bring your family to safety! They tried employing family reasons to return: early September would bring a joint celebration for Cettie's seventy-fifth birthday and a fiftieth wedding anniversary for Senior and Cettie. Furthermore, Cettie was not in good health, suffering from congestive heart failure, pleurisy, and lumbago. She was wheelchair-bound and very weak. Edith's family implored her to come see her mother. But their requests fell on deaf ears. Whether Edith was physically unable to manage the journey or simply did not want to go remains uncertain.

Once war broke out, the family ratcheted up efforts to extract Edith from Europe. Harold and Fowler booked a crossing to fetch her in August, but it was canceled due to threatening submarine attacks.[27] Harold next attempted to hire a private yacht to collect her, an effort that failed on his end but certainly would have been pointless, given her travel phobias.

In August, Edith wrote Senior, "We are in the midst of war preparations and it is an experience of no little interest. Everything is in suspense and uncertain. All the Austrian and German waiters have gone to join their regiments, so that we are all obliged to eat together at the big table. The hotel has laid in provisions for six months. . . . One can buy no more automobile gasoline. . . . The banks will not give money on letters of credit. No one has cash and I do not know what we are going to do. The train connections and mail with Germany and Austria are cut off. All the railroads are being now used to transport the troops. The situation is very serious. We are being calm and generally waiting. We will help where we can and do our best in every way. Do not worry. There is a great power watching over us all. I send you much love."[28]

Harold solved the problem of Edith not being able to get money from the banks by having a Swiss-based International Harvester representative hand-deliver a suitcase full of gold bars.[29] And though gasoline was being rationed, Harold managed to arrange for special deliveries from Italy through International Harvester, and the Swiss government granted Edith special dispensation.[30]

But try as they may, the family couldn't get Edith and her two daughters home. Sister Alta telegrammed Edith prior to the birthday and anniversary celebration: "Mother anxious to have you here on Sept 8. Do try to come."[31] Edith's response: "Not possible to arrive 8 September. Sailing now is difficult and takes much time. I regret this situation."[32]

Senior was not pleased. Edith had now been on what he considered a fool's journey for nearly eighteen months and was badly neglecting her family and responsibilities. She had evolved from her statement just a couple of years earlier in which she preached "what a great influence [a wife] can be in the making or breaking of her husband's life. If for the moment some plan of hers must be given up in order to help along his career, let it be given up, for later, when success has been achieved, the wife finds that she shares her husband's honor by bearing his name."[33] Now, Edith showed no intention of giving up her plan.

Harold was dispatched in September to bring Edith home. This time his crossing went off without a hitch. He reported that two cruisers accompanied his ship for a while in the Atlantic and that a torpedo boat came alongside at Gibraltar, but otherwise it was an uneventful journey.[34] It is possible Harold reveled in risk to the same extent that Edith recoiled from it. He was pleased to be back in Europe, writing his sister Anita that he would do "what Edith feels is best" and that it would be wonderful to see his girls, whom he supposed had "grown as high as office buildings" in his absence.[35]

With the onset of war, Carl Jung had suspended his explorations into his own unconscious and was seeing patients again. While Edith was not back in treatment, Harold began his own therapy. Daughter Muriel, for her part, was being analyzed by Maria Moltzer, in the hopes of stabilizing her mercurial moods.[36]

Harold reported back to his mother, Nettie, "[Edith's] face is almost entirely clear and her step is springy and she walks with her arms free and swinging. She notices all the things of nature and dresses simply and in very artistic taste suitable to her makeup. In the morning we usually take a walk before lunch and in the afternoon also. Then in the evening we sit around the Hotel or go to some moving picture show. . . . Mathilde goes through a regular course of treatment each day and could be discharged by November. . . . One day goes much like another here and the war news absorbs the attention directed towards the outer world."[37]

The burdens on Harold were not insignificant. Aside from playing intermediary between Edith and all her family members, he was trying to steer International Harvester through a major restructuring, continued to oversee the care of his brother Stanley and sister Mary Virginia (including designs for a private Pullman car so she could enjoy train journeys), and was running two households. This was possible only because of his robust sense of duty; just as Harold had promised Santa at the age of seven, he was still trying to be a better boy.

Furthermore, the extended McCormick clan was warring, claiming Harold's father, Cyrus, had taken unfair credit for the reaper invention and that the spoils should be equally divided among all the grandchildren.[38] In decades to come, the Robert McCormick branch of the family would become more well-known for their contributions to Chicago. For now, though, the Cyrus McCormick branch had all the glory, and there was considerable resentment. After all, International Harvester had become the world's largest farm machinery company with over fifty thousand employees worldwide and a worth of more than $400 million.[39]

For Harold, the chance to decompress with Jung was welcome. It wasn't long before he was lured in completely, explaining to Nettie, "Dr. Jung grows on me all the time. You must know him sometime and I hope he will come to America sometime to make us a visit. He would interest you with the many and profound things he knows."[40]

Rather than a triumphant return with Edith on his arm, Harold decided to stay on for a bit, leaving only Fowler back in the States to celebrate Christmas with Senior, Cettie, and other assorted family members. Sixteen-year-old Fowler wrote to Grandma Nettie, "I, too, am deeply disappointed that the entire family is not to-day on this side of the ocean, but I am confident there is some good reason for this not being the case. And I can well understand Mother's feeling about coming back. . . . [She] is very happy in the surroundings and atmosphere of Zurich. She comes and goes and does what she wants, there is ample opportunity and time for study and she has few or no duties imposed on her. Father is divided by his desire to be over here with the business and his friends and family, and his desire to be with Mother. It certainly would simplify matters if Mother could come over. She imagines things worse over here and more difficult than they really are. Don't worry about me!"[41]

For Edith, the transition in allegiance from Senior to Jung was complete, although whether she perceived the analyst as a father figure or as a god could be debated.

In Zurich, an acolyte was at peace. But in New York, a father simmered and a son was cast adrift.

Rockefeller siblings (*clockwise from lower middle*) Bessie, Alta, Edith, and Junior. Courtesy Rockefeller Archive Center.

The Rockefeller family home at Forest Hill, Cleveland.
Courtesy Rockefeller Archive Center.

Brothers Harold (*left*) and Stanley with their father, "Reaper King"
Cyrus McCormick. Courtesy Wisconsin Historical Society, 11079.

Edith and Harold at the time of their wedding.
Courtesy Wisconsin Historical Society, 8374.

The Bastion took up most of a city block. Courtesy
Wisconsin Historical Society, 77204.

The imposing gate that helped make the Bastion feel impenetrable.
Courtesy Chicago History Museum, ICHi-176317; Mildred Mead, photographer.

The Empire Room in the Bastion. Courtesy
Chicago History Museum, ICHi-050403.

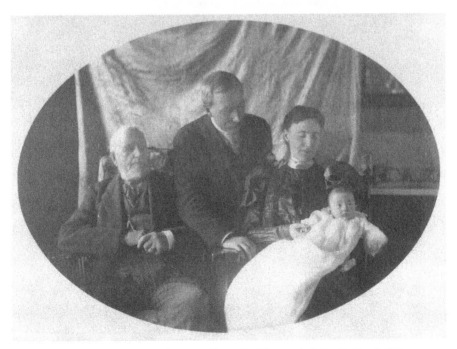

A rare photo of (*from left*) Big Bill Rockefeller with John D. Rockefeller,
Edith, and baby Jack. Courtesy Rockefeller Archive Center.

The happy young family: Harold, Jack, Edith, Fowler.
Courtesy Wisconsin Historical Society, 3631.

The Rockefeller summer home in Pocantico Hills, where
Jack died. Courtesy Rockefeller Archive Center.

(*Back row, from left*) Senior, unidentified young man, Cettie
Rockefeller, and Nettie McCormick, with (*front, from left*) Fowler
and Muriel. Courtesy Wisconsin Historical Society, 8777.

Stanley and Katharine McCormick at their wedding.
Courtesy Wisconsin Historical Society, 11073.

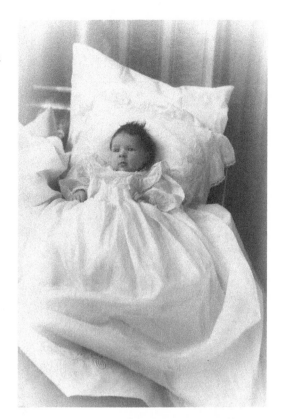

The only known photograph of baby Editha. Courtesy Wisconsin Historical Society, M2002–174.

Frank Lloyd Wright's proposed design for Villa Turicum (not built). Frank Lloyd Wright, *Ausgeführte Bauten und Entwürfe* (Berlin: E. Wasmuth, 1910), Tafel LVIII—Sommer-Wohnsitz für Herrn Harold McCormick, Lake Forest, Illinois (plate 58, summer house for Mr. Harold McCormick, Lake Forest, Illinois), Avery Architectural and Fine Arts Library, Columbia University.

An aerial view of Villa Turicum. Courtesy of the History Center
of Lake Forest–Lake Bluff. Photo by Chicago Aerial Survey.

An interior shot of Villa Turicum. Courtesy
Chicago History Museum, ICHi-176314.

IN FOR THE LONG HAUL

1915–16

Dear Father, Harold's cable informing me of Mother's death came as a surprise for while I knew that Mother was ill I did not know that the end would come so suddenly.

I am sad that I have no longer an earthly Mother, that I shall never be able to sit down and talk with my Mother again. But I am glad that her suffering is now over and that her spirit is at peace. She was always like the Spartan mothers. Everything which came to her, she accepted and she bore her frailty of body with uncomplaining patience. With a quiet determination and with a great will she went right on, and she saw her path clearly. I regret that I did not see her again, but it was meant to be so, and my life will bear witness to my Mother. If a name is not pulled down it is raised and honor is brought to it by the lives of those who bear it.

I wish I could be with you now in these first days of a new adaptation to life. As the great Chinese Philosopher who lived six hundred years before Christ says, We should be like water flowing on, no matter what obstacles have to be overcome, either getting over them, or getting around them, but someway or other always flowing on. You and Mother helped me to adapt myself to life again after Jack died, and I should like to be with you now. But I know that you feel my love and my thoughts near you. I know that Mother's spirit is going on in a beautiful development, so while I am sad that I shall not see her again, I am happy for her.

My love is with you, dear Father. Your loving daughter, Edith.[1]

Edith's letter traveled where she couldn't: across the Atlantic, to New York, to be at her father's side for Cettie's funeral. Harold, temporarily back in the States for his nephew Cyrus's wedding, had been at Cettie's bedside when she died in her sleep, thereby cementing his position as preferred family member. Senior's dissatisfaction with Edith was growing exponentially.

Still, Harold, eager to resume his work with Dr. Jung, traveled back to Zurich in March 1915, choosing to travel on an Italian steamer carrying 142 horses and merely eight passengers. He reported a rough voyage and that they traveled with their lights extinguished as a safety measure.[2] Two months later, the Germans would sink the *Lusitania* and escalate the war. (One of Harold's many McCormick cousins, Harold Stone, was one of the over one thousand fatalities.) Fowler managed to make the crossing in June, and, with the exception of Mathilde, who was still in Davos, the family was together again for the first time in two years. Harold intended to stay only a few months, but that would extend to three years.[3]

While Jung had encouraged Edith to explore her emotions, he suggested the opposite course of action for Harold. As extrovert Harold explained to Senior, "Now I am learning a little the new way, and I am trying to learn to think, for I have always had a superabundance of 'feelings.' With Edith it's just exactly the other way. So it goes."[4]

Under Jung's tutelage, Harold began writing treatises: one on the development of aviation; a personality analysis of longtime family friend Woodrow Wilson; a piece outlining the economic benefits of peace in Europe titled "Cash Value of Ultimate Peace Terms"; and his magnum opus, *Via Pacis,*[5] his peace plan. Edith, the more intellectual of the two, provided editing and advice. They had *Via Pacis* published and sent copies to President Wilson and other top American officials. Then Harold began meeting with European leaders to present his solution to the escalating hostilities. Unfortunately, *Via Pacis* was misconstrued as a pacifist position; people felt its goal was to protest American involvement in the war, and soon the State Department chastised Harold to stop meeting with foreign officials.[6]

By now, word had leaked out that the McCormick clan was in town, and the requests for financial assistance began. One of the prime recipients of their generosity was Jung himself. Firm believers in his methods and philosophy, the McCormicks gave handsomely to underwrite translations of his work into English, French, and Russian. As the years went on, their contributions to his work increased.

Peaceful Zurich was a refuge for artists, and the community thrived with theater, coffee shop performances and discussions, and music recitals as these artistic souls interacted. They were talented but unemployed, and Edith stepped into the breach, providing financial support, usually anonymously. She sponsored numerous musicians and composers, including Ermanno Wolf-Ferrari, Philipp Jarnach, and Otto Luening.

Wisconsin-born Luening described his first meeting with Edith, in her Hotel Baur au Lac suite: "She looked like her father, John D. Rockefeller, Sr. Her face was plain and oval, with remarkable pale-blue eyes. Her glance was sympathetic, warm, and understanding, and she seemed to observe everything that was going on about her. Her skin was like old parchment, only creamy. She seemed either to be skillfully made up or not to use any makeup at all. Her hair was tied in a very plain German style."[7]

As they discussed how America needed more gifted composers, Edith opened the wall safe, removed a wad of Swiss money, placed it in an envelope, and handed it to Luening. She demanded he take a two-month vacation, then return to Zurich to continue his studies. She had one stipulation: he would eventually return to America and settle in Chicago.

Edith supported Luening for several years, having money transferred directly into an account for him at a Swiss bank. They met occasionally to discuss his progress. He summed up their relationship after her death: "Mrs. McCormick never interfered with my studies in any way. . . . She listened to my adventures with obvious interest and was often quite complimentary about my development as a human being. . . . I heard from others— and I agree—that in her relations with many of us she functioned partly as therapist. She let us talk without trying to direct us, but she gave us some guidance, assurance, and reassurance in our work. For me, this was very helpful. She was definitely not a patroness of the ordinary kind. One felt from her a strong understanding and an empathy that were often unspoken. Later, she was appreciative of anything I did that was in any way substantial, and when I had a performance she was pleased and supportive. My relationship with her has had a lasting influence on my life."[8]

Another young artist, a feisty writer from Ireland by the name of James Joyce, received notice from a bank that an account had been set up in his name and that he would be receiving a thousand francs a month from an anonymous donor.[9] Joyce, working on a manuscript called "Ulysses," sought the source and discovered his patroness was Edith. He came to the hotel to thank her in person. She replied, "I know you are a great artist,"[10] and tried to convince him to undergo treatment, which he politely refused.

Edith supported James Joyce for eighteen months before abruptly ending her subsidy. One explanation is that she had learned early on from her father not to let people become too reliant upon her donations. Another is that she sometimes cut off support in order to avoid complacency in the artists.

Or, some historians suggest that perhaps Carl Jung intervened. Having heard reports of the writer's heavy drinking, Jung urged Edith to again attempt to persuade Joyce to begin analysis. When Joyce refused, it is possible Jung took offense and recommended Edith halt her subsidies.[11]

Joyce, however, didn't appreciate the termination. He begged her to see him so he could plead his case; she refused. He sent a portion of the "Ulysses" manuscript in an attempt to change her mind; she refused.[12] "Dear Mr. Joyce," she wrote, "Thank you for the fine manuscript, which I am glad to keep for you with the understanding that, when for any reason, you want it, you have only to write for it. As the Bank told you, I am not able to help you any longer financially. . . . You will find publishers and will come forward yourself, I know."[13]

Once Edith had made up her mind, she would not be swayed. Joyce was frustrated by her denial, writing to a friend, "I wrote a long letter to Mrs. M. asking her very urgently to consider the advisability of the revivability of her aid. That distinguished lady never answered."[14] Scholars speculate that the character of Mrs. Mervyn Talboys in *Ulysses*—a sadistic, haughty society woman—is based on Edith.[15] However, upon Edith's death many years later, James Joyce would strike a tone of forgiveness: "She was very kind to me at a difficult moment and was a woman of considerable distinction."[16]

It is easy to lose sight of the fact that both Carl Jung and James Joyce were yet relative unknowns and that Edith's support buoyed them through critical times.

As to how else Edith and Harold were occupying their time, reports vary. According to chauffeur Emile Ammann, Edith was taking classes in the domestic arts, including knitting and cooking, although the latter came to a sudden halt when Edith found herself disgusted by the feel of shelling hard-boiled eggs. Ammann also reports that Edith wrote incessantly: "She wrote very legibly without even casting a single glance at paper and pen. She wrote while she read the newspaper. She wrote in a traveling automobile while admiring the scenery. She even wrote in her salon while she received visitors."[17]

If true, the amount of journals Edith must have filled is staggering, and their loss somewhere along the way creates a terrible void in reconstructing her life.

There are also indications that perhaps both Harold and Edith were having affairs. Carl Jung invited Harold along on a ten-day walking trip that included both his wife, Emma Jung, and his mistress, Toni Wolff.[18] Jung did not believe in monogamy and likely counseled Harold in overcoming the shame associated with extramarital relationships. There had been speculation in Chicago newspapers for years of Harold's involvement with various opera singers or socialites, and now he was free to act as he wished without worry of word getting back to Senior.

Chauffeur Ammann received the following advice from Edith: "If your subconscious mind causes you to love more than one woman, you mustn't feel guilty. To be sure, you have to respect the existing laws until they are changed. However, psychoanalysis will soon be commonplace and then human laws will be changed accordingly."[19] Her driver took this as her blessing to have an affair with Emmy, Edith's maid, a relationship that continued for several years until Ammann's wife demanded he put an end to it.

Harold had his own suite of rooms, separate from Edith's, which he had personally decorated in bold stripes. After a close encounter with one of Edith's visitors, it is said that Edith demanded, "Harold! You are not to enter my suite without first announcing yourself to Emma [Emmy]."[20] According to Ammann, the sexual liaisons of both McCormicks were daily gossip among the hotel staff and greater Zurich society.[21]

Is it true? Had reserved Edith managed to drop her imperial complex, to allow others close to her? It is easy to imagine her fully engaged in revising Harold's words in *Via Pacis* or overseeing translations of Jung's work into English but considerably harder to believe that she was allowing herself to feel, to take pleasure in her body, to step back into her skin. While there is ample reason to believe Harold's infidelities, whether at his flying parties or at backstage doors, the proof on Edith is sketchier.

Harold resigned from International Harvester in 1916, leaving the reins with very annoyed brother Cyrus. Suffice it to say both Edith's and Harold's families had lost patience with their extended absence, with Harold frequently reassuring Senior—who worried they had joined a cult of sorts—they were not "banqueting" their time away.[22] One of his letters ran nearly two thousand words as he tried to explain the basic tenets of Jung's philosophy.[23] In another, Harold assured, "This is not a tabernacle of joy, but a shrine to which seekers only address themselves, and it is in this spirit that I have again postponed my sailing and that Edith still finds herself held. This is not a place . . . which encourages remaining here beyond the right or the normal time, but the whole question is one of degree at best, for no one who is really interested in analytical psychology and finds it of help ever drops it, because if it is one thing,—it is to be lived, and the more one studies the more one is prepared to live on its basis."[24]

Back in Chicago, few knew of the psychological journeys that Edith and Harold were on—mental disturbances were a subject around which the family maintained strictest secrecy. Newspapers painted a different picture of their time there, including a wealth of misinformation about Edith's activities. The Chicago Daily Tribune reported that the McCormicks were enthralled with Zurich:

> Mrs. McCormick goes boating on the Swiss lakes—she never goes on lake Michigan—she plays tennis daily, and rides, and when at home, her only exercise is walking and dancing.
>
> Then, it seems, she has gathered a very interesting foreign circle at Zurich. Many brilliant Poles, Russians, Greeks, and Serbians are refugees there, and a salon was not difficult to establish; finally both Mr. and Mrs. McCormick are interested in the Red Cross and working for it. So with the war of eleven nations raging on all sides of them the atmosphere is undoubtedly charged with more vital possibilities than Lake Forest in summer.[25]

A more somber newspaper article ran a few months later, after the fatal sinking of the Ancona, an American steamer. Friends who had expected Harold and Edith to return in time for the fall opera season believed the McCormick family was aboard the ill-fated ship. All breathed a sigh of relief to hear they were still safe in Switzerland.[26]

At the end of 1916, Edith summed up her year in a letter to Senior, focusing on emotions, as she'd been coached: "This year has been a year full of problems and full of beauties. As it nears close we look onward with hope, confidence and trust. We know not what is ahead for us, but we do know that we have our love, we have found our paths, so we know that while the road may be a hard one it will have its beauties. You on your path have your philosophy and your religion which guide you. I on my path have my philosophy and my religion which guide me. That they differ makes no harm because we have love which makes the bond between us. I respect the things that you do which I cannot understand, and likewise you respect my individuality and my point of view. So love keeps us close and warm."[27]

PSYCHOLOGICAL CLUB

1916–17

*E*dith and Harold were now in the heart of Jung's inner circle. Jung had built a community of analysts, patients, and believers. For years he'd been giving lectures under a loose organization he called the Psychological Club. Edith encouraged him to take things a step further and obtain a physical location where people could regularly meet to discuss the various aspects of Jung's philosophy.

Jung biographer Richard Noll explains, "Harold and Edith were now zealots when it came to Jung and analytical psychology. And being Rocke-fellers and McCormicks, they knew they had the power to make Jung's influence felt in the world. . . . For Jung and analytical psychology to gain any respectability, it was clear to his American patrons that the Psychological Club needed a building for its lectures, seminars, and other social events and to lodge guests. Plans were made to buy or rent a building in Zurich and renovate it to resemble an American country club."[1]

As usual, Edith had grand plans. She located a desirable property in Feldbach, outside of Zurich proper. However, a railroad ran through it. Much as she had, years earlier, believed she could relocate Jung himself to America by purchasing a house for him, she began efforts to reconfigure the rail line. After much convincing from others, though, she settled instead for a villa with lovely gardens at 1 Loewenstrasse, in the expensive part of Zurich.[2] Edith rented it for a two-year period and provided a hostess, a cook, three servants, and a workman.

The *New York Times* got the wrong impression, reporting that Edith had purchased a Swiss estate with the intent of establishing a hospital for convalescents under the direction of prominent Swiss doctors. The article went on to explain that the Rockefeller Foundation had no knowledge of this undertaking and that the hospital was Edith's own idea and financed entirely by her.[3]

The trouble was, she didn't have the necessary cash. Of the needed $120,000, she borrowed $80,000 from the bank. Then she appealed to Senior for money, specifically Standard Oil stocks: "As a woman of forty-three I should like to have more money to help with. There are causes in which I am interested which are uplifting and of such importance to my development which I cannot help as I should like to because I have not the money. I hope that you will see that as a woman of earnestness of purpose and singleness of spirit I am worthy of more confidence on your part."[4] Her sister Alta, around this time period, also requested more money from Senior, getting in a slight dig at her gallivanting sister: "I think during my whole life I never did anything that you seriously disapproved."[5]

Senior (whose personal fortune was growing at the estimated rate of a hundred dollars a minute)[6] asked for a detailed accounting of Edith's assets and liabilities.[7] In her less-than-thorough reply, she reported that she owned $3 million worth of stocks. Edith indicated her big annual donations were $25,000 to the infectious diseases institute and at least $12,000 to the opera (though she often gave more) and now this one-time gift of $120,000 to establish the Psychological Club. She concluded, "This work is unique in the history of mankind and its far reaching values are inestimable."[8] This was a woefully incomplete tally: adding the Verdi monument, artist stipends, and book translations could have rounded out her philanthropic report.

Her complete list of expenses would have been long indeed, including the Bastion and Villa Turicum, which were still staffed despite the family's absence; several suites in the Hotel Baur au Lac; tuition for the three children; her staff in Switzerland; and regular new additions to her wardrobe. Edith was quick to point out to Senior that she, not Harold, paid for all their Zurich expenses.[9]

In 1913, personal income tax was introduced in the States, a new cost that caused Edith serious headache. By 1919, she owed the IRS $140,000 (equivalent to $2.4 million in 2020). She began selling off some of her securities in order to pay her debts. What she didn't know is that, while she gave Senior limited information about her declining financial situation, the banks were reporting back to him regularly. He, and Junior, knew far more than she thought.

Senior came through with increased stocks for Edith and helped her pay off that IRS bill, but it would, in the years to come, never be enough. Within a few years, she would be nearly a million dollars in debt.

In 1917, Senior restructured his giving to Edith and Alta, doing away with their annual allowances (approximately $30,000 a year) and establishing trusts worth $12 million each. They would have access to the interest (roughly $72,000 a year, minus $7,500 from Edith's allotment that was earmarked for Harold), but not the principal. Senior explained to Edith, "This trust . . . makes very careful provisions for the distribution of the money to your children and to their children, and my belief is that it is better to have the provisions of this paper carried out rather than for you to exercise the power it gives you to dispose of the property at your death by will."[10] In other words, Senior was making sure Edith's children and grandchildren would have money to inherit.

Junior, on the other hand, received well over $400 million as well as the power to manipulate the principal as he wished.[11] There was no such thing as gender equality in the House of Rockefeller. To add insult to injury, Edith's trust was controlled by a committee of five men, including Harold, Junior, and her brother-in-law Parmalee.[12]

In his financial restructuring, Senior had given away the bulk of his fortune to Junior, freeing himself of the burden of most of the charitable giving. He was, after all, nearly eighty, and although he proclaimed he'd live to one hundred, one could never be sure. The average life expectancy for men at the time was fifty-five. One imagines all of his descendants had considered what would happen to his fortune when he died. Edith must have assumed greater wealth was in her future.

For now, all she could do was continue to press for her cause: "Dear Father, I sometimes wish that you could forget that I am a woman, so that you might give to me some of the advantages which John has in administrations. I am very capable, and everyone finds me very resembling you."[13]

Harold added his voice to hers: "In Edith, Father, I see the near counterpart of your personality. I think she is more like you than any other of your children, all attributes considered. . . . Her spirit and beauty of character are to me boundless. She has your purpose and tenacity without one little diminution. Perhaps I should not say these things to you as being out of my province or as being already known to you, but it is quite natural that at this distance and after this length of time you should sometimes find yourself wondering what is being accomplished. I say everything."[14]

Lack of respect from her father and financial inequity with her brother must have rankled Edith, as she sat a world away, studying the great philosophers and pondering the meaning of life. Her duties as mother had fallen yet further away as the children aged; she bore no affiliation to any church anymore; and she had sloughed off her dutiful daughter role by sustained physical absence. Edith was recreating herself in an image of entirely her own making.

The opening of the Psychological Club in 1916 was a triumph for Edith. Before giving a speech to welcome all the members, Carl Jung presented Edith with an inscribed prepublication copy of his *Seven Sermons to the Dead*, which detailed his explorations into his unconscious.[15] Looking around the room, Edith knew everyone and was a vital member of the group. Jung, in a letter to a colleague, explained, "The Club is really originally an idea of Mrs. McCormick. Without the participation of her idea, she would not have condescended so far to our favours."[16]

Whether to reward Edith for her generosity, gain advantage for future "favours," or because he felt she truly warranted the role, Jung anointed her as an analyst. There is no doubt that, while she still had her own unconquered issues, she thoroughly understood his philosophy. Perhaps in an effort to regain her father's respect, she described her work to Senior: "New patients are coming to me all the time, and I have had some fifty cases now. I hear in a year twelve thousand dreams. This work is very concentrated and very difficult,— but so intensely interesting. It is so beautiful to see life and joy come into the eyes of those who have come to me so hopeless and seemingly lost!"[17]

Edith occasionally fell into the role of analyst in her letters with her father, as in a June 1917 letter in which she encouraged him to open up emotionally: "I wish some times that you would let me get nearer to you— you, your real self, so that your heart would feel the warmth of a simple human soul. Perhaps you will let me some day."[18]

And so, her first job, at age forty-three. She would never accept any money for her work as analyst, but it gave her tremendous satisfaction, added a certain element of intrigue to her reputation, and was, she hoped, helpful for her patients.

It was a perfect situation for Edith. Due to wartime restrictions, travel was practically impossible. It rendered her transportation phobias inconsequential. She spent her time studying, hearing other people's dreams, and editing. While the bulk of her time was spent in the Baur au Lac, Edith ventured out for events at the Psychological Club, periodic concerts or theater, and other special occasions. One lecture at the club, on the gospel and Christianity, given by theologian Adolf Keller, would lead to a unique relationship in which she accompanied him on his visits to the poor.

Keller recalled, "One day, she stood before me and declared, 'I want to see other people.' I invited the stiff lady, who wanted out of her ivory tower, to join me on my visits to the poor. For a full year, the daughter of old Rockefeller, perhaps the richest woman in the world, came with me to the small alleyways, where I often led her up the stairs and down the aisles by the hand, such that she had to take out her olfactory bottle, and taught her the life of 'other people' and the phenomenology of poverty. She was passionately interested, even if she could scarcely believe it and seldom spoke."[19] In return, Edith would help support Keller financially.

A believer in numerology and astrology and still an insatiable student of linguistics, Edith became interested in the significance of numbers and letters. She would not have considered it a coincidence that the people in her innermost circle all had names beginning with E. In Greek, the letter eta referred to the quality of being at peace with the world; in old Japanese, it stood for courage; in Hebrew, it was the image of balance. As a student of language, Edith knew names had meaning, and she surrounded herself with the like-minded. There was her maid Emmy; her chauffeur, Emile; her friend Emma Jung; her language tutor, Emil Abegg;[20] and two men who would play pivotal roles in her life: Emil Medtner and Edwin Krenn.

Emil Medtner was a Russian publisher and an influential member of the Russian symbolist movement. The symbolist movement and Jung's thinking were on a similar plane: both stressed spirituality, the individual, and dreams. Emil came to Jung for emotional support and emerged as his friend, even accompanying the family on holidays. He worked closely with Edith both on Russian translations of Jung's work and as the first librarian of the Psychological Club. Intellectual peers and united in their love of Nietzsche, Wagner, and Jung, Edith and Emil became very close. (It must be noted that Emil was an anti-Semite. While Edith was an ardent believer in all things German, there is no evidence that she bore any type of religious prejudice.)

When Edith began to plan for her return to Chicago after the war, her intent was to bring Emil back with her. Medtner's biographer Magnus Ljunggren suggests that Emil considered an offer to travel to the States and become Edith's secretary. While tempted by the possibility of having her serve as a backer for his work, he worried that the offer might ultimately involve marriage, in which he had no interest. Medtner declined Edith's secretarial proposal but accepted her financial assistance for several more years. However, as James Joyce had discovered, Edith was capricious in her giving, causing Medtner untold anxiety. Ljunggren explains, "At times he would still regret not having married her (and the Rockefeller millions), while at others he would write violent tirades ... denouncing her as a 'rabid female,' a cold and unreceptive maternal surrogate who deserved only to be 'whipped.'"[21] He would later consider suing her. Suffice it to say Edith was fortunate they parted ways.

The other significant E was a twenty-five-year-old Austrian by the name of Edwin Krenn. Portly, blond, and always dressed to the nines, Edwin came to Edith for analysis and never left. As Ammann described it, Edwin started with three sessions a week and then gradually increased his visits until he had a daily appointment lasting "'from morning until midnight.' Numerous well-meaning people ... tried to make her understand that the scandal around her was getting bigger and bigger. She answered each time with her favorite phrase: 'This is my problem, and I can do what I please.'"[22]

Edwin Krenn would stay. In the end, he would remain by Edith's side until her death. Whatever his motivations—pure love or pure selfishness—he would be the best friend she ever had. Some historians suggest Edwin was homosexual.[23] Edith helped him obtain Swiss citizenship and maintained forevermore that he was a Swiss architect, a dubious claim at best (Jung biographer Richard Noll claimed Krenn was a gardener).[24] But Austrian or Swiss, architect or gardener, lover or friend, he made Edith happy.

The *New York Evening Journal* would attempt to sum up their relationship years later: "Whether she loved him, there is none can tell, as she never did ... but her cherished companion he was and she paid not the slightest heed to the public's snickers at the spectacle of the middle-aged woman and her youthful escort threading their eventful way through all sorts of social, civic and private ramblings. Their demeanor was always gravely dignified and there was no hint of romancing between them save their constant association."[25]

Perhaps it was all a reaction to Harold's activities, to the orgies it was said he was having in his own suite down the hall. According to Ammann, Harold was living the life his McCormick and Rockefeller relatives forbade in the States, with multiple women, ample amounts of decadent food, and copious quantities of alcohol. He was shaking off decades of responsibility and duty. Ammann relates stories of meeting Harold clandestinely by the loading dock in order to chauffeur him to mysterious engagements, sometimes lasting days or even weeks.[26] Harold's mother Nettie (who found sex immoral except for procreation), Senior, and Junior would have been horrified. Edith's behavior, by comparison, was mild. Was she really engaged in sexual liaisons with Emil and Edwin? It seems likely that her passion was as deeply intellectual as Harold's was wantonly physical.

Since the Jungian community saw no shame in infidelity, perhaps Harold and Edith accepted these new partners, on both sides, with grace. Meanwhile, they were able to present a united front on the issues that mattered to them, including helping those less fortunate. And in wartime there were ample opportunities to do good, to wear those community service hats that fit them so well.

Harold had taken on a role as procurement officer for the United States and spent considerable time at an office handling requests for supplies. This position enabled him to intercede in desperate situations. In August 1917, he received a letter from the American consulate-general in Zurich reading, "Yesterday 40 Americans, men, women and children, refugees from Turkey[,] came through here in a horrible condition, not having had anything to eat for three days and many of them in rags and without underclothing. The world knows of the ready response of your noble and generous hearted wife and yourself to relieve the worthy wants of the poor, made so through this unchristian, uncivilized, and unnecessary war, and I merely present this matter to you for whatever action you might consider just. . . . It does seem like an imposition on the goodness of Mrs. McCormick and yourself and I would not feel the least badly if you reply that you had done enough, for both in Germany and America your generous responses to the demands of the poor and needy are universally known."[27]

A letter dated two days later indicates Harold made a hefty donation to help these refugees, including new clothing for them all.[28] The McCormicks also made large donations to American fund drives, including an ambulance fund organized by Chicago conductor Cleofonte Campanini. Among all the smaller gifts of $1, $5, and $10, Edith's $1,000 contribution stood out.[29]

On another occasion that same year, they hosted fifty-nine American former prisoners of war for dinner at the Baur au Lac. The sailors had been captured by the Germans and tossed aboard the also-captured British freighter the *Yarrowdale*. Bursting at the seams with four hundred prisoners of assorted nationalities, it finally lumbered to Germany, where the men spent three months in the Dulken prison camp. The prisoners had eaten virtually nothing but watery cabbage soup for three months before being released in neutral Switzerland. Harold and Edith fed them generously and also provided fifty francs and new clothing for each of the raggedy young men.[30]

But for sheer excitement, nothing could top their role in the escape of a French flying ace, Lieutenant Eugene Gilbert. Forced to make an emergency landing on Swiss soil, Gilbert was kept under guard in a barracks in Zurich. But one evening, the guard mysteriously wandered off—a startling breach in protocol no proper Swiss could explain. Nearby, a rescuer awaited in a speedy car and whisked the French lieutenant to the city of Lausanne under the cover of darkness. There, on the banks of Lake Geneva, a high-speed motorboat rushed Gilbert to Evian, a French-owned city on the far side. Years later, newspaper reports gave credit for the escape to Edith and Harold, recalling that Gilbert had previously been seen in their presence at dinner dances at the Baur au Lac.[31]

An airplane, a motorboat, and a fast car: it had the mark of Harold on it all along.

A FAMILY IN TATTERS

1917–20

*T*hings began to fall apart. Whereas once the majority of Harold and Edith's family had been in Switzerland, in therapy, working on improving themselves, gradually the family began to splinter.

Perhaps Edith's hands-off approach to child-rearing went overboard, as it appears she had precious little involvement with her children's lives. In keeping with Jung's philosophy, she did not want to interfere with their inherent natures: "I am firmly convinced that perfect freedom in individual development is absolutely necessary. I have observed that in the upbringing of my own children."[1]

Son Fowler began his collegiate career at Princeton, after a stint in France as a Gentleman Volunteer in the Army Ambulance Service and several months in Switzerland.[2] He was an intellectually solid and emotionally balanced young man. While in Zurich, he had furthered his psychological development with Jung and his intellectual awareness by studying Nietzsche, Schopenhauer, and other great German writers. His relationship with Jung would develop into a solid, lifelong friendship.[3]

Mathilde, still breathing the good mountain air in Davos, wrote a letter to Senior, probably at her parents' urging: "Dearest Grandfather: It is a long time since you have heard from me. But they say: 'No news is good news,' so you may be sure that I am getting on famously. Just ten days ago was the fourth year since I came here. Poor little weak thing that I was then. The doctors said that I would not live longer than a few years. And now, four years have gone by, and I am still living, indeed, much healthier and stronger than I ever was. I ride, I skate, I toboggan, I row, and I walk long, long distances, so far and so fast that nobody cares to accompany me."[4]

Six months later, Mathilde sent a follow-up letter: "To me, it is so delightful, so enjoyable to go for long rides in the country with . . . one or the other of the two brothers who own the establishment. I love it and feel it is the only sport I will ever be able to do with all my heart and soul. Both the teachers are very nice gentlemen, one is a very good painter as well as a major in the Swiss army."[5]

Perhaps the family should have paid more attention to their youngest daughter. Mathilde had spent little time in the company of her parents or siblings. While she may have been physically recovered, there were other factors at work in her life that would soon cause family drama.

Senior may have sensed something was afoot, for he sent back a patriotic letter that would prove to be prescient: "We want you all to be true Americans and to love your own country and not to be enamored with the allurements that come especially to our American girls sometimes by the fortune hunters of the world."[6]

Mathilde's older sister, Muriel, had graduated from a German school in Zurich and subsequently enrolled in a French boarding school in Lausanne. She continued to undergo analysis twice a week.[7] Muriel still suffered bouts of temper—Harold reported she was "headstrong and quite perverse"[8]—but was learning to channel her emotions through the arts.

Edith summed up her daughters' personalities in a letter to Senior in 1918. It was one of the last peaceful family reports she would send. "Mathilde leads her class, even though she has to do all her studies in German. She is a lovely girl. Very poised, extremely intelligent, interesting to talk to. Lovable. With Muriel one cannot talk so well—she is not interesting in her thinking for she is the 'doing' type. She plays the piano very well. Then she has a beautiful voice, and sings for her age remarkably. She plays the 'cello. In fact, in music, dancing, and acting she has much talent as also for the languages, speaking four. She has a nature as big as the world, and for this reason she is very difficult at times. But she is learning that this great force in her is to be controlled and used. She is strikingly beautiful."[9]

Harold and Edith's family took their first, and only, full family photographs in 1917 while Mathilde was visiting from Davos.[10] No doubt Senior rejoiced upon getting his copies, knowing that the family was together, albeit briefly. Edith reported to Senior that she was looking for a house to rent, "with the idea of having a little more family life than we have here in the hotel," but she hadn't found anything, in part because she felt they were safer in the hotel.[11]

Jung's Psychological Club was off to a rocky start. While the lectures were useful and well attended, the building was a bad fit. The rates for rental rooms were steep, as were the restaurant costs, and the grand setting was too opulent for most members to feel comfortable. After much discussion, they abandoned the site on Loewenstrasse and chose a more reasonable location on Gemeindestrasse, where the club still exists today.[12]

The other problem was knottier. Something about the chemistry of the group wasn't working. Asking patients who had come to Jung for mental or emotional issues to mingle and socialize was not without risk.

Decades later, Fowler recalled, "I do know that Father and Mother were very instrumental in helping to get the Club started and I also remember very clearly Father feeling how little most of the members at that time (not speaking of Dr. and Mrs. Jung, and not speaking of Miss Wolff to my knowledge) knew about social life and how to have a sociable time. Father used to laugh about some of the efforts to have joyous evenings, and how they fell flat. It was all considered to be trivial and too light."[13]

Gregarious Harold was appointed chair of the Entertainment Committee and organized ping-pong tournaments, billiard matches, and simple party games. A favorite among club members was the keyhole game, where members had to guess the identity of another member on the other side of the door by recognizing his or her eye through the keyhole.[14] These tame entertainments were perhaps not at the level of frivolity to which Harold was accustomed.

Harold's family had been campaigning for him to return for most of the three years he'd been in Zurich. Finally, in June 1918, with the war winding down, he could put it off no longer and returned to the States to assume the presidency of International Harvester, at his brother Cyrus's behest. Nobody knew it yet, but this spelled the beginning of the end for the Rockefeller-McCormick union.

Harold's return meant he was readily available when Anita sent a distress call. Her only child, Emmons Jr., had been stricken with the Spanish flu, a global pandemic that would claim nearly 100 million victims. Harold hopped on a train to Philadelphia to help Anita and the team of nurses she had assembled to tend to Emmons. It was to no avail: he died three days later. The only consolation was that Emmons's new bride, Eleanor, was pregnant with twins. Anita hovered around Eleanor until and during the birth, a mere month after Emmons's death. A baby boy was stillborn, but the little girl, Nancy, was well and would be adored.[15]

Now that he was back in Chicago, Harold was able to rule over the opera again. Opera in wartime had been a hard sell; with rationing in place and so many sacrifices being made, opera was not a high priority. There had even been a bomb threat at the Auditorium Theater the previous year. Conductor Cleofonte Campanini, alerted to the situation, cleverly got the entire audience to stand by launching into an impromptu performance of the national anthem. A fireman rushed in, grabbed the bomb from underneath an empty seat, and ferried it safely outside. Most of the audience hardly knew what was happening, although one man reportedly jumped into the orchestra pit and took shelter behind a cello. The bomb was a dud.[16]

Even with the war over, the audiences were dwindling as the Spanish flu raged; more and more people were opting to simply stay home. By 1919, box seat subscriptions had dropped from 160 to 65. Unsold seats were given free of charge to returning military personnel.[17]

Financially, the Chicago Grand Opera Company was hanging on only thanks to the McCormicks. Edith and Harold provided advances at the beginning of each season to ensure the company had enough money to cover costs while ticket sales trickled in. In 1916 they gave $60,000; in 1917 it was $250,000; in 1918, $317,600; and in 1919 well over $400,000 (equivalent to nearly $6 million in 2020).[18] Some of the money would be recouped through ticket sales, but not all.

Opera was the thing Edith likely missed most about the States, perhaps more than her extended family, homes, or friends. She and Harold took tremendous pride in their role in creating the Chicago Grand Opera, and she hungrily consumed news about the productions from newspapers and letters. One *Tribune* reporter commented that Edith's absence created a "distinct void" at the opera and that "without her support, moral and financial, grand opera would never have become the great civic and social feature it is here today."[19] Cleofonte Campanini and his wife, Eva Tetrazzini (a singer, as was her more famous sister, Luisa Tetrazzini), were good friends with the McCormicks and would visit Edith when they were in Europe

Chauffeur Emile Ammann described Campanini as Edith's idol. Pictures of the conductor adorned the walls of her hotel suite. "Oh! That opera director! How desperately we wished him away! Whenever his arrival was announced, even the garage was turned upside down. All engines had to be subjected to a thorough overhaul. And woe, if we refrained from polishing them! But that's not enough; Mrs. Rockefeller herself put on a big show. She ordered the most beautiful and expensive items from Paris and Wiesbaden. At the very most, she would only ever wear them four or five times."[20]

Edith was eager to please the Campaninis. Back in 1912, Signora Campanini had confided to Edith that she desired a dog she could tuck in her bag when they traveled—"the littlest dog in the world." So Edith sent a representative to a New York dog show to purchase the smallest purebred Pomeranian in the world. Five thousand dollars later, a charming little prize dog named Offley Wee Blackie was brought to Chicago in a special car and presented to Signora Campanini.[21]

A consummate musician and charismatic leader, Campanini was considered one of the world's finest conductors. He was music director at Milan's famous La Scala Opera House for three years and had been head at the Manhattan Opera Company as well. By sheer force of his magnetic personality, Campanini held things together despite the war's impact, presiding over the world's preeminent opera stars. Under his baton, Chicago Grand Opera magically pulled off Wagner's Ring Cycle two seasons in a row. (Anti-German sentiment caused some booing, whereupon it was decided to avoid German operas until the war was over.)[22]

It seemed the disasters had waited for Harold to return to the States. Aside from being thrown back into International Harvester duties and helping his sister Anita with her personal tragedy, he was also present when Cleofonte Campanini suddenly became ill. It began as pneumonia and then, over the course of five agonizing weeks, developed into heart failure with complications of all the major organs. Harold hired the best doctors, paid all medical expenses, and spent hours each day visiting in the hospital. He and Signora Campanini were at the conductor's side when he died just before Christmas 1919. Among his last words to Harold were "Don't hold up the opera for me. Continue right on."[23]

Campanini's death was a tough personal blow for Harold and Edith, who had both adored the man. Harold wrote Edith a nine-page letter with all the details of the sad occasion. Gino Marinuzzi stepped in as artistic director but without the panache that Campanini had embodied. Soprano Mary Garden wrote, "Now, Marinuzzi was a great artist, but nobody could touch Campanini, nobody in the world. He was the most consummate artist in every way, not only as a conductor."[24]

And the loss of Campanini opened another door, a passageway that led to disaster. A few months before Campanini's illness, Harold had accompanied the Chicago Grand Opera to New York for a performance, where he had been approached by a Polish soprano asking to sing with the company. Her name was Ganna Walska (originally Hanna Puacz), and she was a mediocre singer at best. However, she was also ravishingly beautiful and determined.

Harold informed her that he did not make the artistic decisions for the company but that he would happily pass her name to Campanini.[25] Campanini knew of Ganna and quickly declined. But when the maestro died a few months later, the situation changed. Harold tried again, writing a four-page letter to the Executive Committee in which he assured them he would take full responsibility for the booking.[26] It was unprecedented. It was also the beginning of a fiasco.

Neighbor Arthur Meeker described Ganna: "La Walska . . . was so radiantly lovely that everybody present gasped when they saw her. . . . She was one of those rare types of classical beauty so fine, so regular, so overwhelmingly bewitching that none could resist it. Her eyes were large, dark, and flashing; her features pure Greek; her skin of a dazzling pallor. . . . Ganna herself was fully aware of the power of her charms; she was said to have announced that every man proposed to her the second time he met her. 'Yes,' remarked [an observer] . . . 'but she doesn't say what they propose.'"[27]

Driver Ammann, in his book, said there were rumors Ganna was a spy.[28]

Aside from finagling singing roles, Ganna was on the hunt for millionaire husbands. At the time that she met Harold, she was married to Dr. Joseph Fraenkel, an elderly New York endocrinologist. He was her first millionaire (her initial husband had been Russian baron Arcardie d'Eingorn, not particularly wealthy, merely titled). Fraenkel passed away in April 1920, and a grieving Ganna booked herself on a crossing later that summer on the *Aquitania* for a few months of rest in Paris.

Harold had fallen and fallen hard. He managed to persuade the Executive Committee to book Ganna for late in the year to sing the title role in *Zaza*. And then, with that to look forward to on his calendar, now terribly torn between his duty to family and his fervent desire, he was off to do some soul-searching. He went on a retreat with a spiritual healer in Highmount,

New York, presumably to meditate and attempt to sort out his life. From there, he reported to Senior, ambiguously, that he "had done too much thinking and not enough feeling. I was proud of 'thinking' but I outdid it, as that functioning was not my adaptation to life. I am trying to bring back the emotional side of life which I have lost."[29]

To his sister Anita, Harold confided that there was a romantic reason for being in upstate New York: Ganna was there, too. "There is One here who is helping me very much. To be in her presence and to feel her interest in one in its true expression and feeling is one of the big events in my life and so I accept it gladly."[30] Harold was all in, no holds barred. He began sending passionate love letters to Ganna.

Then he, too, boarded the *Aquitania*. And here is where the story takes a decidedly Hollywood turn.

Also on board the *Aquitania* was millionaire bachelor Alexander Smith Cochran, the carpet king, owner of Alexander Smith and Sons Carpet Mills. Recently dubbed "Richest Bachelor in New York," the world knew him as a playboy who loved yachting and hunting.

It must have been an interesting crossing. Femme fatale Ganna, barely just widowed, had two millionaires fawning over her. Perhaps three: it was rumored Chicago plumbing mogul Richard Crane was also in the mix.[31] By the time the ship docked in Europe, both Harold and Alexander were completely smitten. Harold asked Ganna whether she would consider marrying him, if he were available. She declined.

Ganna had been outspoken about her views on marriage: "'I cannot think of marriage. I like the stage better than anything else. Husband? Never again. He is a hindrance to art; he is always in the way and refuses to sacrifice for my sake. Even a fiancé is bad. My husband must be my slave. It is hard to find men in American who are willing to be slaves. They are quick to offer themselves. They see you once on the stage and ask you to wed them the same night.'"[32]

Edith had heard rumors, possibly from Mary Garden,[33] but was not prepared for what happened next. When Harold appeared in Zurich, he asked for a divorce. He was in love with Ganna—he needed to be with her—and wanted out of the marriage.

Edith refused. Repeatedly. Harold persisted. Edith refused some more. But, in time, feeling that she had truly lost him, Edith reluctantly agreed to the divorce.[34]

Harold ran off to the telegram office to cable Ganna, in Paris, the good news. But on the way he collided with a messenger boy who handed him a telegram. It read, "Just married Alexander Smith Cochran. Hope you will understand and that we will always be good friends."[35] Apparently Ganna had found her slave.

Harold hired a private plane to get to Paris as quickly as he could. And there, in Ganna's suite at the Crillon Hotel, the scene was almost operatic. Ganna recalled, "While Mr. Cochran was still sleeping in the next room in his first day of married life, I was pouring the coffee for Mr. McCormick. In a businesslike way, quite naturally, and just as if he would say 'No sugar, please,' he said to me: 'You see, Edith finally consented to give me a divorce. Now you must divorce Mr. Cochran and we will be married as soon as possible.'"[36]

Even Ganna, whose marriages were notoriously short-lived, couldn't face the scandal such a quick widowhood-marriage-divorce-marriage would bring. She again declined Harold's proposal.

This odd trio—Ganna, Alexander, Harold—spent the next several days together in Paris: dining, going to the theater, accompanying Ganna to her dressmaker. And when time came for Mr. and Mrs. Cochran to sail back to the States, a bereft Harold stood on the pier throwing rice at the newlyweds.[37]

Brokenhearted ("I am suffering, I am tortured"),[38] Harold made his way back to Zurich to patch things up with Edith. The McCormick clan began to make plans to return and reunite. That was easier for some members than for others.

Harold wrote to Senior, ambiguously, "I have had a hard summer here with many problems of one sort or another, but now I am coming out of them, and through some, and day after tomorrow Muriel and Mathilde go with me to Paris for two weeks. Muriel returns with me to the U.S.A. and Mathilde returns to Edith. Later in the winter or spring Mathilde may come over. I look forward to having a good talk with you and it is fine to feel we can meet up in understanding, and in exchange of views, and that is friendship, or at least along the road toward it."[39]

In pursuing Ganna and asking Edith for a divorce, Harold had taken the risk of alienating Senior and Junior; his mother, Nettie; and others. Now he needed to mend fences.

Nettie, who had always been fond of Edith and decidedly in awe of Senior, wrote to him in October 1920, trying to assuage any bad feelings toward her son:

I am resting under the delightful news, by cable, that Harold and Muriel are on the ocean, having sailed on the Acquitania [*sic*], Saturday, Oct 23rd. I wish I might be on the dock to welcome this first contingent— expecting the rest to follow;—for my heart longs for the dear family to be together, with Edith the reigning queen, and Mathilde, the sweet child—as in the days when you and our dear Mrs. Rockefeller, blessed them with a visit under their roof.

I have written each of them, that in these crisis days all are needed here, to keep the ship in its course. In union is strength. We must present an unbroken front. We need all the help we can get from this united McCormick-Rockefeller family to pull through, and it needs parents and children, each one to do his or her part.[40]

Ganna's engagement as Zaza with the Chicago Grand Opera was a bust. Anticipation ran high for the sold-out event. But conductor Gino Marinuzzi grew frustrated with Ganna during rehearsals, asking her repeatedly to project, to sing louder. Maestro Marinuzzi finally handed the baton to assistant Pietro Cimini and walked off. Cimini had similar difficulties with her, and finally, three days before the first performance, he asked her to "sing in her natural voice." Ganna replied, "Pig, you would ruin my performance!" She ran off the stage and departed Chicago immediately.[41]

Harold's public statement was, "It is unfortunate. The opera wasn't ready, that's all. Madame Walska has gone to her home in New York for the holidays."[42] After having begged the Executive Committee to book her, Harold's humiliation must have been deep.

Ganna greatly overestimated her own gifts. Frequently she was overcome with terrible stage fright and unable to perform; it was rumored that she'd been pelted with rotten vegetables in Havana.[43] But lovestruck Harold heard and saw none of this. He continued to believe she had tremendous talent.

Maestro Marinuzzi resigned two weeks later, saying he couldn't handle the "wrangling of the stars."[44] As soon as she heard about Marinuzzi, Edith cabled the board, urging them to appoint Mary Garden general director.[45] She had lobbied for this after Campanini's death, but the board was wary of designating a woman. This time Edith insisted, and Mary Garden became one of the first women to head an opera company.

Edith had her own worries. Not only was she aware of the situation with Harold and Ganna, and not only was she trying to muster the courage to cross the ocean, but she also had a major financial debacle on her hands.

The days of Edith hiding quietly in Zurich were long gone. Requests for financial assistance came every day, from every corner. While Harold was in the States in 1919, Edith had been approached by a German inventor about an enterprise he wished Harold and International Harvester to consider. It was a method of impregnating wood so as to make it harder, stronger, able to withstand more pressure. In addition, he had a technique for transforming cheap stones into something resembling diamonds and a chemical treatment that could make a copper-like substance.[46]

Edith cabled Harold numerous times about this gentleman, but, distracted by business, Ganna, and family matters, he didn't respond. Not wanting to miss out on a great opportunity, Edith decided to proceed on her own. She consulted with experts she knew in Switzerland for advice and to oversee testing on these inventions to be sure they were sound. Dr. Jung was involved—skeptical at first, but later supportive—as were a German scientist by the name of Keller Huguenst and Paul Koenig, representing the American Smelting and Refining Company. They witnessed the testing in Switzerland, and while the treatment of the stones and copper was somewhat unreliable, the wood impregnation was convincing.[47]

Senior warned Edith not to get involved: "Please suspend all business investments and commitments until you hear from me further and we can make full and satisfactory examination."[48] He also cabled Harold: "I am opposed to Edith having anything to do with the project at all. I fear it will result in great loss and trouble. I must earnestly entreat her to discontinue this, not only, but not to engage in any business schemes."[49]

Harold replied to his father-in-law, "Dr. Jung in a letter to me wrote, 'Mrs. McCormick has managed the business side in a most admirable way. Sometimes it has been most trying. But she quietly steered the boat through the storm. I went with her through it all in silent collaboration.'"[50]

Proceeding cautiously, Edith decided to have the tests duplicated in America. She cabled Harold to arrange for permits for Paul Koenig and a Swiss scientist to come to Chicago, and Harold did so.[51] Meanwhile, another team of scientists and entrepreneurs, with Edith looking on, tried to reproduce the tests in Zurich, using the instructions Koenig had left behind, and failed. Ultimately the American tests failed as well.[52]

Ammann described the scene:

> They built a laboratory with every imaginable instrument. When the laboratory was finished, they went to work with zeal, even obsession. I had to wait for Madame for seven and eight hour stretches, occasionally even for the night. I often tried to see what was going on in the laboratory, but in vain, because all the windows were glued and tightly closed. Only a small sliding window upstairs in the attic was open, through which constantly streams of smoke escaped.
>
> Finally the important day came. It ended with deeply depressed, defeated faces that I will never forget. I'll never again see anything as pathetic as this inventor and his sponsor when they left the lab. The desperation of my mistress was understandable. The attempt was unsuccessful.[53]

But monies had already been paid. Edith gave the German inventor $100,000. She had also agreed to form and finance three companies: $500,000 for the wood-impregnation company; $500,000 for the metals company; and $75,000 for the stones company. The arrangement was that Edith would hold all the stock; she would provide Herr Koenig with a salary and 20 percent of the earnings from each company; the inventor was to receive 50 percent of the earnings; and the remaining 30 percent would go to Edith.[54]

In the end, all were disappointed. Edith lost $340,000 in the process[55] — and Senior's respect. A steep price to pay. She reassured him, "I am sorry that it happened and I am still suffering the consequences of it, but I feel what is past is past, and I have learned and I shall not have such an experience a second time."[56] She could not have known at the time how this failed endeavor would haunt her.

Senior got in the last "I told you so" in a letter to Harold: "I do sincerely hope Edith will be quite content not to enter into further business schemes."[57] He was remarkably unchanged from the man who had intoned "Edith was greedy" numerous times the day she, as a child, had dared take a second piece of cheese.

TRYING TO FIND
A WAY HOME

1919–21

*I*n the midst of it all, Edith decided to start a zoo.

Right after Harold met Ganna; right before Campanini died; right before the wood-hardening business tanked; right before Harold asked for a divorce; right before the family began to disintegrate, Edith donated land to found a zoo. Even this did not go well.

Back in 1909, Senior had given Edith some land in the western suburbs of Chicago as a gift that he valued at just under half a million dollars. Edith had instructed the McCormicks' business agent, John Chapman, and lawyer, Judson Stone, to divide the land into lots and sell them.

Also in 1909, Daniel Burnham published his widely acclaimed *Plan of Chicago*. Edith was intimately familiar with the book, having worked with Burnham on development ideas for Lake Forest (though they never materialized). Green space was a priority for Burnham,[1] and the push for public parks had resulted in the establishment of the Forest Preserve District of Cook County in 1915. Burnham's cohort, landscape designer Frederick Law Olmsted, had actually configured the community of Riverside, where most of Edith's land lay.

While some of Edith's lots had been sold, the majority sat idle for years and began accumulating serious taxes. In 1917, Edith unloaded thirty-six acres to the Forest Preserve District for $55,000.[2] But by 1919, she owed $20,000 in back taxes.[3]

In October of that year, Edith wrote to family lawyer Stone requesting that her remaining holdings in the town of Riverside be given to the city of Chicago for a zoological park. Stone replied that Riverside was outside the city proper but that the Forest Preserve District would be well suited to accept the properties that would be appropriate (some were in a different part of town) and pay the back taxes in return.[4] The land donation would amount to 83 acres; with the street property thrown in, it totaled 105 acres.[5]

It was a tidy solution. Giving the land away solved her tax problems, might bring her some public goodwill, and could be a lovely boon for the city of Chicago.

Making no reference to her tax benefit, Edith explained that her gift "was born not from my personal love of animals, but from my devotion to human beings. It is important that we have opportunity for scientific study of the processes in animals that we may better understand the processes in ourselves and thus be of material aid to those whom we call neurotics. At present little is known of the science of psychology of animals. When we can make scientific deductions of the actions and reactions of animals, we will find ourselves in a position to reach the human soul."[6]

Had she been inspired by Gilbert Hamilton's primate facility at Riven Rock? Or by animal research being conducted at the Rockefeller Institute for Medical Research, set up by Senior after baby Jack's death? Both were highly unusual for the time, at the forefront of animal behavior studies and medical research. In any case, Edith the analyst was broadening her horizons. And, in typical Edith fashion, she envisioned the world's grandest zoo: a large plot allowing for great variety of species, and, where possible, the animals would be displayed in their natural habitats with moats instead of bars.

But years later, zoo leader John T. McCutcheon would confess that the zoo was "the child of a real estate failure. Mrs. Edith Rockefeller Mc-Cormick had a large tract of land out near Riverside. It was laid out as a subdivision. A few folks bought lots, but the customers weren't standing in line. Each year the tax bill came in, and they kept coming in during Mrs. McCormick's eight years in Switzerland. All in all, things could have been better from her point of view. And as a solution of this situation, she offered her land . . . with the condition that it be used as a great modern zoo such as she had seen abroad. Also the Commissioners were to assume the back taxes. So it was an ill wind that blew us good. It blew a first-class zoo into the lap of Chicagoland."[7]

By January 1920, word was out, and Edith's gift became front-page news: "County to Have Great Zoo: Mrs. McCormick Donates Large Tract of Land near Riverside to Forest Preserve,"[8] "What Do Animals Think? Mrs. McCormick's Gift of Land to Permit Study of Zoo Psychology."[9]

Forest Preserve District president Peter Reinberg quickly assembled a group of prominent Chicago leaders to steer the ship: Charles Hutchinson, Colonel Robert McCormick (a cousin of Harold's), Charles Wacker, Daniel Ryan. They established a governing society to run the institution and appointed beloved *Chicago Tribune* cartoonist John McCutcheon president. The new governing members expanded the list of prominent Chicagoans to include John Borden, Charles Dawes, Samuel Insull, John Pirie, John Shedd, and Martin Ryerson, among others.[10]

Thus, Edith was the godmother of the Chicago Zoological Park—later, more informally, Brookfield Zoo (the property was partially in Riverside, partially in Brookfield). The agreement stipulated that the land would always be used for zoological purposes; that adjacent lands would be purchased to complete the space; that the zoo would open within five years; and that the Forest Preserve District would pay the back taxes. If any of these conditions were unmet, the land would revert to Edith's ownership.[11]

As with most things in Edith's life, things didn't go smoothly. Several of these conditions would become contentious in the years to come. Edith announced her intention to donate the land in 1919; the zoo wouldn't open until 1934. Whereas her gift was initially seen as another generous gesture from the woman who had already given the city grand opera and theater, things would take a decidedly negative turn soon.

There was one other drawback: Senior and Junior learned of Edith's gift in the newspapers and weren't pleased that she had blithely given away the land she'd been given for investment purposes. It was yet another way she had disappointed them.

But for now, it was time to return to Chicago. The Great War was over. Her marriage was quite nearly over as well. It was time. But it wasn't easy.

Dr. Jung was unwilling to accompany Edith on the return voyage. Instead, three doctors were involved with the undertaking, Dr. Zungden, Dr. Meude-Ernst, and Dr. Josef Hartmann, who was to escort her all the way to the Bastion. What exactly they did (medication? hypnosis?) is unclear, but their combined bill would run $50,000.[12] In addition, Edith had to somehow get to the coast to board the ship, and a train was out of the question.

Driver Emile Ammann recalled Edith somberly telling him, "I must return to Chicago. But unfortunately I cannot withstand train travel. I shall have to get used to considerable distances in the automobile. Now you have to drive with me . . . drive . . . I will tell you how much I can endure. Do I make myself clear?"[13]

Several times a day, Edith, Emile, and her maid Emmy went out motoring. Usually they just went a hundred kilometers or so before returning to the Baur au Lac. Occasionally they managed to overnight in a hotel and return the next morning. And so, methodically, spasmodically, Edith chipped away at her fears, her sights set on Chicago.

The plan was for Edith to return in February 1921 with Mathilde. But Edith couldn't manage it, and Mathilde reported to Harold, "Mother terrible making difficulties till last moment." In that same cable, she also indicated that she had personally enjoyed a visit with Ganna in Paris.[14] Mathilde made her way to Chicago without Edith.

A few months later, Harold, Muriel, and Mathilde returned to Zurich as a united front to convince Edith to come home. By this point, what Edith had intended to be a short trip to Zurich had grown to eight years—the children were grown, family members had died, and a world war had come and gone.

The previous year, Harold had assured Senior that all was well in the marriage: "Edith and I have had great personal differences to adjust between ourselves due to our types and our temperaments. These we have met and cleared up and now we stand side by side with a clearness of purpose and a common viewpoint and we recognize those elements in which we differ but through which we are not apart. And we are closer in love . . . than ever."[15]

But by the spring of 1921, Harold had other plans. Ganna's marriage to Alexander Smith Cochran was already in ruins, providing the opening Harold longed for. He engineered a clandestine rendezvous with the diva in the port town of Dieppe, France, hoping to avoid notice.[16] Having confessed to his sister Anita how desperately he needed Ganna, he wrote to Anita repeatedly on this trip describing his desired's loveliness. Anita became his chief coconspirator in how to extricate himself from his marriage without too much familial fallout. On July 4, 1921, Harold and Ganna jointly sent birthday greetings to Anita, a clear sign of which way things were headed.[17]

But first up on the docket for Edith was news about Fowler. Adjacent to Senior's property in Pocantico Hills, New York, was the Stillman estate, owned by Anne (Fifi) and James Stillman Jr., president of National City Bank. The Rockefeller and Stillman families created a knot of relationships: Edith's first cousins Percy and William (sons of Uncle William) had both married sisters of James Stillman, producing a total of ten children carrying both Stillman and Rockefeller genes. To complicate matters, Fifi and James's son Bud was Fowler's best friend, and Fowler had spent considerable time at the Stillman estate.

In 1920, James and Fifi were regular newspaper fodder because of a tumultuous divorce proceeding. James claimed that Fifi's latest child, Guy, was not his but rather the offspring of a Canadian tour guide named Fred Beauvais. It turned out that James had been having an affair of his own with a former chorus girl, which had possibly resulted in a child. In her typical fiery style, Fifi befriended the chorus girl, and they joined forces. Love letters and sordid details were made public, and side-by-side photos let newspaper readers guess who was the more likely parent of the infants in question.[18] The disgrace was so complete that James was forced out of the bank. The story was long and complicated and involved trips to Dr. Jung from both parties. It took several years, but James and Fifi finally reconciled, albeit temporarily.

Fowler was squarely in the middle of this fiasco. In 1921, about to graduate from Princeton, it was rumored that he had become engaged to James and Fifi's daughter, Anne. Even the *New York Times* covered the story, with the headline "Denies He Is Engaged to Miss Anne Stillman."[19] The truth was actually worse, but that wouldn't come out for some time.

For now, scandal-shy Senior wrote to Harold in April, "I read in the papers that Fowly is not engaged to Miss Stillman—that he has denied it. I know, from what Fowly said to me, that he probably had called at the Stillman home. Though it made me sick at heart, I refrained from talking to Fowly about the Stillmans. I am careful about these things. What a calamity it would be for him to be engaged to a daughter of the two who are being paraded in the newspapers today! But whatever else you do, dear Harold, see to it that our dear boy is not permitted to be drawn into this alliance. May the Good Lord spare us and save us from this calamity! And when you have fully absorbed and digested this letter, will you kindly commit it to the flames—but please be sure and not fail to carry out my wish. I know—I know only too well—what I am talking about—dear Harold, do not fail."[20]

Harold, head-over-heels in love with Ganna and ready to accept a scandal when necessary, replied within the week: "From everything I know, there is not a word of truth in the report as published. Moreover, I am absolutely sure that there is no intimacy of feeling in the direction which the newspapers indicated. We must all be true to ourselves, with the development of the individual, taking into full account the values of the collective society element and there is a line between these two concerning which there is no definite period or apostrophe, but which is characterized much more by a semi colon or a question mark; and that, indeed is one of the big questions of life. In principle, speaking for me alone, I cannot avoid any publicity where I feel the circumstances help me to a certain direction where it is all justified. Such publicity is to be regretted, but not to my mind to be shunned. I will consign your letter to the flames, exactly as you desire."[21]

The truth of the matter was more scandalous than Senior had imagined: Fowler was in love with front-page Fifi, his best friend's mother. Did Harold know at this point? That is unclear. Reading between the lines of his April 14 letter, it seems likely. At some point Harold appears to have helped facilitate the relationship. It is doubtful he shared his information with Edith at this early juncture. There was always the danger Edith would share with Senior. Information would be meted out very deliberately, and only when unavoidable, to Senior.

But the bulk of the family was in love—with inconvenient people. Fowler's situation would temporarily blow over, with a much noisier episode to come down the road.

On Harold and the girls' 1921 trip to Zurich, youngest daughter Mathilde had confessed to Harold that she, too, was in love.[22] In her exuberant, sixteen-year-old hormone-driven state, she had fallen in love with her Swiss riding instructor (the one who had been a major in the Swiss army and was fond of painting, as per her letter to Grandfather).[23] Max Oser was forty-four years old. Had Edith been privy to this relationship, she might have warned Mathilde that Oser had also pursued Edith's niece Margaret Strong by sending her love letters.[24] But Edith was out of the loop. Mathilde pressed Harold for approval to marry Oser when she turned seventeen. Harold, who was all about matters of the heart, found her ardor convincing and gave his blessing.[25]

Senior, aware he was operating with severely limited knowledge, wrote Edith (who scarcely knew more), "But, Edith dear, the financial question, while important, is not important when compared to the other question—the great question of your being present with your children. And how sadly they need your presence, and how very solicitous we all are for them! In this connection, I may add that you could have been a great comfort and help to your mother and me. But this sinks into insignificance also, when we consider the dear children, and the importance of the constant, jealous, watch-care of the mother, and the untold sorrow that may be entailed upon us all. Edith dear, you know it all, and so much better than I—indeed, I know so little. The responsibility is with you. I hope it is not too late. . . . I am not lecturing. I am not scolding. I love you, Edith dear, and I am still hoping."[26]

The McCormick clan was a potent stew of forbidden passion.

At this time, Edith was still not ready to travel back to the States, despite an onslaught of cables from every imaginable family member. It would mean she would miss Fowler's graduation from Princeton, but Harold and Muriel returned to the States without her. Mathilde went on vacation to the French seaside with her chaperone, Julia Mangold (conveniently also a distant relative of Max Oser's).

Once back in the States, after Fowler's graduation, Harold went to the Bastion while Muriel and Fowler holed up in Villa Turicum, where they had secret guests: Fifi and her son Bud, who had somehow eluded the press. Only neighbor Grandma Nettie was aware of their visit, and in her eyes, she just saw best friends Fowler and Bud providing shelter to poor, beleaguered Fifi. Nettie wrote to Harold, "Mrs. S. has felt the comfort and advantage of perfect repose in your house. At first she took her meals in her room, feeling unable to do more. Everything goes off well. Not a single outsider has been in the house but me, I think, and your children stand the isolation well."[27] To complete the idyllic scene, they all sang hymns together.

Edith continued to prepare for her return. One thing was certain: she had no intention of returning alone. Her long-term aim was to establish Villa Turicum as an institute for analytical psychology—a branch of Dr. Jung's work in the United States, where she could see patients and hold educational retreats. She wanted a partner. Emil Medtner was her first choice, but he demurred.[28]

Next on her list was Edwin Krenn, her young Austrian-turned-Swiss patient who claimed to be an architect. Not only was he a Jung devotee, but his architectural skills would be perfect for the zoological park. Edith wrote to zoo president John McCutcheon asking that Edwin be appointed as architect, "so that my ideas for the entire plan for the Zoological Gardens may be conveyed through him."[29] If there was a reply, that has gone missing in the zoo files, but her request was ignored.

The return party was finally settled: Edith; maid Emmy; Edwin Krenn; Dr. Josef Hartmann; Mathilde's governess, Louise Beley (but no Mathilde, who was frolicking on the seashore); and twenty-three trunks of Edith's belongings.[30] The crossing was booked, and they were ready to go.

Harold, in the meantime, quietly darted back over to Paris to be with Ganna. He was deep in divorce planning, cabling Anita repeatedly with his thoughts on lawyers, which house he would request in the divorce (Villa Turicum, as he could stay with his mother while in the city), and other details. He deliberately selected a different steamer back to avoid traveling "with other party."[31] He continued his careful correspondence with Senior, laying the groundwork for a future relationship, never mentioning divorce but frequently lacing his letters with mentions of a man-to-man talk and of mutual understanding despite differences.[32]

Then word leaked to the rest of the family that Edith was returning with a male friend and that divorce was imminent.

Harold's older brother, Cyrus, who was as scandal-wary as Edith's father, sounded the alarm in a rare and delicately worded telegram to Senior: "Just learned plan of sailing September tenth. Is there any means you think of to postpone departure thus giving opportunity for mutual mediation and conference to avoid complications which would cause distress to those who would prefer not to be drawn in. Are you communicating along those lines and do you advise me to communicate. Please telegraph me your opinion. Am suggesting this only with desire to help."[33]

This message prompted Senior to cable Edith the next day, "Notwithstanding my urgency for your return there may be reasons why it would be better to delay for a time at least to afford opportunity for deliberate mutual consideration of vital questions rather than possibly precipitating developments resulting from your return just now. You know the whole situation. I know little, but incline to believe it the part of wisdom to delay coming for the present. Tenderest love."[34]

Eight years of begging Edith to return and then an eleventh-hour about-face.

It fell on deaf ears. Having made it as far as Cherbourg, France, the travel party was ready to sail. Her plan now set in motion, it seems unlikely she

could have stayed in France longer in any case, her fears probably dangerously close to breaking through. "Your loving cable brought me warmth
and happiness," she replied to her father. "I am coming as planned. I have
every hope for mutual understanding. Will see you soon. Much love."[35]

While Edith was on board the *George Washington*,[36] Senior received a
letter from a law firm: "Dear Sir, At the suggestion of Mr. Cyrus McCormick, I am writing to suggest that you designate some lawyers in New
York to whom I can talk on behalf of Mr. Harold McCormick regarding
certain questions that have arisen between him and his wife. Mr. Cyrus
McCormick feels that it is to the best interest of all concerned that such
communication should take place before Mrs. Harold McCormick's arrival
in this country."[37]

The crossing would mark her transition from an idyll to a hornet's nest.
Had Edith known what lay ahead, she might never have returned.

ON HER OWN

1921–22

*I*t wasn't exactly a grand welcome. Waiting at the dock were Fowler and Muriel, as well as George Spangler, the business manager of the Chicago Grand Opera.[1] No Senior, no Junior, despite Junior's earlier letter to Harold in which he said, "Please give [Edith] our love and tell her how eagerly we are waiting to welcome her home again."[2]

Oh, there were some reporters.

Edith resolutely denied divorce was imminent: "I can assure you that nothing is further from my mind. I saw Mr. McCormick three times in Zurich two weeks ago and we had some pleasant conversation. I am a psychologist and believe in freedom of action. I am very human, and think that it is a beautiful idea if two people enjoy each other's society and if one can help the other, that they should be permitted to do so. Mr. McCormick has kept me fully informed of all that he is doing, and our correspondence has always been very pleasant. If he finds entertainment in anybody's company it is all right.'"[3]

It seems Harold and Ganna had received her blessing.

After checking in at the Plaza Hotel, Edith quickly sent off a telegram to Senior, informing him she had arrived safely and would appear on his doorstep the following day with her "traveling companion."[4]

The trouble was, her traveling companion was not welcome: "We will be very happy to welcome you and the children tomorrow Thurs the 29th but regrets we cannot arrange for any others excepting your maid. Please telegraph us when you will arrive here. With tenderest love."[5]

There was another volley of telegrams in which both restated their views—and each stood firm.

And yet a third round of telegrams: "I am leaving for Chicago on Saturday and it would make me more happy than I can say to see you after these long years of separation before I go to my home to take up my work there. Will you not permit me, your daughter, to come to Lakewood tomorrow Friday for luncheon and bring with me my two friends, who have been my traveling companions all the way from Zurich. I feel such warm love in my heart for you, that I know that you must feel warm to me."[6]

A curt but clear response: "Dear Daughter: telegram received. Much as I regret it is better we wait until we can have the visit quietly by ourselves. With tenderest love."[7]

Edith relented. Let Senior win this round; she would go visit him with only Emmy. On that September 30, she ventured to the ferry dock for the crossing to New Jersey, where her father was staying at his vacation home at the Lakewood Country Club. But a ferry! Such a fragile little vessel. And then, much as had happened on her wedding day, the Fates intervened in the form of storm clouds.

"Dear Father," Edith wrote again, "Destiny seems to mean that we are not to see each other now. When I could have come to see you, you were not ready to receive me. And today I was, after many delays, at the Staten Island ferry at half past eleven, when the storm turned me back. Well, I am now in America, so that the occasions for us to see each other can be pregnant."[8]

Edith and her troupe packed up and headed to Chicago. She would never see her father again. Nor would she ever leave Chicago.

Harold, meanwhile, traveled back to the States on a separate steamer, with a quick visit to Senior in early October.[9] There is no record of their discussion, but in the race to Senior's loyalty, Harold had the clear inside track, having been with Cettie when she died and successfully maintaining a closer relationship with his father-in-law during the years that Edith lived halfway around the world.

It is easy to imagine Edith's relief to be back in the Bastion, with the massive gates closed behind her, once again surrounded by her books and treasures. The trouble was, she was alone. When Harold returned to Chicago, he took up residence at Villa Turicum and overnighted with his mother, Nettie, just down the street whenever he needed to be in the city. None of the extended McCormick clan—Nettie, Anita, Katharine, Cyrus, the cousins—greeted or even spoke to Edith upon her return.[10] Muriel and Fowler aligned themselves with Harold; Mathilde was still abroad. This, despite Muriel's telegram to Edith during the crossing that she was ready to "welcome you with my heart full of true love."[11] Edwin Krenn had thrown a wrench in the works.

Harold issued a formal statement that appeared in the *New York Times* under the headline "M'Cormicks Live Apart in Chicago": "Mr. Harold McCormick presents his compliments and begs to announce that the report that he and his wife are living apart is true."[12]

For her part, Edith steered the conversations to synthetic psychology: "Let us compare the mind to a house, and its thoughts to the furniture it contains. Some of the furniture is unsightly, covered with dust, broken or ugly. We clear it all out—throw it away, and the mind is clear. But we must replace this furniture or the house is useless."[13] But while she spoke of moving on, her house remained unchanged. She kept Harold's and the children's rooms just as they had been, ready for them to return.

Dr. Hartmann returned to Switzerland, his seemingly impossible mission accomplished and his stipend pocketed. Senior's banker friends reported back to him that Hartmann had requested his payment in cash, perhaps afraid Edith's check would bounce. The bank declined.[14] Edith gave Edwin Krenn $1 million in Standard Oil stocks in order to establish him as a man of independent means,[15] and he was installed across the street from the Bastion, at the Drake Hotel, which had sprung up during Edith's stay in Zurich. In fact, when planners developed the hotel, they approached Harold and asked him to be a sponsor. As they were to be located in the heart of McCormickville, they intended to name it the McCormick Hotel. Harold subscribed $50,000 but declined the naming honor.[16]

Edith had returned to a world vastly changed. Prohibition had begun and Chicago was ground zero for organized crime, with speakeasies on every block and shotgun battles dominating the headlines. Skyscrapers had created a brand-new skyline for Chicago. Hemlines, too, had moved up, a full six inches higher than when Edith left. And, thanks to the efforts of Katharine and so many other determined women, the Nineteenth Amendment had passed, granting women equal voting rights, with Illinois being one of the first states to approve the amendment. Edith became involved with the League of Women Voters and hosted teas and other events to help women register.

Women were bursting out of their preassigned roles: Edith Wharton became the first American woman to win a Pulitzer Prize for her novel *The Age of Innocence*, Marie Curie had already secured two Nobel Prizes, Margaret Sanger opened the first birth control clinic, Loretta Walsh officially enlisted as the first active-duty woman in the U.S. Navy, and Representative Jeannette Rankin became the first woman elected to Congress. Right and left, women were questioning why they had accepted second-class status for so long. In just a couple of years, Alice Paul would propose the Equal Rights Amendment, laying a clear, if bumpy, path forward.

There were new forms of entertainment as well: an automatic gramophone, the moving pictures, and radio. Edith had one of the first gramophones in the city. And diva Mary Garden ushered in the age of radio in Chicago by singing an aria from *Madama Butterfly* on the inaugural broadcast of KYW on November 11.[17] (Edith would speak on the radio too, but not until 1927.)

It was a whole new world.

Edith would need all the entertainment she could find. Harold demanded his divorce. Ganna's marriage to Alexander Smith Cochran was on its last legs, and Harold was determined to be ready this time. He assembled a powerhouse team of lawyers that included a former Illinois Supreme Court chief justice as well as an up-and-coming lawyer named Clarence Darrow, who would become a household name a few years later with his performances at the Scopes Monkey Trial and the Leopold and Loeb case. Harold's legal team tried to reach Edith by letter, by telegram, by telephone.[18] Edith ignored them all, reasoning if they couldn't reach her, Harold couldn't divorce her.

"I feel just as you do that the most natural and beautiful thing is for Harold and I to be together. I am always quietly waiting and hoping for this," Edith wrote to her father on November 19, 1921.[19] After all, she'd come home to save her marriage. She'd come home to reunite her family. But things weren't working out that way.

Unable to contact Edith, Harold's lawyers sent notice to her brother-in-law Parmalee Prentice (sister Alta's husband) at his law firm in New York,[20] using him as a go-between to Senior. Alta explained to Senior, "They have brought one witness from Switzerland and are keeping him here. . . . I am very much afraid that unless Edith can be brought to make an early adjustment there will be actions taken that all must regret, and that no one then can stop."[21] Who the witness was (if anyone) is unclear.

Terrified the divorce would play out in the press like the Stillman case, Senior pressed Edith to move forward. "I think you should be represented by the best legal counsel at once, to avoid disagreeable publicity for yourself, and the rest of us, if possible."[22] Edith seemed to welcome the assistance, responding, "I cannot tell you how happy I am to receive your letter. . . . I have no legal counsel for I have always hoped."[23] She didn't appear to realize that Senior's goal was to avoid negative publicity rather than to secure a good settlement.

Senior, Junior, and Parmalee arranged for Edith to be represented by former judge Charles S. Cutting. Harold's lawyers informed Senior that Harold would agree to a charge of desertion. If Edith didn't agree to this, he would charge adultery.[24] The pressure was on from all sides. Edith would need to settle quietly and on Harold's terms. That she didn't want a divorce was immaterial. That Harold had been in hot pursuit of Ganna also seemed irrelevant.

The fact that Edith's lawyer, Judge Cutting, was secretly corresponding on the side with Senior, Junior, and Parmalee[25] seems not only unfair but likely unethical, as Junior acknowledged: "It is important that Mrs. McCormick should not, for the present at least and until we have agreed that it is wise, know that I have written you or that you may know any of these facts."[26]

Cutting replied, "I am writing you . . . because both you and your father are necessarily very much interested in the outcome of this very unfortunate situation. As you know, and as Mrs. McCormick has indicated in her letter to her father, she is not anxious for the separation and it would not take very much to have her mind recur to its former determination not to proceed. . . . Of course, your letter has not been shown to her."[27]

Edith asked for alimony. It was rejected. Edith asked for the Bastion free and clear. That was rejected. Edith had to pay off Harold's half of the Bastion. Harold was awarded Villa Turicum and Edith agreed to buy it from him, in part to keep Ganna from enjoying it. In addition, she paid Harold for two lots he had purchased adjoining the Bastion, to avoid having immediate neighbors. Edith wrote to her father, "This is too one sided, especially when one considers that I do not want a divorce."[28]

In the end, Harold received not only his divorce but a small fortune from Edith. Both were in debt at the time, Harold to the tune of $1.25 million and Edith about $700,000.[29]

The proceedings took a mere fifty minutes. Edith didn't even remove her coat. Harold hadn't bothered to appear. The papers reported the total exchange:

Judge Charles McDonald: State your name in full.
Edith Rockefeller McCormick.
Where do you reside?
1000 Lake Shore Drive.
How long have you resided there?
Since August 1897, except for periods which I have spent abroad.
When were you married and to whom?
November 26, 1895, to Harold F. McCormick.
How long did you live with him?
Until May 27, 1918.
On that date what happened?
He left me.
Where were you on that occasion?
In Zurich, in Switzerland.
Did he give any reason for leaving you?
He gave no reason at all and there was no reason.
What was the name of the hotel in Zurich at which you lived?
The Baur au Lac.
Has he supported you since, or contributed any money for your
    support?
He has not supported me.
Has he contributed anything at all to your support?
Not one cent.
How did you conduct yourself toward him during the time you lived
    together?
In the manner a wife should.
Thank you. That is all.[30]

Edith wrote to Senior and Junior on December 27, 1921, informing them that she'd signed the papers and that the divorce would be granted the following morning. She outlined the financial details: she owed Harold $450,000 for the Bastion; $1,958,916.50 for Villa Turicum; and $50,000 for the two lots adjoining the Bastion. She went on to detail her four-year payment schedule, then wrote, "This is a heavy burden that I have taken upon my shoulders, but there is nothing to do but to go on and do the best I can. I wanted to be fair and generous to Harold, for I love him."[31]

Junior agreed it was a burden but sidestepped elegantly, "Of course you would not have assumed these obligations had you not seen in advance how you would be able to meet them."[32]

If Edith had hoped for help from Senior or Junior, that would not be forthcoming. Junior wrote to Senior, "I may be doing Edith an injustice but I fancy that she is hoping that you or I will help her in making these payments. Had she advised with me I should have strongly urged her not to consider the purchase of the country house in addition to the city house. Since she has acted without seeking advice and I assume she did not communicate with you in advance of closing the contract it would seem to me as though she ought to work out her own financial problem as best she can. If she should ask you to help her financially I am hoping very much that whatever you may do, if anything, will be predicated on an absolute agreement on her part to terminate all further contact with the Austrian who came over with her and whose continued presence in Chicago has caused so much unfavorable comment. . . . I assume you will destroy this letter when you have read it."[33]

For all of her concern about how Senior would react, Edith may have failed to consider the backlash of Junior's heavy disapproval. She wasn't aware that, by now, Senior had transferred the vast majority of wealth to his son, and Junior was calling the financial shots. Junior did not condone Edith's return with Edwin or Harold's wanton behavior, as indicated in a particularly honest letter he wrote to Muriel: "Every effort that I could put forth was exerted to persuade your father to seek a reconciliation and avoid this sorrowful ending. Failing in that I urged him to let matters rest as they were and not widen and make irreparable the breach, but in that also I failed. Who that knows thinks for a moment that either your mother or your father are happy! They were never more unhappy!"[34]

In choosing a very different life path, Edith had lost her childhood confidant and closest friend. Junior, having worked assiduously to rebuild the Rockefeller family name through careful philanthropic work for the past decade, was appalled at the scandal. Offended by his sister's choices over the last decade, Junior now turned his back on Edith. Their relationship was fractured, and she would never be able to win him back.

In the meantime, she had to figure out her finances. It was a terrible deal for a divorce she never wanted. Edith had been railroaded.

Back in 1917, when Senior restructured his annual giving to Edith, he had built in a yearly allowance for Harold, which had grown to $30,000.[35] While there was some discussion of ending this, it wasn't clearly stipulated in the divorce. Since Senior had given Fowler a large amount of securities, currently yielding an annual income of $20,000, Senior suggested splitting the $30,000 between Mathilde and Muriel instead.[36] But the final agreement did not put an end to the gift, and Harold and Edith would argue about who had the right to that money in the months and years to come. But that was chump change compared to the $2.5 million Edith now owed Harold.

Shortly after the divorce, Senior tallied up the money he had given Edith, an impressive list including every birthday and Christmas gift, shares of Standard Oil stocks, cash, and other miscellaneous remittances dating back to 1903. The grand total by 1922, according to Senior, was a staggering $13,213,023.55.[37] Someone was keeping score. Meticulously.

Just to be perfectly clear about his loyalties, during all the divorce negotiations, Senior sent Harold his annual $1,000 check for Christmas. They continued their loving correspondence as if nothing had changed. Harold's thank you letter also mentions, "It was good to see John and Parmalee out here."[38] While the newspapers noted that Junior's family stopped in Chicago on their way back from a trip to the Orient, there is no record of whether he visited Edith. Apparently, though, he saw Harold.

Senior replied to Harold's thank you note with clear forgiveness: "The past is past, and now we will address ourselves to doing the best each day, as it comes, with all the changes and all the cares and responsibilities."[39]

It seems it was fine for Harold to have Ganna but not for Edith to have Edwin.

Harold may have had a tough go of the situation with his mother, Nettie, who had always liked Edith and feared losing favor with Senior, though Nettie was beginning to show signs of dementia. Nettie's biographer Stella Virginia Roderick states, "It was a grief to Mrs. [Nettie] McCormick, not only for the break in her son's life, but for the loss to her of Edith with whom in earlier years she had been so congenial and whom she loved."[40]

One day after the divorce was final, the Grand Opera performed *Salome*, with Mary Garden again in the title role. Both Harold and Edith were present, this time in opposite boxes. Muriel sat with Harold, pointedly ignoring Edith.[41] *Salome*, of all things. An opera of those gone mad. A story of lust, seduction, betrayal. Eleven years earlier, they'd had to cancel the last performance. This time, the newspapers allotted more inches to the demise of the marriage than to the opera.

Edith was on her own. And the whole world knew.

A YEAR IN THE LIFE

1922–23

*I*f 1921 seemed crazy, it was merely a warmup for 1922.

The year Edith would turn fifty began with Mathilde returning from Europe, settling in with Harold and pointedly ignoring her mother.[1] Then, at a moment when Harold had been called to New York to attend to an ill Muriel, the Swiss newspapers notified the family they were running a story about Mathilde and Max Oser's engagement.[2] Mathilde invited a few newspapermen to tea. And all hell broke loose.

While Harold rushed home from the East Coast, Mathilde cabled Edith just before the news broke: "Dear Mother: I would like to tell you myself of my engagement to Mr. Oser. I have not felt that I have been able to ask your advice about it but I want you to know it from me."[3]

Edith replied, "Dear Mathilde: Your letter gives me much sorrow because I love you and because I want you to be happy. Will you not reconsider before it is too late?"[4]

Harold invited Edith to the announcement, hoping they could be unified parents, but she refused to be party to this relationship, scolding Harold, "I cannot understand how you can be so blind—a young girl not yet of age. I do not give my consent, for it would mean great sadness for beautiful Mathilde as time goes on. May I ask you, why do you want to get Mathilde out of the way?"[5]

All family members fired off missives to Senior: Edith (please help me oppose this engagement),[6] Harold (I feel that Mathilde's life happiness depends upon this),[7] Fowler (I do not support this),[8] Muriel (something must be done to stop this nonsense),[9] and Mathilde herself (he is a very wonderful man).[10] Senior replied to Edith that he hoped Mathilde would "hear our counsels and in any event . . . put aside the question for the present. Only think how sad it would make Grandmother Rockefeller feel if she were here."[11] Also in New York, another family member, Junior, cringed with the news and pleaded futilely with Harold to do what he could to stop the relationship.[12]

The front page of the *New York Times* announced the engagement, adding, "Whether Mrs. Edith Rockefeller McCormick . . . attended the family conference is not known. It is believed, however, that she has not interested herself in the matter since her single brief statement several days ago that 'Mrs. McCormick would not discuss the matter either one way or the other.'"[13]

Unable to get Mathilde to talk about the situation, Edith sent a note, remarkable in all that it reveals about family issues:

Dearest Mathilde, I miss not seeing you very much. What your problems are which keep you from coming to me as one human being to another, you must know. What can it harm to come to talk to one's Mother. We can always listen to what those who love us say—it does not mean that we have to follow and certainly we do not unless we find understanding in the words spoken. I am not only thinking of today and this year for you, but I am thinking of the future. Do you want to bring children into the world knowing that they will be insane? And this is what happens when a much older man marries a young girl. You find an example of this in our own family. Grandfather McCormick was forty-nine and Grandmother was twenty-three—twenty-six years difference in age. Seven children were born to them. Two died young and two are insane. Do you see how unjust it is to bring children into the world doomed to insanity? And do you see how the girl who does this brings on herself hours of suffering and anguish? Ask Grandmother McCormick how many nights she has cried through the whole night in her despair over her poor sick children.

Dearest Mathilde, you are not doing anything remarkable or unusual in wanting to force through a marriage with an older man of another generation. Girls are marrying secretly older men every day. It is, I am sorry to say, quite the fashion at the present time. Some marry their money. Some marry their name. Some marry them on account of the father complex (and this is your case). None of them marry for the manhood—for the older men have not got it as the young men of twenty. Of course, as the girls experience this their eyes are opened and they see what they have done. I am writing you these facts because young girls do not know them, and Mothers are here to tell them—to teach them. I would so love to see you. Ever your devoted and loving Mother.[14]

Edith had hoped to enroll Mathilde in an American boarding school (Muriel too; Westover was on the docket)[15] where she would meet new people and hopefully embrace her U.S. citizenship rather than pine for Switzerland. Edith appealed to Senior to help her in this quest, knowing he was nothing if not a proud American.[16] Having finally succeeded in getting the McCormick clan back from Europe, Senior would not have been keen on losing Mathilde to a Swiss riding master nearly thirty years her elder.

Another letter went off from Edith to her Swiss lawyers, asking them to inform Max that she would never approve of this marriage and that they would never get a dime from her. Certain Max was a fortune hunter, Edith asked her lawyers to remind him that she had helped draft her niece Margaret Strong's rejection to the love letter Max had previously sent her.[17]

Harold, for his part, sent a long, heartfelt letter to a Swiss connection asking him to very covertly investigate Max. He stressed that he liked Max and felt him to be a fine gentleman but that he wanted no surprises down the line.[18]

Mathilde found support not only in Harold but also in Aunt Anita, who tried to assume a motherly role in a friendly letter to Max: "There are deep places that we should go into all together—I mean you and M[athilde] and Harold and I. I only say 'I' because M has no mother near her and although I cannot be all of that, I can be some of it—and I love her dearly."[19]

Harold whisked his three children off to Walnut Grove, the old McCormick farm in Virginia, for some quality time. And to brighten the mood and ensure favorite parent status, he brought back a playful Irish terrier puppy, of championship stock, full of joy and mischief.

Edith reluctantly agreed to allow Harold sole guardianship of Mathilde in a bargain intended to keep her from marrying until she was eighteen,[20] believing that time away from Max would temper the flames of love.

In the middle of the posturing, legal wrangling over guardianship, and emotional pleas for Mathilde to reconsider, the *Chicago Daily Tribune* ran a story implying that Fowler intended to marry Fifi Stillman once her high-profile divorce was complete: "'Isn't that the worst piffle you ever heard?' Young McCormick said when 'Bud' Stillman showed him the headlines of an evening paper. 'I knew they would publish such a story, but I did not know just when, so when "Bud" showed me the story he said, 'Well, it's come at last.' I learned that reporters were working on such a report in Chicago. It looks like pure malice to me to print such a story at a time like this, even it were true. I wish to take this occasion to deny it, every word of it.'"[21]

But Fowler's story wasn't fully cooked yet; there would be more to come. In the meantime, Harold himself took center stage.

Just as Alexander Smith Cochran was getting divorced from Ganna Walska in June 1922, Harold underwent a controversial medical procedure that promised sexual rejuvenation. Ganna was twenty years younger than Harold, and although he took pride in being in good physical shape, he feared his libido might be waning (as Edith had implied when she told Mathilde that older men haven't "got it" as do young men). His physician informed him that the gymnastic exercise he'd been doing—he was able to complete fifteen handsprings in a row—was too strenuous for his age and suggested he look into the new field of gland transplantation.[22]

And so it came to be that, for $50,000, Harold allowed himself to be implanted with glands from a monkey in an attempt to restore his sexual potency. While everyone involved—from surgeon Victor Lespinasse (the country's leading expert on gland transplants), to the hospital staff, to all family members—was sworn to secrecy, the press had tapped into telephone lines, so soon the news was out.[23] Nationwide. A juicy story such as this could not be contained.

At first the rumor spread—from sources ranging from the *New York Times* to small rural papers—that in the same hospital was a virile but impoverished young blacksmith, who had been paid handsomely for his glands. This inspired a barroom ditty:

> Under the spreading chestnut tree,
> The village smithy stands;
> The smith a gloomy man is he,
> McCormick has his glands.[24]

Harold summoned cousin and *Chicago Tribune* publisher Robert Mc-Cormick to his bedside and asked him to put out a statement that lawsuits would be filed if the articles didn't stop.[25] The articles kept coming, though most now with the monkey gland story instead, but no lawsuits ever materialized.

Some articles had more fun with it than others. The *Belleville News Democrat* went all in, under a headline "Lost Manhood Restored. Putting a New Carburetor into a Petered-Out Chicago Millionaire."

> Will Harold F. Mccormick be able to deliver the goods after the wound heals? This great American millionaire and plutocrat has just had an extremely delicate surgical operation performed on his body to cure him of his impotency and to restore his manhood. . . .
>
> He remained, even after his marriage to Rockefeller's girl, a carousing sport and a regular devil with some mighty fast women, and in his ambition to cut capers, hewed a little into and over the line, leaving himself a petered-out physical wreck. . . .
>
> M'Cormick is now free to marry his Polish song-bird, but he realizes that in his present senility the marriage contract entered into with any woman would be a hollow mockery and laughable farce. . . .
>
> Go to it Harold, you big stiff![26]

The *Belleville News Democrat* was inundated with so many requests for this juicy editorial that it printed a second run of 2,500 copies.

Even in this deeply embarrassed state, Harold could not contain his perennially happy-go-lucky personality and wired Ganna in Paris that he felt rejuvenated, like a new man.

The board of International Harvester was not amused. They requested Harold's resignation, which he happily supplied, never having wanted the mantle initially. It did mean that for the first time, the company would be led by a non-McCormick: longtime executive Alexander Legge.[27]

Harold sailed for Paris once fully recovered, where he married Ganna in August.[28] At the time, it was illegal in the States to remarry until a full twelve months after one's divorce, so they did the deed in Paris and had a second ceremony in Lake Forest in February 1923.[29] Ganna was now Ganna Puacz d'Eingorn Fraenkel Cochran McCormick. (More surnames were still to come.)

There was, of course, the problem of Senior. Harold sent a telegram on August 13: "Mrs. Cochran and I were married today. Am very happy and know you are glad for me. Want send this direct word to you." A note is typed on Senior's copy of the telegram by an assistant: "Read the attached cable to him at Mr R's direction, and upon his instruction make this memorandum: 'No answer to this telegram. File it away.'"[30]

One can only imagine what Katharine's reaction might have been to all this news. One brother underwent gland transplantation to increase his virility while the other was locked away for life, prone to violent sexual attacks. Stanley's medical team recorded his almost maniacal episodes of masturbation. Katharine's pleas for endocrine testing for Stanley continued to go unheeded, his medical team stating that "his age is such that his glandular defects are likely to have assumed permanent form."[31] If hormones could help with the one case, why not the other?

But as for Harold, he felt rejuvenated and free and eagerly looked forward to his new life. Harold and Ganna and Mathilde and Max were all in Europe, where Max had managed to tuck Mathilde into a remote hideaway cabin in the Alps, and the couple was quietly living together. Harold wrote to Senior glowingly about the times they spent together, roasting marshmallows, deep in conversation, planning Mathilde's wedding,[32] which would be in London in April.[33] Essentially, Harold and Max were contemporaries, and Mathilde and Ganna not terribly far apart. After Mathilde's wedding, Harold was quick to report to Senior that Mathilde and Max had signed "separation contracts" to neatly divide their wealth in case the marriage did not last.[34]

There was scarcely a week in 1922 when the McCormick family did not make headlines for one scandal or another. Edith somehow managed to maintain her emotional homeostasis, explaining years later to a reporter, "You are like a craft that is caught in the current of a stream. You must learn to keep your craft in the center but you have nothing to do with the current. It will bear you downstream whether you will or not."[35]

Also in the news was the continuing debate over James Joyce's *Ulysses*. Originally distributed as a serial in the *Little Review* over the course of several years, a masturbation scene led to an obscenity designation, and the book was banned in the United States. It was published on Joyce's birthday, February 2, 1922, in Paris, but it would take many years before it was readily available in the United States. While T. S. Eliot would state, "I hold this book to be the most important expression which the present age has found; it is a book to which we are all indebted, and from which none of us can escape,"[36] having provided key funding for a book deemed obscene probably didn't help Edith's image with her straitlaced family.

The year ended with a flurry of expectation among the press that Edith was now free to marry her friend Edwin Krenn, since twelve months had passed since her divorce from Harold. Excitement peaked on December 31, with reporters stationed at both Edith's house and across the street at the Drake Hotel. Some climbed trees for a better vantage point. All seemed promising, particularly after two uniformed footmen unrolled a red carpet down the front walk and installed a gaily striped awning over it. Edwin was tailed by a posse of reporters as he went about his day's chores. Several friends arrived at the Bastion and then were whisked off, along with Edith and Edwin, but merely to the opera. Meanwhile, over at the Drake, Edwin's business partner Edward Dato spent a tense day: industrious reporters seeking a comment from him had been slipping notes under his door, only to have rival correspondents snatch them out. He'd spent the afternoon "vainly trying to catch the elusive envelopes as they appeared and disappeared."[37]

All in all, it seemed like a fitting way to end the year.

PARTNERSHIP

1921-25

*W*hile Harold and Mathilde were pursuing their new loves in Europe, while Fowler and Muriel steadfastly ignored their mother, and while Senior opted to keep his silence rather than get involved in the fray, one person stood quietly and faithfully by Edith's side: Edwin Krenn.

Edwin appeared at the Bastion every day, often twice, at his appointed times, always dressed to the nines, including spats, and unfailingly bearing a small corsage for Edith. He maintained a card file to keep track of which of his two hundred hand-tailored suits he had worn on each day.[1] Edwin was Edith's usual escort to the opera, the theater, and numerous other social engagements.

Friend Arthur Meeker described Edwin: "Poor little Mr. Krenn could not have had an easy life. Small and blond, with pudgy, dimpled fingers, he always reminded me of a newly hatched duckling. There was a tentative quality in his smile, as well there might be—Chicago society definitely disapproved of Edwin Krenn. Who were they to judge? But they did judge, with the terrible finality of a tight, small community with uncompromisingly Bourgeois standards. His public relations with his employer, more than discreet, were dignified to the point of stateliness. She was a woman deserted in humiliating circumstances by her husband, estranged, as far as one could tell, from her children, immensely rich, immensely lonely— what wonder if she needed a friend she could trust to share her intellectual interests, someone happily outside the limited group of Middlewestern millionaires and their frantically extroverted wives with whom, otherwise, her lot was unalterably cast?"[2]

Chicago knew Edwin Krenn as Edith's silent but constant companion. She had ostensibly brought him back to help design the zoo, but the zoo leaders had opted for a different architect. Instead, Edith and Edwin started a new enterprise that, for a while, was a tremendous success.

One day late in 1921, as Edith was battling through her divorce negotiations, Edwin Krenn had an unexpected visitor at his Drake Hotel suite: Edward Dato, originally from Ukraine but a classmate of Edwin's from his Zurich prep school days. He was working (ironically) at International Harvester when he read a newspaper article that mentioned his old classmate.[3] Edward and his wife, Minnie, were proud parents of a newborn son named Harold; their next two children would be named Edith and Edwin.[4]

Delighted to find his old classmate, Edwin introduced Edward to Edith, and the three Es hit it off such that they decided to start a small real estate firm with Edith's remaining Riverside land holdings. Years later, Edward Dato recalled that at the inaugural meeting in the Bastion, Edith handed over $5.2 million worth of securities, already endorsed, with the directions that they should be used to establish the Edith Rockefeller McCormick Trust to fund the business. Dato claims he walked out of the meeting nervously clutching that small fortune, flagged down a cab, and locked the papers in a flimsy safe in his office.[5] The public was invited to buy into the trust, and thousands of small investors jumped at the chance, with the sterling Rockefeller name a virtual guarantee of financial success.

Edward and Edwin put in $1,500 each. Accordingly, Edith held fifty-two thousand shares while the men each had fifteen.[6] They started in a one-room ground-floor office at Michigan Avenue and Ohio Street, just down from the Bastion.[7] And so Krenn & Dato was born.

The Riverside lots now sold like magic. Edith had owned them since 1909 and had them subdivided and utilities laid, but the lots hadn't sold. But now, with the promise of a splendid new zoo to come and with shiny Krenn & Dato signs in the yards, the lots began to disappear. The first few sold for $800 each. Then, a stroke of luck: a local banker inquired about a large corner lot, and Edward sold it to him for an astronomical $9,000. Cleverly, Edward had the banker help with publicity, and that did the trick. An advertisement in the next day's paper included a quote from the banker predicting great profits for investors. And the people came. There was a snowstorm the day the ad ran, but people stood in line for hours to buy the lots. Edward raised the price from $800 to $5,000, and still they sold.[8]

The Riverside sites were just the beginning. Krenn & Dato expanded rapidly. Using free entertainment and refreshments as a lure, the partners ushered potential salesmen into classroom settings,[9] hiring them in bunches of a hundred or more and providing group training.[10] Eventually they would employ 1,500 people—salesmen, architects, engineers, property managers. They issued a monthly magazine, the *Krenn & Dato Times*, complete with its own comic strip featuring punny character Iona Lott, had baseball tournaments, and ran salesman-of-the-month (Top-Notchers) contests.[11] The one-room office on Michigan Avenue grew to include the entire three-story building, plus an additional site on LaSalle Street. It became known as the Rockefeller block (deep in the heart of McCormickville).[12] The timing was perfect; it was the very beginning of the real estate boom. Everyone, it seemed, was buying land either to live on or for investment purposes.

The *New York Herald* noted, "It will be interesting to learn how Mrs. McCormick's ventures turn out and how well she is able to hold her own with the male real estate dealers of Chicago who have been accustomed to purely masculine competition."[13] The Krenn & Dato newsletter shows the firm employed female realtors as well as male.

Edith's goal was to provide affordable real estate for first-time buyers. A new rail line had been established running north out of the city, and Krenn & Dato gobbled up huge tracts of land and set to work subdividing, developing, and selling. The firm owned property from the northernmost suburbs (Waukegan), to the western suburbs of LaGrange and Berwyn, to the southern areas in Calumet.[14] Selling off $11 million of her Standard Oil stocks, Edith bought land in Niles Center (today Skokie), where they built a massive apartment building dubbed Meadow Lane Garden Apartments and a subdivision called Devonshire Manor. Edwin designed an administrative office in Niles Center, an eye-catcher meant to resemble a Greek temple, which was their logo.[15]

Cashing in an additional half million worth of stocks, Edith purchased the old polo grounds bounded by Lincoln, Peterson, and California Avenues.[16] She and her partners had a sixteen-floor skyscraper constructed at 3300 Lake Shore Drive overlooking the lake.[17] Up north, in Highland Park, they laid out the two-hundred-acre Highland Park Highlands, as close to

Edith's Lake Forest home as Edith "could possibly select,"[18] including streets named Dato and Krenn.[19]

Within a few frenetic years, Krenn & Dato was one of the nation's largest real estate firms, boasting over sixteen thousand proud new property owners.[20] The grand triumvirate of Es was making home ownership possible for the middle class. They owned land mostly around Chicago and its suburbs but also in other parts of the United States and Canada. The Krenn & Dato advertisements, with the firm's slogan "The Mark of Security," sported the tagline "Exclusive Agents for Mrs. Rockefeller McCormick Properties." One ad boasted "Developments Exceeding a Hundred Million Dollars,"[21] representing their worth if all the properties sold. In very short order, it had become an empire.

Edith provided the money; Edwin and Edward purchased the land and ran the business. Edith vowed to stay out of the office, so any meetings of the three partners took place in the Bastion, out of sight.[22] Edwin and Edward each received $40,000 in annual salary; all profits went back into the company.[23]

At long last, Edith had the satisfaction of a successful business—not only one that was raking in money but one that positively impacted people's lives. Yet, if she had expected praise from her father, that would never come.

Senior cautioned, "I shall expect later on that you will have great disappointment in connection with these real estate transactions, and it would give us all great humiliation to find a duplication of the experience which you have already had in your business adventures with foreigners."[24]

Senior kept at it, too, never praising, always warning, and rubbing her nose in her failure with the wood-hardening business: "You will recall that in another affair of business some time ago, I gave you words of warning, and you found at last that my apprehensions were correct, and that these transactions resulted in a large loss to you. It will be a fatal mistake for you to close your eyes to what is so apparent to others in the business world, who naturally are getting more or less information about the business you do and the way it is being conducted. I am expecting you will have sad disappointments along these lines, and I only regret that you do not seem sensitive to the danger. . . . Please read and carefully ponder, and keep all this communication to yourself and destroy it after you have thoroughly saturated yourself with its meaning."[25]

Senior sent compatriot Junior a copy of the letter. Junior responded, "I hope it will cause Edith to stop and . . . ponder well the question of her financial associates. But even if it should fail of accomplishment along that line, it seems to me a very important letter for you to have written, as a record and as a protection, in the event that the disaster which we all fear should overtake Edith and she should come back to you or me with the question why we had not warned her, if we had information which caused us uneasiness."[26]

Whether they were fearing or actually hoping for disaster is unclear.

Edith kept up the facade of intending to visit her father, writing numerous times that "her trunks were packed" or she "planned to come" for Senior's birthday, but somehow her plans were always scuttled.[27] It seems likely that she knew a visit might help patch up their fractured relationship, but her travel fears prevented such endeavors. For his part, Senior declared he was too old to travel to Chicago.

Whereas Senior ignored her success, the public took notice, and not in a good way. Her gift of land for a zoo had been contingent on the Forest Preserve District paying for the construction and maintenance of the buildings out of tax revenues. The Forest Preserve District proposed a bond issue that would provide $500,000 a year for five years to finance construction, followed by $250,000 a year for maintenance. For the average homeowner, this came down to an approximately forty-cent tax raise the first five years and thirteen cents thereafter.[28] It was hardly a fortune.

But also on the ballot of the November 1923 election was a tax increase for schools. Perceived, erroneously, as being mutually exclusive, a cry of "schools not monkeys" became loud and clear.[29] When it became known that Krenn & Dato had sold the remaining Riverside lots for over $1 million, people cried foul. Had the zoo gift been a calculated real estate maneuver from the get-go? Were ordinary citizens being asked to finance a zoo while a multimillionaire padded her pockets with real estate gains? The *Chicago Journal* ran back-to-back editorials, "Real Estate and the Zoo"[30] and "Not a Good Time for Zoos," declaring "school seats are worth more than monkeys. . . . The voters of this county should bury the zoo proposition at the polls."[31]

Chicago Zoological Society president John McCutcheon was perfectly placed to mount the counteroffensive. In his role as *Chicago Tribune* cartoonist, he created pro-zoo comics, one of which ran right in the middle of the front page, above the fold, two days before the election.[32]

But the zoo bill was roundly defeated by a margin of over two to one. The Forest Preserve District had land, a governing body, architectural plans (designed by Edwin Clark, not Edwin Krenn), and a newly hired director but no money to move forward.

Just as it had taken many years for the John R. McCormick Memorial Institute for Infectious Diseases to gain traction, so it was for the Chicago Zoological Society. The new director, without a park to run, moved on to oversee the new Shedd Aquarium; a number of trustees and governing members resigned; and those stalwarts who remained regrouped in order to figure out how to proceed.[33] Edith's direct involvement with the zoo was minimal. While she was present at the 1926 planning meeting,[34] she hadn't bothered to attend most board meetings or even the ceremonial ground-breaking on October 27, 1922.[35] Whether this was because of the media frenzy that surrounded her, her travel fears, or a lack of real interest is unknown.

Edith was always somewhat on edge in public. She was frequently peppered with questions about her family's scandals or her relationship with Edwin. Plus, she never lost her fear of suffering a panic attack in public, despite her profound belief in psychoanalysis and many years with Carl Jung. Jung, for his part, publicly declared Edith fit: "Mrs. McCormick was cured years ago. She is a splendidly balanced woman who took advantage of her years of residence in Zurich to store away an immense amount of knowledge in all fields from Sanskrit to psychology. Mrs. McCormick today is one of the most learned women I know. I have made her as perfect as possible, according to the qualities with which she is gifted by nature. I could not make her any different, as I do not claim to create anything, but I certainly claim that she is perfectly balanced, according to her nature."[36] The same article surmised that Jung believed an unhappy marriage had been the root of Edith's depression.

Leaving Chicago proper was stressful for Edith, and she did it only in carefully controlled circumstances, with her own driver, in her own vehicle. Though only thirty-four miles away, Villa Turicum staff recalled that Edith spent limited time at her beautiful summer home. Superintendent John Dunford reported that she never dined or slept at Villa Turicum following her return from Switzerland: "Mrs. McCormick used to come out several times a week and stay an hour or two. She said it was the beauty spot of the world."[37]

When she did go out in public, the papers nearly always reported what she wore, including specific jewelry, and in whose company she was (usually Edwin). In February 1923, she attended a party where conversation centered on Howard Carter's recent discovery of King Tutankhamun's tomb. Edith's dinner comments made news: "I had long known that I had a previous incarnation, but I did not know who I had been. When they began to dig in Luxor I had a vague sense of something impending. As they approached the inner chamber of the tomb the feeling grew stronger, until I felt that a curtain was about to be lifted in my life. Then they opened the mummy chamber, and when I saw the pictures of it, I knew. There was my little chair. I was Ankh-es-en-pa-Aten."[38] A year later, Edith would host a luncheon at the Bastion for archaeologist Howard Carter.[39]

While Edith's comment that she'd been King Tut's child bride was amusing for some, Spiritualism was all the rage. Her daughter Muriel was a fierce believer as well.

Muriel was on a path all her own. Having publicly stated that she was opposed to her sister Mathilde's marriage to Max Oser,[40] and rolling her eyes at her father's wooing of Ganna Walska Cochran,[41] Muriel took a decidedly different route. Her passion had always been the arts, an acceptable outlet for her fiery emotions. Having enjoyed a host of nicknames in childhood, including Menia, Mosie, Mackie, and Princess Mju, she took the stage name Nawanna Micor.[42] (Her preferred letter was clearly M.) In 1922, she had her public debut as the male lead in La Passant at Chicago's Modern French Theater, wearing costumes she'd created and using sets she had designed. Edith was in the front row, alone, having left Edwin behind this time. Except for a brief acknowledgment when Edith handed Muriel a giant basket of pink roses at the end, there was no interaction between mother and daughter.[43] Muriel wrote to her grandfather that they just bowed to one another in public.[44]

A rumor circulated that Muriel had been offered $1 million to star in four moving pictures.[45] But Muriel was a purist, saying she would not be bought by anybody. This resolution applied to her grandfather as well. Muriel returned Senior's annual birthday check with a note: "I really can't understand what prompted you to express your loving feeling in such a materialistic manner. . . . I could never cash that check. Please do not misunderstand. Had it been a million, I would react in the same manner, for I accept money from nobody."[46]

She was a free spirit, Muriel. A dog lover all her life, in 1927 she would argue with a policeman over licensing her dogs, particularly the smallest, Wu-si-woo, a Pekingese standing a mere three inches high. "Why, a license tag would almost break his neck. He's so small, and he's always in my sight. In winter I carry him in my muff or in my pocket.'"[47]

Muriel's approach to marriage was also unique. Her godparents, George and Marian McKinlock, believing Muriel had been cast adrift by Edith and Harold, took her under their care, even going so far as to move Muriel into a cottage on their Lake Forest estate. While at a séance, Muriel was visited by their dead son, George Alexander McKinlock Jr., who had been killed in the war. A "curious sort of spiritual wooing followed,"[48] and after more psychic sessions, Muriel became convinced she and George were soulmates. Announcing a spiritual engagement to George Jr., Muriel spent many hours with mother Marian devotedly grieving at his grave. Chicago history buffs may know that, to honor their son, the McKinlocks pledged nine acres of downtown land to Northwestern University for the creation of a medical school.

There is a further twist to this tale. The *Chicago Tribune* announced in 1925 that Muriel underwent emergency surgery resulting from complications of appendicitis.[49] However, the attending surgeon was an obstetrician/gynecologist, and Muriel's appendix had been removed when she was a toddler. One can only speculate what type of procedure was done. Sitting by her side in the hospital were her ersatz mothers, Aunt Anita and Marian McKinlock. The papers reported Muriel and Marian's relationship was almost like mother and daughter.[50] Later in life, Muriel would adopt children, unwilling or unable to become pregnant herself.

Muriel had also attracted an undesirable suitor by the name of Arthur Sears, a lunatic who had become convinced that he and Muriel were destined to be together and had set April 15, 1926, as their wedding date. He sent her over 350 letters professing his love. Number 347 reads, "To me, the Dearest, Sweetest, Best & Beautifullest one of these here flappers south of the Mason and Dixon Line. I mean Muriel McCormick who has just 10 more days until she is no longer Miss but Mrs. if that there little flapper thinks she aint going to start paying me those 24 hours of love interest on April 15th she has another think coming, she sure going to suffer when I colect [sic] my interest yes Sir, Ain't she?"[51]

Frustrated by Muriel's lack of response, Sears began, unwisely, sending letters to Senior, who promptly instructed his lawyers to take action. Sears was committed to a state institution and prohibited from further contact with Muriel.[52]

Similarly, a familiar figure had appeared on Edith's doorstep: her Swiss chauffeur, Emile Ammann. Following his years of service to Edith in Zurich, Ammann had moved to Mauritius to recommit himself to his family. But that didn't go well, so he traced Edith to Chicago. Claiming he was under her hypnotic influence, Ammann wrote her, and Edwin, multiple letters asking to see her. Receiving no response, he came to her door.[53]

Mentally unwell people frequently sought out Edith. It was common knowledge that she analyzed her patients free of charge; her household staff had become accustomed to unbalanced individuals asking for help. One man who wrote threatened machine gun violence and acid torture unless he received $50,000.[54] It was at such times that her security team justified its worth and Edith's perennial fears of the outside world were reinforced. Her guards were armed, and one unfortunate watchman lost his life late one night in Edith's kitchen because his gun accidentally discharged when he bent over to pick up a towel.[55]

Another time, a young soprano, Charlotte Caillies, frustrated that she couldn't get a role with the Chicago Grand Opera, took a concoction of codeine, veronal, and chloroform, intending to take her life—fortunately unsuccessfully. But she had left a note requesting that Edith (who had never met the young woman) send her body to her parents' grave in New York and that her pet parrot be given chloroform so it could be her faithful companion in her coffin.[56] After all, Edith was known for her benevolence and interest in people's psychic well-being. The role came with these sorts of dangers.

But chauffeur Ammann was a more serious threat. He wasn't asking for money or work, just to be released from Edith's hypnotic influence. Ammann recalled his first meeting with Edith: "Her oversized, piercing eyes never left me during the interview! Was that a hypnotic look? In the end, does Mrs. Rockefeller use her servants and her visitors as guinea pigs for hypnotic experiments?"[57]

The superintendent of Chicago's psychopathic hospital was summoned to collar Ammann, who was deemed dangerously insane. The issue went before the court, and after having spent four weeks in a psych ward, Ammann was released with the stipulation that he leave the country. One of the people who testified on his behalf was Edith's maid Emmy, with whom Ammann claimed to have had an affair lasting several years.[58]

Amman wrote, "That I was in Chicago made them very uncomfortable; no doubt they were afraid of my tattling. Mrs. Rockefeller, like many other Americans, believed that everything in Europe was permissible for her, even disrespect for decency and morality; whereas in the United States she was very prude and discreet. Therefore, it was necessary to delete me—the eyewitness of their Zurich escapades—from the list of the living."[59]

Either version of this story is plausible. Perhaps Ammann was unbalanced, or perhaps Edith tucked him away so he couldn't tattle. His autobiography is outrageous but does not read as the words of a madman, although some of his claims stand at odds with the facts. It is also possible his book was retaliation for his temporary incarceration. Four weeks in a psychiatric ward couldn't have been easy.

In 1948, many years after Edith's death, Ammann wrote to Junior, complaining of dreams he'd been having at regular intervals over several months. In the dreams, Edith stood before him, begging him to write to Junior. After a particularly vivid dream, in which Edith demanded angrily, "This time it is necessary to write to my brother, I want this done," Ammann complied. A handwritten note on the letter indicates Junior did not answer.[60]

ELDER STATESWOMAN

1925-28

*N*ow comfortably in her fifties, divorced, and successful in a business venture, Edith was secure and unapologetic in her beliefs and approach to life. In a way, she had little left to lose: her family had abandoned her and she had been publicly humiliated by her husband, so why not go for broke? She began to finally use her voice to speak out about the role of the individual, and in particular women, though not always in a fashion the greater majority could understand.

One example was her speech at a Cordon Club luncheon, just one month after her divorce was finalized:

> After many years of study I have concluded that the whole happiness of life and what brings poise and serenity to the soul consists in an understanding of one's self, why that self is placed in the world, and how to use it to the best advantage. . . .
>
> In all human activities there are negative and positive forces. Woman is a negative force; man, a positive. It is when women try to be other than they are by nature and play the game according to the man's rules that they are apt to fail. The negative position of a woman does not prevent her from being creative or having ideas that are original and progressive. She is creatively negative. Her ability is fully as much of a force as is the man's positiveness, but, being differently constructed, she expresses it in a different manner.[1]

It could be argued that Edith expressed herself "in a different manner" than most. Whatever her emotional or social shortcomings, she was mentally on a higher level than virtually everyone in her orbit. As a result, she usually spoke above their heads.

She referenced self-sufficiency and finding happiness within: "We are everything within ourselves. Everything comes from within us and not outside of us. . . . It is time we began to grow within us so that we will be so rich with good, so overflowing that the overflow will pick up our fallen brothers without any detriment to ourselves."[2]

Edith was on an intellectual quest, devoting part of each day to furthering her understanding of the leading philosophers, the world's religions, and the great writers, a habit begun while she was in Zurich. She preferred to read in the author's language, believing too much was lost in translation, and would annotate her personal copies with handwritten notes (in that language) on virtually every page.[3] Her lifetime of study in languages had served her well, and she continued her language studies up until the end of her life.

Her 15,000-volume library[4] rivaled the collections of some universities, including 143 volumes of Goethe, 30 volumes of Hugo, 24 volumes of Eliot, over 400 psychology books (340 of them in German), 29 volumes of Maupassant, 50 volumes of Balzac, and the world's largest collection of works by Ruskin.[5] Her collection of writings by Kant and his commentators, such as Heidegger, Chamberlain, and Wundt, indicated a profound mastery of his philosophy. These were not library sets merely for display; these books were heavily notated. As S. M. Melamed put it, "Her Kantiens was sufficient to satisfy the needs of any Kantian scholar."[6]

In addition, Edith was an inveterate collector of first editions, illuminated books, and copies that had once belonged to royalty. This woman valued books and had spent a small fortune on her library. Edith owned a first edition of the English Bible; original handwritten verses from writers such as Longfellow, Browning, Rousseau, and Lamb; a first English translation of Ovid dating back to 1640; an illuminated book of hours from the fifteenth century; and volumes containing bookplates from Napoleon, Marie Antoinette, Charles II, Louis XIV, and Louis XV. Some of her editions dated back to the 1500s and were printed on vellum, including a 1512 first English version of *Lohengrin*, for which she had paid $21,000.[7] There were also large sections on gardens, furniture, astrology, lace, and Chinese art.[8]

Melamed summed up Edith's interests: "The marginal notes in the major books which she studied indicate clearly that she was deeply interested in epistemology, ethics, psychology, sociology, Christian dogma, history of mysticism and of the church, comparative religion, Judaism, Buddhism, Plato, Kant, and Goethe. Her Goethe collection was probably the richest in the country, and her interest in his works and personality was a match to her predilection for Kant." Melamed concluded, "But only recently … did it come to light that a Rockefeller was as versed in philosophical and theological thought as any American university professor. This representative of a great family was that dame extraordinaire, the late Edith Rockefeller McCormick."[9]

Let there be no doubt: Edith was an intellectual powerhouse. In contrast, Harold was gadding about Europe with Ganna, finally free of the intense philosophical conversations Edith may have wanted to share with him. Jung had been right: one was a thinker, the other, a feeler.

Edith once told a reporter that her role was that of a giver. A reporter explained, "By this she did not mean to imply that she was philanthropic in the sense that she doles out her vast wealth to others who need it. On the contrary, she gives of her mind. She thinks out the problems of others, counsels them and encourages their efforts toward advancement. 'My object in the world is to think new thoughts,' she said."[10]

Edith, ever trying to teach and inspire, often laced her speeches with historical references. Shortly after Mathilde announced her engagement to Max Oser, Edith gave a speech to the Chicago College Club with thinly veiled remarks about the match but also interesting commentary on the role of women: "If a woman marries outside her own clan or tribe, she'll be a slave. History proves it. In olden days, if a man were bored with the women in his own tribe, he went and stole a wife from another clan and brought her back with him. But the stolen bride had a sorry time of it, for the women of the men's tribe would hate the foreign bride, who would have to depend for happiness entirely upon her husband, to whom she would be virtually a slave. From this condition, there grew up a kind of serfdom for women which enmeshed women who married outside their own tribe. This period of serfdom was an era of down curves for women, but it was sandwiched between two up-curves, the ancient and the modern. In the very ancient period, it was a woman who was the first architect, the first creator of pottery, the first specialist in mixing herbs, the first exponent of cookery."[11]

This notion of the woman historically being the leader came back in other speeches."Formerly it was the woman who ruled. She made the laws, man kept them. It was women who first built houses, made gardens, invented water pots and cooking utensils. But the pendulum swung too far in that direction, and nature, who loves an even keel, adjusted it."[12]

Edith, again and again, stressed that men and women are fundamentally different in how they approach problems but that both should be equally valued. While she hadn't joined sister-in-law Katharine at the forefront of the woman suffrage movement, Edith now applauded the progress: "Women are now victors. But they are much more than victors, for they have done much more than fight for their place. Their place has been won through sociological development and growth. All the modern woman wants is to be let alone, to develop, to demonstrate and to expand. Mother love is important, but it is not everything. Woman's universal love is a bigger thing."[13]

Having grown aware that her brother, Junior, now presided over the bulk of the Rockefeller fortune, Edith attempted again to get involved with the family philanthropies: "I could help you in solving and disposing of some of the questions which are brought to you for your consideration. It would be interesting to me and it would take some of the responsibility and burden from your shoulders. We have the same inheritances, we are both constructive in our point of view of life and in our feeling of responsibility towards our brother."[14] But Junior had no interest in involving his errant sister.

Perhaps only now fully realizing the inequities in her life stemming from gender roles, Edith agreed to serve on the planning board for the Women's World's Fair, adding her intellectual star power to the event (she was advertised as the "keenly intellectual" board member).[15] The inaugural kickoff took place on April 18, 1925, when "Paulette Revere" galloped on horseback through downtown Chicago, congratulating women on their progress over 150 years (Paul Revere's ride having taken place 150 years prior, to the day). President Calvin Coolidge gave a radio speech opening the fair, and his wife, Grace, pushed a button in Washington telegraphing a signal to open the doors and declare the fair begun. The eight-day event featured women politicians, inventors, journalists, artists, physicians, authors—over one hundred different occupations were represented in the three hundred booths (including one for Krenn & Dato, who proudly employed women across many departments).[16] Over two hundred thousand attended in the first year.[17]

Though the fair wasn't her idea initially, *Time* magazine gave her some of the credit: "Overtopping all others was the name of a curiously engrossing personality—Edith Rockefeller McCormick. Sapient in the arcana of psychoanalysis, lavish in support of opera, eccentric in her choice of good works which include a zoo, Mrs. Rockefeller McCormick adheres to no party, cult or faction of her own. She has, of late, taken up women. And whether or not she originated the women's first all-woman fair, it is certain that she was its preeminent prophetess." The article included a quote from Edith: "The Women's World Fair marks the passing of the drooping, useless hothouse lily of Queen Victoria's reign and glorifies that nonetheless beautiful flower, the red rose of modern woman, eager, joyous, purposeful."[18]

Had Edith felt like a useless hothouse flower while restricted by marriage and family roles? If so, she was finally coming into her own, speaking out on issues that mattered to her, planning for future endeavors far greater than anything she'd already accomplished, and not giving a damn what anyone thought of her.

Historian Dianne MacLeod argues that Edith "was in the vanguard in seeking individual stability through psychoanalysis, condoning divorce, and supporting women's equality, but she nostalgically valued the principle of community, women's role as nurturers, the visual arts of previous eras, and the power of dreams to effect change. . . . McCormick progressively adopted a worldview that superseded her needs as an individual and embraced the broader concerns of humanity. She grew from an introspective, passive matron who adhered to the Gilded Age's ideals of refinement and domestic femininity into a crusader for human rights and world peace."[19]

Chicago hosted the Women's World's Fair for several consecutive years, and as the fourth year kicked off, Edith expressed delight that young women were choosing careers based on professionals they had seen at the fair. "There, where they met women lawyers and physicians and realtors with years of experience concentrated in one place, they had an opportunity to select and to reject and to choose the one they proposed to follow." She felt the fair was a "marker on the path of progress."[20]

Seeking to capitalize on the idea of women's equality, on the tails of the fair Edith sent a mass mailing through her real estate firm: "What thought, what idea, was emphasized by the recently held Women's World's

Fair? Isn't it this:—Woman has at last demonstrated her actual equality in the Professions, in Art, in Literature, in Business and in Finance."[21] She'd moved well beyond her mother's maxim that a woman's greatest privilege was being a good wife and mother.

Edith ventured into all sorts of new endeavors, including supporting an effort to widen Lake Shore Drive into two lanes in each direction to reduce congestion, despite the opposition of many of her Gold Coast neighbors.[22]

She even edged into Harold's territory, aviation, with a project that raised eyebrows across the country. She backed a proposal for a passenger airline that would provide regular service from Chicago to New York. When she announced that each plane would cost $2 million, have a capacity of two hundred passengers, and be able to make the one-way flight in ten hours, skepticism ran high.[23] Though she was right on target with this idea, there is no record that she was involved beyond her initial investment. (As a historical marker, it is interesting to note that Amelia Earhart was making her own aviation headlines around this time.)

Krenn & Dato was at the heart of one of Edith's grandest plans. For just under $2 million, Edith bought eighteen hundred acres just across the state line, outside the city of Kenosha, Wisconsin. Beautiful rolling hills abutting over three miles of Lake Michigan coastline would offer large beach homes, a marina, even an airport.[24] Krenn & Dato ran a full-page announcement: "A thorough believer in the doctrine of work, Mrs. Mc-Cormick has proven that women are as great a factor as men in the sphere of modern art, commerce, and civic progress. And now Mrs. McCormick proposes to build a model recreation city on the North Shore."[25] Krenn & Dato hyped the project by running a naming contest, offering a grand prize of $1,500 and a hundred smaller prizes. Amid the eighty thousand entries with such suggestions as Elysiana, Krenosha, Edithsdream, and Edithwatha was the winner: Edithton Beach.[26]

What somehow got lost in the coverage was the nobler intention Edith had for the land. Alongside the well-to-do suburb, she had sketched out plans for a unique university campus that complemented other educational institutions. She called it National University, and the plan was for it to be a vacation center for all the other colleges in the country.

Whereas most of the language in the Krenn & Dato brochures was written by marketing professionals, the National University materials have Edith's unmistakable voice. "Picture the leading professors and scholars in any given department of learning becoming lecturers in their special sub-jects during the summer months. Scholars and noted teachers from all over the world may be induced to find much pleasure amidst such environments as the National University Campus only can provide. Exchange of views on methods of teaching can be accomplished more fully by an exchange of professors from the various universities lecturing in the halls of the campus during the summer than in any other way known. In other words, the very best from every university can become the property of everyone interested. . . . Progress and enlightenment in any community is in inverse ratio to its ignorance and provincialism."[27]

National University was Edith's attempt to push society along the evo-lutionary path: to share knowledge, to combine wisdom, to embrace Jung's notion of individuation. No expense was to be spared. On its 3.5 miles of lakefront property, the university would have state-of-the-art everything: radio station, auditorium, open-air concert stadium, library, lecture halls, housing for faculty and students. Houses for the professors' families were to be given prime location on the lakefront and around the golf course. The athletic grounds—including tennis courts, riding stables, baseball and polo fields, gymnastics halls, swimming pools—would be sufficient to host a future American Olympic games.[28] Krenn & Dato asked the Olmsted brothers, famous landscape architects, to consider being involved in the planning.[29] However, when the Olmsted brothers contacted Junior for a reference on the firm, he declined to comment.[30]

Senior and Junior, ears to the ground, had been quietly gathering infor-mation about Edwin Krenn and Edward Dato, such as when adviser Frank Staley reported that "Krenn hasn't much in a business way while Datto [sic] has a jew's tricks and speaks very brokenly."[31] Senior warned Edith repeatedly that she should have a trusted adviser overseeing the business, but she replied with full faith in her partners. Had she been privy to their correspondence, she would have been pleased with Junior's report to Senior in 1925 that the "situation is far better than we had feared."[32]

Krenn & Dato began with the infrastructure work at Edithton, laying roads and utilities, building a welcome arch, and pouring huge amounts of money into the project that lay in the sand dunes of Wisconsin. Noble intentions—but, like so many of Edith's projects, doomed.

The Chicago Zoological Society, meanwhile, had finally managed to pass a tax referendum in the spring of 1926, and the board was able to begin construction. The first few buildings popped up in 1927, a new director was hired, and optimism and energy were running high.[33] The aim was to open in time for the 1933 Century of Progress Exposition, which would be held in Chicago (Edith served as honorary chairman of the Enrollment Committee for the exposition).[34] Edith kept herself abreast of the zoo's progress but always at arm's length; she never seemed fully invested.

There were plans, too, to expand the Bastion. While already too large for a family of just one, Edith had other ideas for it. She hired her Villa Turicum architect, Charles Adams Platt, to draw up plans for additions that would turn the 1880s stone castle into an Italian-style palazzo, four stories tall and an entire city block in size, to be used as an art museum and mayor's mansion upon her death.[35] Architectural historian Keith Morgan claims that, had the house been built, it "would have rivaled the scale of its Renaissance palazzo models."[36]

Edith spelled out her wishes for the space in her first will, dated July 1931: "Rockefeller McCormick Museum of Chicago, which institution shall be a gallery of art, a museum of antiques and other rare and beautiful articles, in order that it may aid in encouraging and developing the study of the fine arts and of advancing the general knowledge of kindred subjects. It is my wish that said Museum shall be for the use and benefit of all persons whomsoever, to the end that the same shall be an institution to which the entire public shall forever have access."[37] She also stipulated that Villa Turicum should become the Rockefeller McCormick Museum of Lake Forest, with similar purposes.

Despite huge sums of money flowing out to purchase property and pay off her divorce settlement, Edith was collecting treasures without pause. She explained her passion: "A collector is always filled with the joyful expectancy that just around the corner awaits that for which he has spent years searching."[38]

In 1928, she became the owner of a particularly important item, a Byzantine New Testament. Historians dated the interior from the 1200s, originating from the city of Constantinople; the stunning cover, done in hammered silver, was added in the 1500s. It was the sheer number of illuminations that made the piece so staggering, nearly a hundred, an unheard of amount.[39]

Professor Edgar Goodspeed, chairman of the New Testament department of the University of Chicago, found it in a little antique shop in Paris. He wrote, "The most amazing thing about it was that it seemed to have a painting illustrating the action of the text on almost every page. I had never seen such a manuscript or anything even remotely approaching it. And no wonder, for there was not another like it in the world! It was . . . no mere curiosity but a serious document for the history of Byzantine art in its last renaissance. . . . We saw in it therefore the promise of a definite contribution to the history of Byzantine iconography and we realized that in no circumstances must it be permitted to disappear again from scholarly scrutiny."[40]

Edith admired Goodspeed, commenting that having heard him lecture in 1924 "will remain as a mile stone in my religious development."[41]

Aware that he'd found a bona fide treasure, Goodspeed contacted Edith immediately, hoping she would champion a fund drive to raise money for the purchase. Instead, Edith bought it outright, stating, "I can see that this is a very distinguished thing. Would it meet your wishes if I authorized you—I do now authorize you—to buy the manuscript for me, and you and your department can have it for study and publication as long as you like."[42]

Quickly, a University of Chicago representative was designated to go purchase the codex. He traveled with two checks from Edith: an initial $20,000, and a second one in the amount of $5,000 should the former prove insufficient.[43] In the end, both were needed. When the newly named Rockefeller McCormick New Testament arrived in Chicago, it was unveiled at an open meeting at the University of Chicago, whereupon a representative of the Newberry Library declared that it "marked the beginning of a new era in the cultural life of the city."[44] Edith also authorized up to $16,000 to have the university reproduce color copies of the entire document for study purposes.[45]

While Edith had no qualms about buying an ancient Bible, she refrained from making donations to religious organizations. This was in stark contrast to Senior and Junior, who gave millions to Baptist organizations. Though Edith was an earnest scholar of religion, she did not adhere to any formal religion.

Edith explained her reluctance in a 1932 interview with reporter Mary Dougherty. "I never heard a Baptist minister say anything from a pulpit that convinced me he was Divinely inspired. What drove me from the church was the fact that to be considered a good church member I had to sit through services regularly and listen with unchallenging mind to the mouthing of the minister whatever matter he chose to discourse, whether it was his interpretation of the Bible, his rules of life or his opinions of society, always expressed with a smug self-assertive manner, denouncing everything which he did not personally approve and implying emphatically that those who did not agree with him could not by any chance be saved."

She continued, explaining that one day she walked out of the church vowing never to return, "and with a profound and sincere desire to find my own way to God, I stepped out, and since have found serenity through my own researches and in the depths of my own soul."[46]

Edith's break with the church was yet another black mark in Senior's unforgiving record book. In *Titan*, Ron Chernow concluded that Edith's decision to leave the church "allowed her to map her own route to salvation, yet it also estranged her from a family spoon-fed on simple Baptist pieties."[47]

For Edith's entire adult life, Senior had routinely given her money as gifts. On the occasions of her birthday, his own birthday, and the anniversary of Cettie's birthday, Edith always received $1,000. But in 1925, a wrapped package appeared at the Bastion. It was Camille Corot's painting *The Crayfish Hole*, valued at $12,000.[48] It depicts a lone boy, white shirt and red cap, searching for shrimp in a deserted pond. The colors are muted: greens, browns, a gray sky. The scene cries solitude. One can only wonder about Senior's intentions.

FULL STEAM AHEAD, BLINDLY

1926–28

The mid-1920s were a high for Edith, as her business venture soared, the infectious diseases institute was going strong, the zoo began coming together, and her plans for the future multiplied.

There were other prominent women high in the social structure of Chicago, but none merited the gravitas Edith held, despite the public embarrassments that had haunted her past. While she entertained less frequently than during her marriage, her invitations were rarely turned down, and she made good use of the Napoleonic tableware with such guests as Queen Marie of Romania, Prince William of Sweden,[1] Lady Spencer-Churchill (Winston Churchill's aunt),[2] and Prince Mozaffar Firouz of the Persian Embassy. *Time* magazine reported of the Persian representative, "Tidily he ate off the McCormick plate of gold, creating fewer crumbs than many another guest."[3] Of the dinner for eighty to honor the Romanian queen, the *Chicago Daily Tribune* said, "The gold service was used at the long table in the dining room—some one remarked it had never served a more appropriate purpose than yesterday—while a great T shaped table laden with the famous Napoleonic silver was set out in the drawing room."[4]

They were hardly enough hours in the day: language lessons, study, committee meetings, dress fittings, realty business discussions, a mounting pile of correspondence, browsing antique catalogs, and, always, a daily walk. Having learned the value of a strict schedule in childhood, routine seemed crucial to her sense of well-being. She took the same route north toward

Lincoln Park every day, deep in thought, with her gold-toothed security guard, Captain McNamara, walking a few steps behind.[5] When someone suggested varying her path, she replied, "It doesn't matter, I'm not really here."[6] On her Christmas Day strolls, she handed out five-dollar gold coins to the policemen she encountered—a step up from the shiny dime Senior was known to distribute to random strangers.

A good chunk of the day was devoted to seeing patients. Still an ardent believer in Jung's techniques, Edith delighted in bringing this new philosophy to Chicago. Calling it "surgery of the soul," she believed that studying dreams was the only way to "pierce the unconscious mind and see what it contains."[7] The *Chicago Daily News* stated, "Mrs. McCormick's belief in psychoanalysis was immutable. She never accepted a cent from any one whom she helped, even from the patients who came daily with attending nurses. Each morning she would sit quietly, allowing the patient to pour out all his thoughts and nodding sympathetically in silence. When he was quite 'emptied' of all disquieting ideas she would gently suggest constructive thoughts to take their place."[8]

Her calendar was full. The opera was a given, as were certain chamber and symphony concerts, art openings, and theater events. Edith frequently hosted lectures on theater, literature, gardening, and other topics at the Bastion. She served on the planning committee for any endeavor she felt would benefit the city, and there were many such undertakings, such as the Chicago Civic Theater, an attempt to establish a playhouse with strong performances but modest prices. For many years, she hosted an annual contest through the Drama League for the best new American play. She never failed to give generously of her time and money.

Theater, music, art, literature: it was all about culture for Edith. Culture for the masses. Just as with Krenn & Dato, her focus was to improve life for the middle and lower classes. Despite her imperial complex, Edith had never been an elitist. Asked in 1911 to define the difference between rich girls and poor girls, Edith wrote, "The girl of wealth can have the advantages of an education which trains the mind to work for itself, grasping the vital things in life and understanding which are the real things. Her self-reliance and judgment can be developed by travel and by the broadening influences of coming in contact with many varied customs and forms of living." However, she pointed out that the advantaged woman can be shown up by the poorer sister "who has just hard, straight ahead work before her from the beginning." Ideally, "the girl rich in worldly possessions and the girl rich in intellect and spirit should go forward side by side into the problems bound to come equally into their lives in the one road of life."[9] She never stopped trying to provide enriching opportunities for those less fortunate.

The Art Institute of Chicago was one of the beneficiaries of Edith's goodwill. She was one of three private benefactors who served as founders for its School of Industrial Arts for young designers.[10] The museum also occasionally showcased some of Edith's private treasures. Edith's collection of fine laces was unparalleled except for those in the Vatican. Primarily Flemish and Italian in origin, the collection was easily worth over $100,000. After loaning them to various museums as traveling exhibits, she placed them at the Art Institute on permanent loan.[11] The institute would also display a particularly famous carpet. In 1928, Edith, at a price of $125,000, acquired Peter the Great's Persian carpet. Created in Iran in the 1500s, Peter the Great presented it to Austria's Emperor Leopold I in the late 1600s. The *Chicago Tribune* declared it ranked sixth in importance of the world's historical carpets.[12] Edith sent Dr. Arthur Upham Pope, an expert in Oriental carpets, to bid on it in auction. It was a spirited bidding session, and while the newspapers reported the next day that the second highest bidder had been Junior, he denied having been involved.[13]

When not at a concert, Edith's evenings were devoted to movies. It was not unusual for her and Edwin to attend three movies in one evening, her Rolls Royce with gold-plated fittings[14] waiting outside one theater ready to usher them to the next. Prior to their arrival, her staff roped off seats in the back row, where she and Edwin would converse quietly in German.

Edwin was an agreeable escort. Whether the choice of activities was mutual or dictated by Edith is unknown, but Arthur Meeker's report is perhaps telling: "Once, upon a male companion's remarking that his wife had a box for Mondays in the [opera] season and he didn't know how he'd be able to stand it, the little man's [Krenn's] voice cracked on a high note of anguish: 'Aie! You should complain about Mondays—I've got to go to the opera every single night!'"[15]

Meeker, a neighbor and member of Edith's social circle, was obviously fond of her. He gave this insightful description of his friend: "It was easy to smile—and people did smile—at her peculiarities and pomposities. She took herself, and everything that concerned her, with tremendous serious-ness; light touches she utterly lacked, likewise a sense of humour. One of my quaintest recollections is of a supper party she gave at the Drake. . . . The room was full of balloons; there was Edith, unsmiling, stiff as a poker, gravely batting them back and forth across our table, because that was what was expected of her."[16]

And what of Harold? Perhaps unsurprisingly, his marriage to Ganna did not last long. If his beautiful bride had banked on his connections to help establish her opera career, that attempt failed. Mathilde reported that the pair "bounced around the Continent like a rubber ball,"[17] darting from opera house to opera house, with Harold providing hefty financial donations in exchange for starring roles. But the reviews were unkind, the audiences even more so, and it soon became clear that good looks and money were not enough to launch a diva; apparently some talent was required as well. If this sounds familiar, it is because Orson Welles took inspiration from their story for his film *Citizen Kane*.[18]

Chicago music critic Claudia Cassidy remarked, "Her voice smites the ear with the cackling impact of the witch in 'Hansel and Gretel.' When she sings . . . it is sacrilege, yet it is done so winsomely that you are puzzled rather than outraged."[19] Influential conductor Walter Damrosch, longtime director of the New York Symphony Orchestra, was married to Margaret Blaine, the sister-in-law of Harold's sister Anita. Ganna's ties to his family put him in a tricky situation; Damrosch once had to explain why he wouldn't employ her: "From the 'absolutely unanimous accounts of my musician friends who have heard her, her voice is absolutely devoid of charm.' 'What a tragedy,' he wrote to Anita, 'if only she would leave art alone, she would be much happier.'"[20]

By 1926, Harold and Ganna were living separate lives, he in Chicago, she in Paris, nearly always in the cozy company of orchestra director Walther Straram.[21] In 1925, there were rumors of trouble when Harold suddenly bolted from a steamer ten minutes before departure. It was noted that the couple had booked separate cabins (she in a suite, he in a single) and that Straram was also aboard.[22] But Harold still loved Ganna, sending her affectionate letters and even, for her birthday in 1930, sending her one of each of the machines International Harvester produced. In her autobiography, Ganna recalled looking out the window in the morning and seeing "a whole regiment of robot-soldiers standing there on exhibition."[23]

Their divorce would take a few more years to come through. Neither had gotten what they wanted out of the union: Harold's heart had been trampled, and Ganna's career had faltered. Perhaps even Ganna had begun to understand that her talents were limited: "'This year . . . the costumes and jewels I shall wear will be so interesting that it will not matter how I sing . . . or whether I sing at all!'"[24]

Ganna was off in search of her next millionaire. In her autobiography, she described Harold: "One of the most beautiful souls I ever encountered . . . was the delicately perfumed soul of Harold McCormick. It was most exquisite, indeed, but unfortunately thickly veiled by the hypocrisy of wrongly applied goodness and by that modern discovery, the inferiority complex. Harold's mind was especially confused by an abnormal sense of what he thought were his responsibilities, almost a mental complex of his duties, and an entirely misguided idea of what his part should be as an important citizen of his beloved city, Chicago."

She also bluntly covered his apparently useless gland transplant: "When still very young, Harold's pockets were already filled with pills of every kind. In the later years his blind submission to the disciples of Aesculapius became absolute to the point of hypochondria. Unfortunately, that same idiosyncrasy led him to idolize the physical expression of love and he became insatiable in his search for the realization of the physical demands—insatiable because they were unattainable for him any more. Nature, in her wisdom, having fulfilled him by giving him four children, had chosen for his second wife an idealist who was able to put so much value on the richness of his soul that she could not even imagine the possibility of his preferring to seek further for a gross and limited pleasure rather than being satisfied with the divine companionship of the spiritual love she was willing to share with him."[25]

As for Harold, he was seeking a new love. The newspapers occasionally reported broken engagements or other rumors. He had taken over his mother Nettie's house (she had since passed) but spent most of his time in California, a better climate for the arthritis that was beginning to plague him and closer to his troubled brother, Stanley.

Edith kept Harold's room ready for him, untouched except by the feather duster. He sent her a single yellow rose every year on her birthday[26] and occasionally stopped by the Bastion or her box at the opera for a visit. In 1931, after his second divorce was final, he visited several times in a short period of time, causing dozens of papers across the country to announce they might remarry,[27] but that was unfounded speculation.

While Edith had always been the more cerebral of the two, she had taken to preaching about love. To over a thousand attendees at a Krenn & Dato banquet, she spoke of passion in the widest sense: "We are entering into another year, and when we have before us clearly the wonderful power of Love—when we are at work, if we will love to work; when we are at play, if we will love to play; when we are at home, if we will love our homes; when we are with our companions or our friends or co-workers, if we will love to be with them, to cooperate with them . . ."[28]

Adding a colorful feather to her burgeoning hat, Edith also had song-writing credits. She penned the lyrics and her friend Eleanor Everest Freer composed the music for a six-song cycle. With titles such as "Love," "Thou," "It Was Spoken," "I Write Not to Thee, Dearest," and "Between," all the pieces were odes to love. Though never popular hits, they may have served to help Edith express her emotions. "How Can We Know" speaks to a trust one only hopes Edith truly felt.

> How can we know when we gaze into the starlit skies
> And feel the attracting force of those twinkling eyes
> And think we are reading the same open book,
> How can we know, how can we know?
> We know by the silence of like-satisfied hearts
> We know by the clarified glance which darts
> From the longing but joyful face on the One
> To the joyful and longing face of the Other.
> And no earth-stained judgment of man,
> And no fireproofed power of the gods,
> Can take this knowledge from us,
> For we know through the trust born of love.[29]

But the frenzy of the 1920s couldn't last—not for the nation, not for Edith. The years passed quickly, full of present-time entertainments and resplendent wishes for the future. But as the decade approached its end, serious problems lay ahead. For those, like Edith, who hadn't seen them coming, it would spell disaster.

DISASTER

1928-32

*D*isaster came in the form of a one-two punch. The first punch was business-related.

Krenn & Dato had been buying up every bit of desirable land, the partners certain they could turn it around for a nice profit. Edith borrowed against her securities whenever more cash was needed, and their empire grew. The firm owned huge amounts of property, was paying out to develop infrastructure and build homes, and also financed mortgages to its new homeowners. The scope was truly impressive. It was a full-service enterprise for middle-class families looking to buy their first home.

In 1926, business was going gangbusters, and Edith, Edwin, and Edward ended the year $500,000 ahead of where they were in January. But the real estate market abruptly stopped in 1927—a temporary correction, they were sure—and the record books suddenly showed a million dollar debt.[1] They were confident they could ride out this lull. Edith wrote to Junior, "As you know yourself from your own real estate holdings . . . this is a time of inactivity in Real Estate and therefore a time of some losses. We are cutting down expenses where possible and looking forward to the time when we shall make money again."[2]

Only it was more than a lull. The real estate market didn't bounce back, and when the stock market crashed in 1929, it spelled absolute disaster for the firm of Krenn & Dato and for Edith personally. They were stuck with thousands of acres no one could buy, mortgages that weren't being paid, and astronomical property taxes. The value of the Edith Rockefeller McCormick Trust plummeted.

Hundreds of clients forfeited on their mortgages, simply unable to pay. Edith, instead of heartlessly reclaiming their properties, allowed them to stay and absorbed the financial blow herself.[3] She was left holding the bag, and the bag dragged her down.

The second punch came in the form of a lump in her right breast. While frantically transferring funds between accounts, borrowing from one pot to save another, she received dire news: cancer in her breast and armpit. Her doctors recommended a mastectomy, which was performed in June 1930 at Chicago's Passavant Memorial Hospital. In a small-world situation, one of the doctors attending to Edith was Lathan Crandall Jr., the son of the Cleveland minister Senior had forbidden Alta to marry so many years ago.[4]

Some malignancy remained—a fact the doctors shared with Senior and Junior but not with Edith.[5] They elected to keep that information from her, not wanting to worry her. She was merely informed that she would have to undergo radiation treatments every five days as a protective measure.

She was fifty-seven years old, and yet the men around her decided she was not to be privy to her own medical information. Even Edwin Krenn determined he needed to shield Edith, although it is doubtful he knew the extent of her prognosis. He wrote to one of Senior's business associates, "The doctors pointed out to me that worries should be kept from her as much as possible and I feel sure that Messrs. Rockefeller, Sr. and Jr. will help in this respect."[6]

Not only did Senior and Junior now have the satisfaction of telling Edith they had been right all along about her business ventures, but now they could also withhold critical personal information from her. Whether it was a kindness or cruelty can be debated.

Radiation treatments curtailed Edith's activities. She had an X-ray apparatus installed in the Bastion and dutifully continued her studies, psychoanalysis practice, and business efforts, but on a severely restricted basis. Her body needed rest. She kept up the pretense of wanting to see Senior, but now she had a bona fide excuse: "I have been looking forward to celebrating your ninety-first birthday at Pocantico Hills with you but on account of the X ray treatments which they are giving me after my major operation for cancer, it is not possible for me to carry out this most cherished plan. So my visit with you will have to be postponed until later."[7]

One more tragedy was added to Edith's list of sorrows, the shuttering of the Chicago Grand Opera.[8] It had struggled financially for years, with Harold and Edith always providing the monetary fallback. After the divorce, they stepped back from their leadership roles. A new opera house had been built, at great expense,[9] and the current economic climate simply did not allow for this luxury. Nor could Edith afford to underwrite it further, despite her comment vowing to buy tickets even in the difficult financial times: "I may come to the opera with holes in my clothes, but I will sign for 3 years."[10] Though opera would eventually rebound in Chicago, Edith would not see it. The liquidation of the company must have been a terrible loss for her.

Edith's income from investments in 1931 was a mere $370,000.[11] On the other side of the ledger was $33,000 in real estate taxes; $44,000 in interest on her mortgages; $90,000 in income tax; $36,000 to the John R. McCormick Memorial Institute for Infectious Diseases; $38,000 in payments on her pearls; $6,000 in other charitable gifts; $2,000 for her visiting nurses; and daily expenses involved in running two large households.[12] Edith also listed $12,000 a year in clothing expenses, a figure that would have horrified her frugal mother, who had been fond of saying a woman only really needed two dresses.[13]

She had completed her $2.5 million divorce payments to Harold and now owned the two homes, though it had required taking on a $500,000 mortgage for the Bastion (worth $2.5 million) and one for $250,000 for Villa Turicum[14] (worth $3.4 million).[15] Her jewelry, antique collections, artwork, and other belongings were worth millions, but in the height of the Depression, that was all meaningless. Things have actual value only if people are willing to buy them.

A parade of bankers and advisers began arriving at the Bastion: suggesting, requesting, demanding.

Swallowing her pride, Edith sent a series of letters to Senior and Junior, appealing for help. Could they just loan her some money? Or purchase her properties from her? They refused. In tandem. In unison. Repeatedly. Their reasoning was that "it would not be a kindness"[16] to Edith in the long run. No doubt they were shielding themselves from having to assume the burden of her debts, for behind the scenes, they were receiving a flurry of communication from their own bankers and advisers.

Edith also asked Harold—three times—if he would buy Villa Turicum or take out a mortgage on it for her, but he refused. She begged, saying she "thought he owed her something, that he had never given her anything, that he had given millions of dollars to others and that now when she needed money she thought he ought to at least give her $50,000."[17] Harold—generous Harold, who it seemed had never denied anyone anything—turned her down.

In the course of her discussions with Junior, Edith learned that Senior had been under the false impression that she refused to visit him when passing through New York on her way back from Europe with Edwin in 1921. She hurried to explain to her father that she had been on her way to him when a thunderstorm intervened and sent her scurrying back to the hotel.[18] But he had been living with this misunderstanding for too many years to let go of it fully. Father and daughter were never to completely mend their relationship.

On Christmas Eve of 1931, Junior wrote to Senior, "It would be in Edith's interest in the long run to liquidate her real estate business now if necessary and close up the relationship she has had with these men [Krenn and Dato], rather than to go on for years trying to nurse back to health an enterprise which, however intrinsically valuable it may be, will require considerable time and much money if it is to be an ultimate success. We felt that for us to put money into the enterprise, however desperate its condition, would be only a beginning of a long, painful relationship with Edith's representatives, who would naturally feel that once we had come in with them the burden would be gradually put on us and they let out ultimately from responsibility."[19]

They may have just been protecting their own fortunes, but it seems like the ultimate "I told you so."

Of course, the men knew something Edith didn't: she was dying. They didn't want to be left holding her debts. So they left her hanging out to dry.

While he denied his sister any assistance, Junior was single-handedly financing the Rockefeller Center construction project in downtown Manhattan, employing an estimated 225,000 men in building that major enterprise.[20] As his sibling faced bankruptcy, he donated property and funds to open the Museum of Modern Art in New York.[21] Although in letters to colleagues he would explain that he needed to "be cruel to be kind,"[22] it does appear that, in this instance, he regarded civic duty before blood.

Senior, at ninety-one, was still hale and hearty, healthier than his youngest daughter. He announced his intention to live to one hundred.[23] His fortune resided mainly with his son but otherwise was neatly tucked away, unavailable to his daughter.

Edith was on her own.

It is ironic that Edith, who had spent her life most fearing madness, would face bankruptcy, whereas her sister Bessie had needlessly worried about pennilessness and succumbed to mental illness.

Cartier agreed to buy some of her jewels: one hundred pearls for $741,000 as well as $180,000 worth of emeralds.[24] Edith attempted to interest Marshall Field and Sears Roebuck in the land around the Bastion,[25] as the business district now bordered her land, but nothing came of it. Edith tried selling anything she could—Peter the Great's rug, Napoleon's dinner set. Her treasures. But no one was buying. There was no money anywhere. She let go of nonessential staff and closed the gardens at Villa Turicum, dismissing numbers of gardeners.[26] She must have known this came as a terrible blow to their families, but she had no choice.

Edwin gave back the $1 million Edith had given him when he came to Chicago,[27] a drop in the bucket of what she needed, but a sweet gesture. He also drew up his own will, leaving everything he had to Edith.[28] She needed more.

There was nothing left to do but write Junior and beg again, as in this heartbreaking letter from June 4, 1932: "You do not realize how your reply on the twelfth of May affected me in the desperate situation in which you know I can find no way out for myself. Even with my greatest efforts, you know that the times are just against me and I feel myself crushed. I realize that much of my present situation is caused by my own fault. I would give much if I could do things differently than I have done them but can you not forgive me and try to help me and think about the days when we were happy together. You know I am so alone in this world now, and in these difficult times need your advise [sic] and your assistance. I have gone through so much in my life and am so tired and weary and need some encouragement from your helping hand. You can understand that the fear of recurring cancer can make the life of the strongest person miserable and is not that enough punishment in your eyes for things which you think that I have done in my life which do not agree with your principles. In all your answers, you express the thought that you do not believe that you would be helping me in the long run. Now please, brother, knowing in your heart that you would like to help me, tell me what do you want me to do in order that you can come to my rescue by which you will prevent me from going into receivership and eventually into bankruptcy. Any way in which you can prevent that will be satisfactory to me. But all alone in this terrible depression with no outlook of being able to dispose of any of my possessions even with great financial sacrifices, with no hope in the near future of an increased income and the increasing taxes, I feel absolutely hopeless."[29]

Junior asked his financial advisers to assess the situation. The first report was of an emotional meeting with Edith and Edwin, during which Edwin broke down repeatedly. Distraught over his role in Edith's downfall, Edwin offered to leave the country if that meant Junior would step forward to help.[30] Ultimately, however, the advisers came to the conclusion that Krenn & Dato had been well-run but that the firm was simply overextended in a terrible market.[31] That was the good news; the bad news was they had no solution.

A local banker, a Mr. Harris, tried to counsel Edith through this mess. He told the Rockefeller advisers he wasn't charging for his services "because last summer when his boy was killed, Mrs. McCormick was at his home when he reached there and came three times a day thereafter. 'She did more for us than any one can ever know and she is doing good for people all the time. When she came to me and said she was in trouble, I felt it would be a great pleasure to do all I could for her.'" When Mr. Harris asked why Edith didn't just hightail it out of the country, skipping out on her financial responsibilities, she replied, "I am having the best experience of my life. I have had everything before and have never known what it is to want to anything and not be able to satisfy my longing. I am learning and having a much greater feeling toward others."[32]

It takes a certain type of mind to appreciate the knowledge acquisition aspect of bankruptcy.

Edith justified her spending as a responsibility of the wealthy. "Only the thoughtless must put down such expenditures as I have made in this way to sheer extravagance. It was on the contrary, and I say this with sincerity, generosity of the finest sort. I never put it down to charity, because it was not charity—it was merely the creation of something that gave me a genuine happiness. Rather than feeling selfish in indulging and expensive tastes which I have cultivated, I have, on the contrary, felt always a glow of satisfaction in being able to satisfy my own artistic cravings and at the same time allow others to share in the advantages of my wealth. Had I hoarded my money for the miserly satisfaction of seeing it grow, I feel I would have been subject to criticism, as according to my standards money should be kept in circulation, and those possessing great amounts of it should realize a corresponding obligation."[33]

Edith had been too successful at keeping her money "in circulation." Whether through greed or generosity, ambition or oversight, she had managed to redistribute her fortune down to the last cent.

While financially frantic and medically unwell, Edith never gave in to desperation, writing an article for the *Chicago Daily News* explaining her viewpoint on the nationwide economic crisis. She attributed the tumultuous world events to a shift in astrological houses, a correction necessary for civilization to move forward. Her concluding statement must have been a personal rallying cry as she maneuvered through her last months:"With head erect and eyes wide open, we take the next step forward, ready to grasp the new values and to feel the understanding love of the laws of universal life."[34]

Similarly, she wrote to Junior suggesting that she recognized certain benefits in aging: "The advantages of youth with life ahead of us are compensated by the advantages of middle age with greater understanding and wider grasp of life."[35]

In the meantime, Edith's surgeon Dr. Lewis McArthur reported back to Junior to say that the cancer had invaded Edith's liver and bone, and "while she has not been informed of this finding, it has been deemed wise that some near relative be advised of this situation."[36] It does seem that by June 1932, Edith was at least aware that additional masses had been found.

For Junior, it became apparent that Edith had precious little time. At this eleventh hour, he stepped up, offering to finance her personal debts, taking her remaining jewelry as collateral, with the stipulation that she close up both residences and move into the Drake Hotel. Junior allowed her to keep her maid Marie Pfaeffle, her secretary Gertrude Hellenthal, and a chauffeur but continued to refuse any involvement in her business enterprises.[37]

So it came to be that in the final summer of her life, on July 6, 1932, Edith was forced to move to a four-room suite in the northwest corner of the Drake Hotel, where she could gaze out the window at her beloved Bastion, now shuttered. She brought along only her piano, her radio, and a few favorite vases.[38]

Also at the Drake was Edwin Krenn—and, in a curious twist of fate, Edith's son, Fowler, and his new bride, Fifi Stillman. The contentious, front-page divorce between Fifi and James Stillman was finally settled, having taken a full decade. The very same day, Fifi and Fowler went to court to marry, thereby making official the third Rockefeller–Stillman union.[39]

Edith had clearly had her suspicions. Way back in 1922, she had written to Senior, "I am hoping that Fowler will decide soon to take up his serious work. I know that he has been of great value to Mrs. Stillman in these two years and a half of her divorce proceedings, but I feel that he should begin to seriously concentrate his energies on his own further development and on his life work. There is always a pitfall for a rich young man in a much older, designing and fascinating woman."[40]

After briefly trying his hand in the stock market,[41] Fowler settled into what clearly was expected of him: a career at International Harvester. He took a menial position under the assumed name "Mac" at the plant in Milwaukee to learn the ropes. He lived quietly on his fifteen-dollar weekly salary, no one knowing he was actually worth millions.

Fowler's true identity was revealed by Fifi herself, who came to visit in Wisconsin. Irrepressible, she greeted him at the factory with a joyful "Fowler!" Fifi told the newspapers, "I knew that Fowler would be lonesome up here at the plant. I thought it my duty to come and see the boy. No doubt many people will comment about my being here, but I want it understood that I am a friend of his best friend, my son Bud."

Fifi continued, "Last night Fowler and I had dinner together, and he told me he was getting a lot of valuable experience. But the poor boy was so tired that his lids were drooping as we talked. And his hands—O, my! Imagine, those hands that had never done anything harder than to hold a mashie, doing that terrible work. They are all calloused now!"[42]

The sudden wedding in 1931 was a replay of the Mathilde-Max story. Harold was supportive,[43] Edith opposed,[44] and the newspapers went wild, with pictures of the couple on front pages around the country. While Harold cabled Stanley that "Mrs. Stillman is a good many years older than Fowler and that might make it seem a drawback but when I see you I want to talk with you about their long friendship and many mutual interests and I feel very happy about it,"[45] Edith wrote to Senior, "I have done all I can to prevent the marriage but without success. I have tried to get his father to try to stop it but without success."[46] Senior begged Fowler to postpone, but Fowler disregarded his plea.[47] Fowler was thirty-two; Fifi was fifty-two.

The age disparity in marriage was one that all three McCormick children would experience. A mere three months later, twenty-nine-year-old Muriel suddenly informed family members that she was engaged to Major Elisha Dyer Hubbard, a fifty-three-year-old war veteran.

After a brief stint in Chicago theater in the mid-1920s, Muriel had a minor breakdown, and the McKinlock family took her with them down to Palm Beach, Florida, to recuperate. She recovered enough to briefly attend the Eastman School of Music in Rochester but did not earn a degree. In 1929 she opened the Palm Beach Playhouse Theater, overseeing construction and presiding over an eleven-week season. Muriel occasionally appeared on stage herself, most notably as Saint Joan in George Bernard Shaw's masterpiece.

The McKinlocks also introduced her to Elisha Hubbard, apparently having decided her spiritual engagement to their deceased son had run its course. Despite the age disparity, this was a match the family could rally around, as both Edith and Junior had known the Hubbard family for years. Having reconciled with her mother in 1929—reporting back to Senior after a visit that Edith "seemed more human to me"[48]—Muriel asked Edith to make the engagement announcement. Perhaps Edith was hopeful that settling down might provide her emotionally unstable daughter some security. Of course, Edith did not attend the ceremony in Maine. It is notable that Edith was not present at any of her children's weddings.

As for Mathilde and Max Oser, they came to visit in 1929, staying with Harold at Nettie's old house, bringing with them their children Anita (named after Harold's sister) and Peter. Edith summoned Mathilde but refused to see Max. When Mathilde asked if she would like to meet her grandchildren, Edith demurred, stating, "Children really aren't at all important, they're just necessary for procreation."[49] Mathilde brought Anita anyway.

During their stay in Chicago, a rumor swirled that there had been a kidnapping attempt on the Oser children, based on the large retinue of security guards around Harold's home.[50] Though there was no merit to the threat, it was a sober reminder of how careful all Rockefeller offspring needed to be.

The Osers swung through New York where Senior welcomed the entire clan, including Max, despite Edith's plea, "I would appreciate very much if you did not receive the fortune hunter Mr. Oser in your home."[51]

Thus the summer of 1932 found Edith installed in the Drake Hotel, mostly reconciled with her children and their new spouses, financially and physically spent. Her fall from grace had been swift and brutal. *Time* magazine called the move "a heartbreaking acquiescence to the condition she always speaks of as 'the change.'"[52] All that remained was to pass with a modicum of dignity.

Edith's formal portrait by Friedrich August von
Kaulbach. Courtesy Rockefeller Archive Center.

Edith's magnificent wrap made of one hundred chinchilla skins with a silver fox collar. American Art Association, *Collection of the Late Edith Rockefeller McCormick*; author's collection.

Edith's platinum breastplate, containing 1,801 diamonds. In this photo, the large central stone is missing. American Art Association, *Collection of the Late Edith Rockefeller McCormick*; author's collection.

A bronze bust of Napoleon atop Edith's writing table with gilded bronze figures. American Art Association, *Collection of the Late Edith Rockefeller McCormick*; author's collection.

A rare opportunity for a family portrait in Zurich (*clockwise from left*): Muriel, Mathilde, Fowler, Harold, and Edith. Courtesy Wisconsin Historical Society, 102045.

(*From right*) Playful Harold, Muriel, and Mathilde posing on a sled. Courtesy Wisconsin Historical Society, 114385.

Harold designed his own room in the Hotel Baur au
Lac. Courtesy Wisconsin Historical Society, 77250.

Edith and Harold were major donors for the Verdi
arch in Parma, Italy. Author's collection.

The diva Ganna Walska. Courtesy
Wisconsin Historical Society, 8787.

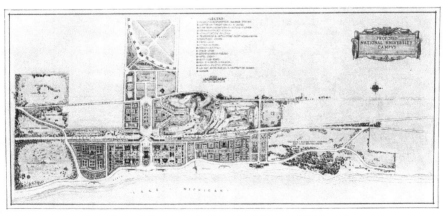

Plans for Edithton, including the National University
campus. Courtesy Rockefeller Archive Center.

The hammered cover of the Rockefeller McCormick New Testament. Courtesy Special Collections Research Center, University of Chicago Library.

Edith giving a speech at the annual Krenn & Dato banquet. Courtesy Chicago History Museum, ICHi-176313.

Brookfield Zoo aerial shot, 1934. Courtesy Chicago Zoological Society.

Senior welcomed Mathilde and, despite Edith's request, Max Oser and their children, Peter and Anita. Courtesy Rockefeller Archive Center.

Edith's last portrait shows a mature woman gazing
directly at the camera, a far cry from her earlier demure
poses. Author's collection. Photo by Kellogg Studios.

DEATH

1932

*E*dith's illness accomplished what she had been unable to do: bring her family together. She moved into the Drake Hotel in July 1932; by August it was clear to her family, if not to her, that the end was near.

Muriel came to town with her new husband, Elisha, and expressed her fear that Edith was dying, to which Edith replied, "I am going to live," and explained that her mind could override her ailing body. Believing that Jung had managed to cure the tuberculosis that had plagued her in earlier years, she voiced her intention to battle cancer through psychoanalysis.

Letters of cheer came from family members. One came from Senior, though actually drafted by Junior: "The problems which the last year or two have brought have been a tax on many people. It is not strange that you are feeling the strain. You have been courageous and resourceful in meeting your personal problems. I am sure that better days are ahead. I shall keep informed of how you are."[1]

Fowler and Fifi, fellow Drake residents, were frequent visitors. Harold flew in from California and visited several times, even posting cables to his mentally unwell siblings, Stanley and Mary Virginia, that read, "Lovely visit with Edith this morning. Beautiful talk of the past and the present."[2] His older brother, Cyrus, also stopped to pay his respects. Edith's sister Alta and her husband, Parmalee, came to town to say their farewells.[3] Edwin, of course, was there every day.

Edith hadn't been this popular in years. Junior wrote to a friend "that there was the completest and most beautiful reconciliation between her and her children and former husband and his family, [which] has turned our sorrow into rejoicing."[4]

Fowler provided an excellent nurse, Florence Everett, whom all came to know as "Aunt Flo." She had just finished tending to Fifi's son Alexander Stillman, who had been injured in a plane crash. (It was quite the soap opera: when Alexander crashed, Fowler and Fifi rushed to the site, also crashing on their landing, though they were not seriously hurt in the incident.)[5]

Reporters took up positions outside the Drake, pressing all who exited for information, which was then duly reported in the daily papers. Aunt Flo was quoted, "Mrs. McCormick has put up the bravest fight I've ever seen. I admire her courage utterly. Never have I seen a patient with such a will to live."[6]

Mathilde had been summoned from Switzerland. That was no overnight trip, and it took some time for her to arrive, days during which Edith slipped in and out of consciousness. Max and the children stayed at Pocantico. By the time Mathilde's train pulled into Chicago, Edith had slipped into a coma, and the doctors had determined nothing more could be done. Fifi went to the train station to meet Mathilde, and they raced back to the Drake with a police escort to usher them through city traffic.

Meanwhile, Aunt Flo was packing, scheduled to leave on the 2:00 train, convinced nothing more could be done. Fowler interrupted her packing to beg her to attempt one more trick to see if Edith could be revived for Mathilde. She agreed, and while Mathilde and Fifi fought through the crowded streets of Chicago, Aunt Flo patiently worked her hydrotherapy cure for over an hour.[7]

It worked. Edith briefly mustered her way out of the haze and spoke a few words to her youngest daughter, even placing her hand on top of Mathilde's head. Then Edith asked for Edwin, who came rushing from his suite, shirt unbuttoned, tie askew.[8]

After that miraculous recovery, Edith rallied for a few days. She was alert when Junior, his wife, Abby, and their son John Rockefeller III came to visit.[9] They returned to New York, but Edith's immediate family stayed, all slights and arguments set aside as they sat vigil.

On August 25, 1932, all three children, Harold, and Edwin were with Edith as she passed, just a few days before her sixtieth birthday. The newspapers stated, "Mrs. McCormick died as serenely as she had lived. No commotion of any kind was perceptible to the reporters who had gathered in the corridor leading into the northwest wing of the Drake for the customary bulletin at 4:30 o'clock. They had no suspicion that the end, so long awaited, had come, until the chief physician appeared bearing a written statement instead of his usual oral report. 'Mrs. McCormick died at 4:40 o'clock,' the statement read. 'Death came peacefully. All members of her family were with her at the end.'"[10]

Edith slipped away quietly, fully embraced by her discordant family for perhaps the only time in her life.

AFTERMATH

1932

*E*dith's body remained in the suite at the Drake for two days, was placed in a bronze casket, and was moved across the street to the Bastion, where her funeral was held on August 27. Harold took the lead in planning the funeral arrangements.

The *Chicago Daily Tribune* reported that twenty policemen stood guard around the Bastion, where "hundreds of men and women anxious for a view of the proceedings, were herded to the north side of the street, where they appropriated places on the curb and on the steps of the . . . adjoining homes."[1] This article indicates the crowd grew to 2,000; other reports had the crowd at over 20,000.[2]

With the sidewalks and streets crowded with onlookers observing a respectful silence, the family and friends gathered in the Bastion. Over $10,000 had been spent on flowers from every available Chicago florist, and some were flown in from New York. The house held 5,000 roses; 12,000 lilies of the valley; 400 orchids; 1,000 gardenias; 750 tuberoses. In the Empire Room the lilies of the valley blanketed the casket; potted palms and large tropical ferns created a backdrop. Edith's favorite flower, the Pernet rose, was present in baskets and bowls strategically placed in several rooms.[3] Senior had personally sent five dozen of the Pernet roses, with Junior sending another three dozen.[4] It was reminiscent of the floral display Edith had planned for her wedding before the venue was abruptly changed. The floral scent was overpowering.

Only forty-four people had been invited to the ceremony, including family members, Edwin, and friends such as composer John Alden Carpenter, Mrs. Waller Borden, and Mrs. Chauncey Borland.

A string quartet played softly behind drapes as mourners were seated. To begin the ceremony, a quartet from the Presbyterian church sang "Peace, Perfect Peace," followed by a Bach aria by the string quartet. A Presbyterian reverend read selections from the Psalms and the Gospels and led a prayer. After a few more songs and prayers, the deed was done. Aside from the final piece, Bizet's "Andante," none of the service seemed to have anything to do with Edith's wishes. A more meaningful tribute would be given by the Friends of the Opera a few weeks later, when hundreds gathered to honor "perhaps the greatest patroness of music Chicago has had" with a short recital of her favorite pieces. Similarly, some of Edith's own songs as well as excerpts from her protégé Otto Luening's opera *Evangeline* would be performed at a memorial concert given by the American Opera Society of Chicago later that year. But the family event bore no reflection of Edith's beliefs or passions.

Following the short service, eight pallbearers (there were technically sixteen, but not all were present), including Edwin, Colonel Robert McCormick, Stanley Field, John McCutcheon, Arthur Meeker, and Augustus Peabody, struggled to maneuver the heavy bronze casket out the door. The hearse, preceded by seven carloads of flowers, made its way to Graceland Cemetery accompanied by her closest family, who must have been stunned to see the thousands of people lining the streets, anxious for a final glimpse of Chicago's patron saint.[5]

Tributes began pouring in, from James Joyce and Carl Jung, to ordinary citizens she had helped. From Daniel Burnham came a resolution from the board of A Century of Progress: "In the death of Edith Rockefeller McCormick the Century of Progress has lost a staunch friend and the city a valued citizen. No one loved Chicago more loyally than she. The founding of important enterprises in science, in the arts, and in high civic projects such as the John McCormick Institute for Infectious Diseases, the Civic opera, and the Zoological gardens was made possible by her initiative and her generosity. To any plan looking to the best advancement of her city she gave the support of her acute and enthusiastic interest. With deepest appreciation, therefore, of her vital contribution toward an era of true progress in Chicago, be it resolved that this expression of our profound regret at the irreparable loss of a great personality be spread upon the records and copies thereof sent to members of her family."[6]

Carl Jung's wife, Emma, wrote to Harold, "Hers seems a tragic fate. . . . I feel great pity for her. . . . And of course the Club will always be a living and lasting expression of her great and generous personality, to which we owe it."[7]

The trustees of the John R. McCormick Memorial Institute for Infectious Diseases sent a tribute detailing their advances in treatment and concluding, "She has won for herself a secure name in the history of medical research and philanthropy."[8]

Dianne MacLeod, in *Enchanted Lives, Enchanted Objects*, states, "Although her male relatives dismissed her as an impractical idealist, her efforts not only were applauded by the thousands of Chicagoans who attended her funeral, but also served to bolster the resolve of the legions of American women who set their sights beyond the home and worked to improve their communities during the Progressive Era."[9]

It is believed that following the funeral, Harold and Junior burned Edith's correspondence and notes.[10] Whether they were trying to protect her and her patients or whether they were merely looking to protect their own families will never be known. But, if true, it is curious that two families that took utmost care to set up family archives and properly document the efforts of their family members took this drastic measure. It would explain the dearth of materials on Edith as compared with other family members.

The newspapers ran tributes for days, full-page spreads of Edith and her family. There was plenty of material to choose from, and it was an invitation to revisit all the scandals. However, it was also a rare opportunity to credit Edith for all she had given the city. The *New York Times* proclaimed, "Mrs. McCormick's leadership in Chicago society . . . remained unchallenged throughout her lifetime, partly due to an attitude born of her position as the richest woman in Chicago and the daughter of the richest man in the world."[11] *Time* magazine ran an article titled "End of a Princess," declaring Edith had been "as near to royalty as it is possible to come in the U.S."[12]

There was, of course, considerable interest in Edith's will and the ensuing lawsuits. In accordance with need, Edith had allocated 4/12 of her estate to Muriel, 2/12 to Mathilde, and 1/12 to Fowler, giving the remaining 5/12 to Edwin.[13] The trouble was, that didn't really amount to anything.

While public reports estimated Edith's worth at $40 million, with all her debts and idle property, it was essentially nothing.

An earlier version of her will had earmarked merely $10,000 for each child ("as my father has provided amply for them") and $2 million for the museums in addition to all her furnishings, books, and collections. The major beneficiary of that first will would have been Edwin Krenn, who was to have received $2 million, the proceeds from the sale of her jewels, and a favorite lacquer Buddha.[14]

As it was, Edwin would never see much of anything financially from Edith's will. A few weeks before her death, under pressure from Junior and Parmalee Prentice, Edwin signed an agreement waiving all claims to the estate as well as his interest in Krenn & Dato in exchange for a guarantee of $2,000 per month for life. The agreement seems to have been engineered to separate Edith's real estate debts from her personal ones, leaving Dato holding the Krenn & Dato disaster and giving loyal Edwin a decent income for life.[15] Edith and Edwin's relations with Edward Dato had become strained, and Dato was suspected of having quietly tucked away nearly half a million dollars' worth of gold bonds.[16]

However, the agreement was canceled after Edith's death, and Krenn was reinstated as chief heir.[17] This would be bad news for him, as tax officials, creditors, and mortgage holders were collecting whatever remained of the estate.

Instead of serving as the basis for new Chicago museums, Edith's carefully collected treasures were auctioned off to pay her debts. A life dismantled. Auctions were held in Chicago, Lake Forest, and New York.[18] But it was the Depression; officials calculated that buyers were able to collect items at the rate of two cents on the dollar, as opposed to original purchase price. A lace coverlet Edith had purchased for nearly $10,000 sold for $650; an Oriental rose quartz vase worth $1,750 went for only $55. In total, the three auctions brought in merely $400,000 on items worth approximately $3 million.[19] Many of the items didn't sell at all.

The auctions were mayhem. Whereas the New York auction was reserved, the Villa Turicum event drew 14,000 public gawkers[20]—not there to buy, merely to look. They trampled the gardens in Lake Forest. Seven people fell into the white marble fountain at Villa Turicum in their push to get closer to the bidding.[21] An admission fee of $10 was charged at the Bastion auction to avoid overcrowding.[22]

Muriel attended all three auctions, weeping. She purchased $97,000 worth of items: anything with Edith's monogram, her bedroom set, the two hunting tapestries, Edith's favorite chinchilla and ermine coats, and several of her mother's favorite jewels.[23] Muriel also attempted to buy Napoleon's silver dinner service—she offered $20,000 for the whole set—but, sadly, it was broken up and the pieces sold for $57,000.[24] Unfortunately, Muriel didn't have the cash to pay the bill for all the items she had bought. She had to request $100,000 from Junior, either from the principal of the trust in her name or from a direct loan from him.

Edwin attended but did not buy anything.[25] Edith had quietly gifted a few personal items to him before her death, including a few Buddhas to add to his massive collection. Edward Dato bought a few table lamps and other miscellaneous items.[26]

Edith's necklace of 1,801 diamonds sold to a New York buyer for $15,000.[27] The Catherine the Great emeralds were broken up and returned to Cartier for $480,000; they later wound up with socialite Barbara Hutton.[28] The Corot painting went to a private buyer. Several items ended up in John Cuneo's estate; a few other items landed in museums and galleries. Since many were bought through buyers or under fictitious names, the vast majority quietly disappeared, unable to be traced. Piecemeal, Edith's collection was disbursed. The auctioneers went so far as to dismantle and sell the paneling on the walls.[29]

No buyer was found for the Emperor's Carpet until 1943, when it finally sold for $75,000. It now resides at the Metropolitan Museum of Art.

Her diamond tiara, her wedding gift from Harold, containing 479 diamonds and an additional 194 rose-cut diamonds, was valued at $25,538. Reports describe it as broken, missing 108 stones—a perfect metaphor for the ruins of her marriage and social standing.[30]

As for the Byzantine New Testament, the color reproductions were completed just days before Edith died, and she was able to see them while on her deathbed. She asked the University of Chicago to buy the codex from her, but the university was not able to provide an amount she felt suitable.[31] Following her death, Harold presented Senior with the three-volume set describing the masterpiece.[32] The codex remained in the estate until 1942, when niece Elizabeth Day McCormick purchased it as a donation to the university.[33]

Edith's estate took nineteen years to settle.[34] After her debts had been paid, there was virtually nothing for her heirs. Her children would benefit only from the trust Senior had established in 1917. During her lifetime, Edith had received annual income from the trust, but the principal had been earmarked for her children. Therefore, it was spared the pillaging all her other monies suffered after her death. Each of her children received an average of $120,000 a year from the trust for their lifetimes. If they wanted access to the principal, they needed to run their request past a board of trustees. While Fowler and Mathilde accepted this agreement and rarely requested funds, Muriel wanted control of the principal and fought with Junior over the terms.[35] It would be a bone of contention between the two, whose relationship would in many ways mirror that of Edith with her brother.

When establishing Krenn & Dato, Edith had set up the Edith Rockefeller McCormick Trust. Thousands of small investors had participated, believing the Rockefeller name to be a sure bet. After Edith's death, the trust failed, unable to provide its investors with the interest and, ultimately, principal they had been promised. Senior and Junior were flooded with heartbreaking letters from small investors, begging the Rockefeller family to honor the commitments of the trust. All were denied. Junior responded to each request with a polite but firm letter, stating they were unable to help.[36]

In the end, the Rockefeller family was in no way held responsible for the demise of Krenn & Dato or the Edith Rockefeller McCormick Trust. The family continued to support her descendants financially and emotionally.

Once estimated to be the nation's wealthiest woman, Edith had somehow, inadvertently, destroyed her fortune.

Longtime neighbor, friend, and ultimately pallbearer Arthur Meeker commented, "Mrs. McCormick's death marked the end of an era. No one again could afford to live as she had lived—nor, perhaps, even if they could, would they have wanted to. By the public, alas, she was quickly forgotten. I find myself occasionally thinking of her with affection. She was a great original, and we have never had too many of those. It seems to me I can see her now pacing the Drive she loved so well, in her brown, short-skirted suit, with her hands in the inevitable muff. I'd know her step in a million, that extraordinary gait, half strut, half sidle. If there are ghosts in Chicago, surely one of the most curious and touching must be that of Edith Rockefeller McCormick."[37]

LEGACY

*E*dith spent her life trying to make a difference, attempting to move humanity forward along the evolutionary axis, helping others, and funding projects she thought could effect change. While some of her efforts—Edithton and the National University, the wood-hardening business, affordable housing for the middle class—may not have fully succeeded, there is still lasting evidence of her work.

SCARLET FEVER

Baby Jack, dead before he truly had a chance to live, made a difference for others. A pair of researchers, Gladys and George Dick, had been studying scarlet fever at Evanston Hospital, just north of Chicago. In the early 1920s, they came to the John R. McCormick Memorial Institute for Infectious Diseases, where they determined hemolytic streptococcus to be the cause of scarlet fever. They invented what became known as the Dick Skin Test and worked on vaccines to prevent the disease.[1] In later years, penicillin was ultimately adopted as the treatment of choice.

A 1933 report indicates that in its first twenty years, the institute treated over 14,000 patients. Fully one-third were suffering from scarlet fever; of those, it is noteworthy that only 142 died. The Dick Skin Test and ensuing immunization protocol were critical in protecting the nursing staff; prior to the implementation of this protection, it had been hard to find people willing to work in the highly contagious environment.[2] The institute was eventually absorbed into the University of Chicago, despite Edith's strong resistance to that idea while she was alive.

The *Journal of Infectious Diseases*, which Harold and Edith launched, is still a respected journal for medical researchers and physicians.[3]

BROOKFIELD ZOO

The Chicago Zoological Park, or Brookfield Zoo, as it became known, opened in 1934. Edith had stipulated in her initial agreement with the Forest Preserve District of Cook County that it needed to open by July 1, 1934, or the land would revert to her estate. It opened on precisely that day. Not everything was finished, but it was enough to satisfy a curious public. Some fifty-eight thousand people attended on that grand opening day; an additional estimated twenty-five thousand were turned away due to traffic and parking problems. Always intended to be the greatest zoo in the world, it lived up to the public's expectation from the first day. The barless exhibits—using moats and rock walls instead of cages—were a novelty and proved to have staying power. Eventually most respectable zoos would utilize this form of display.

Newspaper reports in the 1920s indicate Edith donated the land so people could "get nearer animals to reach the human soul." Brookfield Zoo became a leader in research—the first to employ a full-time curator of research, a pioneer in conservation research, and an inspiration to zoological parks around the world. Brookfield Zoo led the way for zoos, away from menageries, and toward the notion of a true conservation park, where visitors are inspired by the animals before them as well as by the signage to take action to protect the natural world. Edith was the unlikely mother of all these innovations.[4]

CARL JUNG

Dr. Jung, of course, went on to become nearly as famous as his colleague Sigmund Freud. As the "Father of Psychotherapy," his philosophies and techniques helped millions of people live fuller, happier lives. The translations of his work into English and other languages, funded by Edith, helped spread this message.

The Psychological Club in Zurich, begun with Edith's urging and funds, is still in operation, serving as a hub for Jungians around the world, just as she envisioned.

ARTISTS

James Joyce became known as one of the world's finest writers, and *Ulysses* is generally considered to be his masterpiece. When published, it was considered obscene and censored in the United States. Yet it stands today as a brilliant work of stream-of-consciousness thinking—a hallmark of Carl Jung's treatment. Though Joyce never submitted to therapy, as Edith had suggested, his daughter, Lucia, who suffered from severe schizophrenia, worked with Jung.

Otto Luening became an electronic music pioneer. He was a founder of the Columbia-Princeton Electronic Music Center and an early advocate for the use of synthesizers and special editing techniques. He also continued to conduct and compose operas.

Philipp Jarnach continued to work as a pianist, composer, and conductor. A leading composer of modern music in the 1920s, he went on to found the Hamburg Music Academy and had many notable students, among them the future composer Kurt Weill.

Opera in Chicago limped along without Edith and Harold at the helm. Samuel Insull, head of Commonwealth Edison, took over the leadership and oversaw construction of the new Civic Opera House. Sadly, the Depression crushed Insull, and he died with debts of over $14 million. The Chicago Grand Opera Company struggled, as it had from the beginning. It wasn't until the 1950s, with the establishment of the Lyric Opera, that opera finally gained firm footing in Chicago. Today, that stands as one of the nation's leading opera houses.[5] The twenty-plus English translations of operas that Edith underwrote still exist.

HOMES AND PROPERTIES

Edith's homes did not become museums, nor were they ever properly resided in again. 1000 Lake Shore Drive was briefly considered as the site for a restaurant, but the zoning board denied the request. Her mortgage eventually defaulted, and no one stepped forward to buy the home. The Bastion stood empty for years and was finally torn down in 1953. Today, a skyscraper stands in its footprint.

Villa Turicum suffered a similar fate. It was a frequent target of vandals in the 1940s, who stole everything they could dismantle, smashing the marble columns and fountains for good measure. Graffiti proliferated.

In the 1950s, a developer bought the property for a mere $150,000 plus $600,000 in tax debts. He had noble intentions of restoring it but soon discovered the vandalism was too extreme. He eventually tore down the buildings, except for the teahouse, which still stands, and subdivided the land. Today, near the intersection of Rockefeller and McCormick Streets in the Villa Turicum subdivision of Lake Forest, the former reflecting pond and portions of the elaborate beach staircase remain.

Edithton went into foreclosure and was eventually sold off into lots. Future homeowners discovered it wasn't a good site for building—the uneven ground, the sand dunes, and the shifting lands led to creeks running through basements and destroying foundations.

Several of the Krenn & Dato properties in the Chicago area remain. There are eight in Highland Park, lovely family homes. A desirable high-rise just north of downtown Chicago, at 3300 Lake Shore Drive, has a beautiful view of the lakefront. The Meadow Lane Garden Apartments, in what is now Skokie, are still standing. The Roosevelt Hotel in Cedar Rapids, Iowa, reopened in 2010 as an affordable ninety-six-unit apartment complex. The Union National Bank Building in Wichita, Kansas, has recently been thoroughly renovated; in the 1950s, it played a part in civil rights history when sit-ins were held at its drugstore counter.

The Krenn & Dato firm did have a hand in shaping Chicago, although clearly Edith had hoped for greater: "By ever keeping before us the welfare of our city and by planning and working for her betterment we will be making a worthy contribution to American civilization. In the pages of future history which will record the names of those who had vision—who planned and worked for Chicago's greatness—not the least of these will be the name of Krenn & Dato."[6]

VERDI ARCH

Unfortunately, the Verdi arch to which Harold and Edith donated significant funding was bombed in Allied attacks during World War II. Though the monument was reparable, the city of Parma decided to dismantle it in favor of redevelopment of the area. Several of the pillars were tossed in the river, and fragments can still be found nearby. The bas relief of Verdi surrounded by Muses still stands, and several of the statues are on exhibit in a local theater.[7]

MATHILDE

Because all three of Harold and Edith's children married spouses decades older than themselves, there are few blood descendants.

Mathilde, in that hotly disputed union with Max Oser, had two children, Anita and Peter. Perhaps Edith would not have been as vehement in her disapproval had she known they would be the only descendants to carry forth her genes. However, she was right in predicting an unhappy marriage for Mathilde. She and Max seemed content for just a few years before the marriage began to crumble. The couple eventually parted ways, though they never divorced.

Mathilde feared the press, preferred to live quietly in her Swiss chalet, believed obedience was the most desirable trait in children, and was not well balanced emotionally. Given that she was raised largely in an institution, with minimal parental involvement, perhaps this is not surprising. Children Anita and Peter stayed with Mathilde after the separation. Mathilde took on a male companion, a blond ski instructor who went with her everywhere, not unlike Edwin Krenn. Max traveled considerably (perhaps with a lady companion), always writing the children of his adventures. Sadly, Mathilde didn't share those letters with them; they found the letters after Max's death. The children remembered Max as a sweet, gentle man but were forbidden to be with him. He died of a heart attack in 1942.

Mathilde came to the United States with the children in 1939. Terrified of publicity, she traveled third class under an assumed name, instructed her children to pretend she was their nanny, and brought only two dresses for the entire trip (a true descendant of Cettie Rockefeller, who had declared that a woman needs only two dresses). Mathilde intended to return to Switzerland after two weeks but daughter Anita broke out in chicken pox, delaying the trip. By the time all were healthy and ready to travel, World War II was threatening. They would stay in California for the remainder of Mathilde's life.[8]

She had a house built in California but, much like Edith with Villa Turicum, never fully moved in. The furniture, ordered from New York, remained in boxes in the garage, waiting for occupants who never arrived. Mathilde died in 1947 following surgery for cancer. She was only forty-one.[9]

Mathilde's children, Anita and Peter, were delightful people. Anita was vibrant, intelligent, caring. She married Linus Pauling Jr., son of the double Nobel Prize scientist. Together they had five children. Kind, intelligent, unassuming, these five great-grandchildren of Edith carry on the Rockefeller–McCormick genes.

Anita (named after Harold's sister, who had tried to be a motherly figure for Mathilde) took after Edith in her love of the arts. She had the Rockefeller and McCormick philanthropic streak and donated to many European arts organizations. Upon hearing that the Orchestra de la Suisse Romande was to travel to China in the summer, she purchased lightweight suits for the entire ensemble. In the 1960s, she created an arts community called the Études et Rencontres Artistiques in Geneva, Switzerland. It was an institution where dance, theater, and music could thrive under one umbrella. Anita died in 2009.[10]

Mathilde's son, Peter, was a bon vivant with a brilliant mind and a sparkling personality. He lived in a house made of stone and glass in Switzerland—not a right angle in the entire building but containing a round fireplace, a suspended table, a ramp instead of stairs, and a mosaic bathtub. He was full of life, an original thinker, and more than a touch rebellious. Peter died of a heart attack while in his forties. He married three times but had no biological children to carry on the line.[11]

FOWLER

Everyone liked Fowler. He was warm, kind, and remarkably well adjusted. His relatives were fond of his bear hugs and smiles and recall him as an immaculate dresser (as Harold also had been) with monogrammed cuffs.[12] He served as president of International Harvester from 1941 to 1951, where he worked to improve labor-management relations. His philanthropies were mainly in support of African American rights.

Fowler and Fifi had a long marriage, perhaps not perfect but surprisingly sound. Fifi was a domineering mother. Fowler would have no biological children but was a dignified, stabilizing force for Fifi's children and grandchildren (though there were those who wondered if Guy, the youngest child, was Fowler's, not James Stillman's or the rumored Canadian tour guide's). Of Fifi's four children, three married and had numerous offspring, now spread out in the United States and Switzerland. Fifi's son Bud named his third child Fowler McCormick Stillman. When Bud's first marriage disintegrated, Fowler stepped into the breach to look after his namesake.[13]

Throughout his life, Fowler kept journals of his dreams, a Jung devotee to the end. He spent his summers in Zurich at the Hotel Baur au Lac while

Fifi traveled to Quebec. Fowler enjoyed driving Dr. Jung around Europe and traveling with him to farther-flung places, including the American West, as Jung had a particular interest in Native Americans.[14]

Fowler and Fifi lived briefly on a farm in Barrington, Illinois, then purchased a six-thousand-acre cattle ranch in Arizona. Fifi began collecting Southwest Indian art, hoping to establish a museum.[15] Much like Edith's experience, however, after her death in 1969 at age eighty-nine, her collections were auctioned off. Fowler died in 1973.[16]

MURIEL

Fowler's relationships with everyone—Rockefellers, McCormicks, Stillmans—were excellent except for the one he had with Muriel. Temperamental from her very first breath, Muriel grew more difficult as the years went by.

Her husband, Elisha, died in 1936. By then, Muriel had a severe alcohol problem. Following Elisha's death, she adopted two children. The first, a four-year-old girl, was named Edith McCormick Hubbard. The second, a little boy, was named Elisha. Fowler became aware that Muriel was drinking heavily and being abusive to her children and the housekeeper. Little Edith reported that she was being spanked daily (and had the bruises to show for it) and shared bizarre stories such as having to hop on one foot a hundred times as punishment. There were allegations that Muriel may have whipped them. Muriel served in the Women's Army Corps for nearly three years, becoming a sergeant. During her tour of duty, she appointed her housekeeper as guardian. The housekeeper later reported terrible incidents of drunkenness and abuse. In 1944, Fowler sued Muriel to relinquish control of the children. The lawsuit took five years to settle. The children finally went to reside with a loving family in Illinois.

But several years later, Muriel managed to adopt again—four children over the course of four years. Despite the protests of Fowler and Junior, she named them John D. Rockefeller McCormick Hubbard, Harold Fowler McCormick Hubbard, Elisha Dyer Hubbard Jr., and Anna Jones Dyer Hubbard.

Muriel died less than a year after adopting little Anna, and the children were raised by Katherine Dwyer, Muriel's longtime companion and, according to rumor, her lover. She left an estate worth $9 million, the basis of which had been Senior's trust fund to Edith. This estate became contentious. Muriel intended to leave it to her four adopted children. However, Junior's son John D. Rockefeller III was head of the trust committee, and he argued that since her children were not her birth children, they were not entitled to the money. He wished the money to go to Lincoln Center, a new arts center being built in New York City, under his initiative. The court case dragged on for years. By the time it was settled, the $9 million had grown to $13 million, and it was decided to split the money among the children and Lincoln Center.[17]

HAROLD

Harold continued his search for love. He had many rumored romances, among them actress Pola Negri, Betty Noble, Rhoda Tanner Doubleday (who filed a 1933 breach of promise to marry suit and won a $65,000 settlement),[18] and longtime friend Olive Colby (who filed a similar suit).[19] Harold eventually married Adah Wilson, a nurse who took care of him following a heart attack. By then, he was spending most of his time in California. He suffered from debilitating arthritis, intestinal problems, and heart issues. Following the example set by his children, Adah was thirty-two years younger than Harold.

He continued his whistling, even performing on the radio.[20] He maintained good relations with all three children and their spouses. Harold kept up his friendly correspondence with Senior and Junior and continued to be involved in overseeing brother Stanley's and sister Mary Virginia's medical care. He arranged for artist Harold Gaze to paint portraits of his grandchildren as participants in famous fairy tales[21] and commissioned painter Salvador Dali to paint Adah.[22]

Harold's second wife, Ganna, opened a perfume shop in Paris, which failed fairly quickly. She also ran the Théâtre des Champs-Elysées and delighted in entertaining artists and intellectuals. She bought a winter home in Santa Barbara, California, which she converted into a garden showcase named Lotusland. She remarried twice, once to a weapons designer and then to a maharaja who shared her passion for spiritual matters.[23]

Harold died of a cerebral brain hemorrhage in 1941. All three children attended his funeral.[24] Adah remarried—unhappily; she obtained a divorce citing cruelty—and had a son.[25] She died in 1970 in a fall into the Grand Canyon near Navajo Bridge.[26]

THE MCCORMICKS

Cyrus McCormick Jr. died in 1936. He had married Alice Holt after the death of his beloved first wife, Harriet, and lived a very responsible, diligent, oldest-son lifestyle until his death.

Stanley died in 1947, leaving a $33 million estate to loyal wife Katharine. He never did emerge from his Riven Rock estate, except for closely guarded car rides, several trips to the beach, and a couple of frenzied escape attempts. Mathilde and Muriel had occasional contact with him in carefully monitored outings. Katharine, who would have preferred an heir to whom to leave her fortunes, donated millions to her causes: nearly $2 million to fund Gregory Pincus's work on the birth control pill, $5 million to Planned Parenthood, and monies to many other cultural and social institutions. She also subsidized the journal *Endocrinology*, established the Neuroendocrine Research Foundation at Harvard, and funded Stanley McCormick Hall (a female dormitory at MIT). The Stanley McCormick Courtyard at the northwest corner of Chicago's Art Institute was her gift as well. Through Katharine, Stanley's life benefited a great many others.[27]

Several years after Stanley's death, research concluded a definite link between chemical imbalances and schizophrenia, just as Katharine had unsuccessfully argued for decades.[28]

Mary Virginia, also under constant medical surveillance, died the same year as Harold. Her days passed quietly, with a daily routine that included croquet, drives, and movies. She exclaimed, "I love to think what I will tell Jesus when I see him," shortly before she died.[29]

Sister Anita outlived them all, dying at the age of eighty-seven in 1954. She continued to be a dominant force in Chicago school reform, did everything in her power to advocate for world peace, gave millions to her charities, and presided over her grandchildren.[30]

THE ROCKEFELLERS

Senior did not achieve his goal of living to one hundred. He died at the age of ninety-seven, in 1937.[31] His life is well examined in numerous books.

The Rockefeller drive for civic duty endured with Junior's branch of the family. Having inherited the vast majority of Senior's money, he was responsible for overseeing the Rockefeller philanthropies. Through his diligent money management and carefully crafted public image, he helped restore his family's long-tainted reputation. Many of Junior's children and grandchildren went on to assume positions of civic prominence: Nelson Rockefeller was the forty-first vice president of the United States; Winthrop Rockefeller was governor of Arkansas; David Rockefeller served for over twenty years as CEO of Chase Bank; grandson John D. Rockefeller IV became senator from West Virginia; and grandson Winthrop Paul Rockefeller was lieutenant governor of Arkansas.

The Rockefeller line remains strong, with regular reunions among "The Cousins," although Edith's descendants are not considered part of the pack. Ron Chernow commented, "A profound dichotomy now opened in the Rockefeller family between the dutiful son and the wayward daughters and sons-in-law—a dichotomy so deep that the world would think of Junior's descendants alone as the real Rockefellers."[32]

EDWIN KRENN

Edwin married an art student named Mae Clayton two years after Edith's death.[33] They were divorced seven years later—she alleged cruelty, citing an incident where he flung a deck of cards at her during a bridge party as well as an occasion when he pushed her.[34] Edwin went on to run a lighting fixture company and later a biochemical laboratory. He never again neared the success he had enjoyed with Krenn & Dato. He died in 1965.[35]

EMILE AMMANN

After being released from the psychiatric hospital, Edith's chauffeur Emile Ammann made good on his promise to leave the country. But his story only got more bizarre. Passing through New York City on his one night before boarding a cross-Atlantic steamer, he claims he barely avoided being shot by random gunfire. Upon disembarking in France, he discovered his family was still abroad, so he set sail again, headed for Havana. But on his first night on the ship, a fellow passenger stabbed him in the groin, necessitating fourteen days of bed rest. Then, upon arrival in Cuba, the authorities gassed below-deck cabins to eradicate rats, not realizing people were still down there. Ammann claims to have rescued one man and was on his way back in to rescue another when he passed out, hit his head, and was knocked unconscious. Assumed dead, he was taken to the morgue, where someone finally noticed he was still breathing. Ammann was eventually reunited with his wife and children and continued his life of travel and inexplicable adventure. Or so he claims.[36] Rockefeller advisers discovered there were investigations pending on him in both France and Switzerland in the 1930s.[37]

EDITH'S GRAVESITE

Edith's body lay in the Graceland Cemetery vault for decades, until Fowler arranged for final burial.[38] Little Jack and baby Editha were buried with her at a discreet site near a pond. Harold was buried in the same cemetery but near his parents and other family members.

In death, as in life, Edith is separate from both the Rockefellers and the McCormicks. She forged her own path, a task that could not have been easy, given the personalities and forces around her. For this—if not for her generosity, intelligence, and fierce determination to change the world—she should have our respect.

Though cut short, there is no question that Edith had lived a full life. May her philosophy of life serve as inspiration: "No one is too rich nor too poor, too nobly born, nor too humble to escape responsibility for living to the fullest every hour of his life. Living not only physically, though care of one's health and the fullest development of one's strength is one of the first rules of life . . . but living spiritually, socially, intellectually and honestly is the duty of every individual."[39]

ACKNOWLEDGMENTS

NOTES

SOURCES

AUTHOR INTERVIEW

BOOK CLUB DISCUSSION GUIDE

INDEX

ACKNOWLEDGMENTS

Edith demanded ten years of my time. First there was considerable research, including dozens of archives, historical societies, and libraries in the Chicago area and beyond, as I tried to fit together the pieces of her life. And then came the drafts: over eight years I wrote six different manuscripts about Edith. It was a demoralizing period of writing, rejection, writing, and more rejection. I would not have persisted if not for so many people who insisted this story had merit.

Along the way, I developed a great respect for librarians and archivists, most notably Amy Fitch at the Rockefeller Archive Center and Lee Grady at the McCormick Family Archives. Carla Owens, formerly at the Brookfield Zoo archives, provided friendship alongside information.

Edith's great-granddaughter Ramona and her wonderful husband, Steve, couldn't have been more gracious about sharing their stories or more supportive of my efforts. Likewise, Sabrina Pauling, Fowler McCormick Stillman, and Alex Stillman were kind and trusting. I hope they feel I have done Edith's story justice. In a work of this type, it is inevitable that some things may be misconstrued or just plain wrong—for such errors I apologize to the reader, the family, and, most of all, Edith.

I will always be indebted to Steven Rockefeller for the tour of Kykuit and for being willing to talk about his great-aunt. Based on my time with him and what I know of Edith, I consider Rockefellers highly intelligent, deeply thoughtful, and refreshingly open to new ideas.

In Zurich, Dr. Ruth Frehner of the James Joyce Foundation was unbelievably kind and helpful, Vincente de Moura helped facilitate a delightful visit to the Jung Institute, and Eva-Marie Hein at the Hotel Baur au Lac was a perfect hostess. Marianne Jehle was gracious in providing information about Adolf Keller, and Georgina Seel's friendly tour of the Psychological Club felt like walking back in time. I am also grateful to Francesco Campanini and Magnus Ljunggren for their assistance.

Anne Devlin, agent at Max Gartenberg Literary Agency, has been kind, supportive, and helpful since my very first interaction with her. Sylvia Frank Rodrigue at Southern Illinois University Press championed this project, and her insightful comments made the manuscript more meaningful. I am deeply grateful to editors Wayne Larsen and Julie Bush, whose careful reading caught errors and glitches, as well as to Jennifer Egan and all the SIU Press staff.

My boss, mentor, and friend George Rabb was responsible for first introducing me to Edith's story and for giving me the courage to write. His trust was a gift that I will always treasure. This book wouldn't exist without his encouragement. I am also thankful for the support of Brookfield Zoo.

My writing friends Ellen Hummel, Judy Cates, Traci Failla, Dale Wyant, Shannon Anderson, Karla Kroeplin, Kimberli Bindschatel, Valerie Biel, Jim Ballowe, and Christine DeSmet deserve my deepest thanks. They inspired me, encouraged me, and held my hand. I promise to stop complaining now.

My wonderful friends kept me sane. What would I do without them? Honestly. I am me because of them.

Unlike Edith, I am blessed with a deeply caring family. I am rich in ways Edith never was. Peter Friederici, Michele James, Liam Friederici, Claudia Petersen, Rick Petersen, Anneliese Petersen, and Erika Petersen will always be home to me. My father, Hartmann Friederici, instilled a work ethic that kept me tethered to this project until it was done. My mother, Erica Friederici, gave me, well . . . everything. I miss her every day.

To Jim, who paid the bills while I was incessantly researching, writing, querying, and starting over again and again, thank you.

To Greg and Annie, you are the world to me. Being your mother is the greatest honor of my life.

NOTES

AMB   Anita McCormick Blaine
CZS   Chicago Zoological Society
ERM   Edith Rockefeller McCormick
HFM   Harold Fowler McCormick
JDR   John D. Rockefeller (Sr.)
JR   John D. Rockefeller Jr.
NFM   Nettie Fowler McCormick
RAC   Rockefeller Archive Center
       OMR   Office of the Messrs Rockefeller, followed by series letter
       B/F   box/folder
SRM   Stanley Robert McCormick
WHS   Wisconsin Historical Society

PREFACE

1. Manchester, *Rockefeller Family Portrait*, 30, 102.
2. "Mrs. McCormick's Philosophy of Control of Man's Destiny as Revealed in an Interview," *Chicago Daily News*, August 30, 1932.

GROWING UP ROCKEFELLER, 1872–88

1. Fosdick, *John D. Rockefeller, Jr.*, 5.
2. Stasz, *Rockefeller Women*, 75.
3. Chernow, *Titan*, 140.
4. Stasz, *Rockefeller Women*, 79.
5. JR account books, RAC/OMR/Z/B11/F109.
6. Fosdick, *John D. Rockefeller, Jr.*, 32.
7. Manchester, *Rockefeller Family Portrait*, 70.
8. Stasz, *Rockefeller Women*, 77.
9. Fosdick, *John D. Rockefeller, Jr.*, 9.
10. Manchester, *Rockefeller Family Portrait*, 160.
11. Chernow, *Titan*, 123.
12. Manchester, *Rockefeller Family Portrait*, 50.

13. JR account books, RAC/OMR/Z/B11/F109.
14. Reverend Ralph Walker, "Sixty Years a Sunday School Superintendent," *Watchman's Examiner*, November 1932.
15. Stasz, *Rockefeller Women*, 83.
16. Chernow, *Titan*, 125.
17. Manchester, *Rockefeller Family Portrait*, 101.
18. Chernow, *Titan*, 188.
19. Mary Dougherty, "'Life as It Seemed to Me,' Described by Mrs. McCormick," *New York Evening Journal*, August 30, 1932. This was a series published over several days; the title varies slightly by day.
20. Manchester, *Rockefeller Family Portrait*, 65.
21. Chernow, *Titan*, 193.
22. Fosdick, *John D. Rockefeller, Jr.*, 27.
23. Fosdick, 21.
24. Manchester, *Rockefeller Family Portrait*, 113.
25. JR account books, RAC/OMR/Z/B11/F108.
26. Chernow, *Titan*, 188.
27. Harr and Johnson, *Rockefeller Century*, 40.
28. "Mrs. McCormick's Philosophy of Control of Man's Destiny as Revealed in an Interview," *Chicago Daily News*, August 30, 1932.
29. Mary Dougherty, "'Life as It Seemed to Me,' Told by Mrs. McCormick," *New York Evening Journal*, August 29, 1932.
30. Stasz, *Rockefeller Women*, 101.
31. Chernow, *Titan*, 220.
32. Samuel Melamed to JR, February 28, 1934, RAC/OMR/H/B80/F609.

THE PRINCE OF MCCORMICK REAPER, 1888–95

1. Harrison, *Timeless Affair*, 20.
2. Stasz, *Rockefeller Women*, 103–4.
3. Harrison, *Timeless Affair*, 29.
4. HFM to AMB, September 20, 1898, WHS, AMB Collection, Box 440, HFM /1898 folder.
5. Roderick, *Nettie Fowler McCormick*, 179.
6. HFM to Santa Claus, WHS, AMB Collection, Box 440, HFM/1879 folder.
7. History of Rye Country Day School, https://www.ryecountryday.org/about /history.
8. Stasz, *Rockefeller Women*, 102.
9. MacLeod, *Enchanted Lives*, 210.
10. Stasz, *Rockefeller Women*, 108.
11. ERM/JR correspondence, RAC/OMR/H/B79/F607.
12. Chernow, *Titan*, 127.
13. E. McCormick, "Four Family Divisions," 259.

14. Fields, *Katharine Dexter McCormick*, 41.
15. JR to Fowler McCormick, November 27, 1941, RAC/OMR/H/B181/F1381.
16. "The Gossip of Gotham," *Akron Beacon Journal*, February 9, 1895, 5.
17. ERM to NFM, May 27, 1895, WHS, NFM Collection, Box 66.
18. Roderick, *Nettie Fowler McCormick*, 188.
19. HFM to JDR, May 1, 1908, RAC/OMR/H/B79/F605.
20. HFM to AMB, June 3, 1895, WHS, AMB Collection, HFM/1895 folder.
21. "Women: End of a Princess," *Time*, September 5, 1932.
22. Chernow, *Titan*, 416.
23. "Miss Edith Rockefeller Is to Wed," *Chicago Daily Tribune*, June 4, 1895.
24. "Society—Amusements," *Chicago Tribune*, June 7, 1895.
25. Stasz, *Rockefeller Women*, 125.
26. "No Ceremony in Church . . . Illness Causes Change of Plans," *New York Times*, November 25, 1895.
27. "Wed among Kinsfolk," *Chicago Daily Tribune*, November 27, 1895.
28. Mary Dougherty, "'Life as It Seemed to Me,' by Mrs. McCormick," *New York Evening Journal*, August 31, 1932.
29. Chernow, *Titan*, 415.
30. Chernow, 417.
31. "May Wed at Bedside," *Chicago Daily Tribune*, November 26, 1895.
32. Roderick, *Nettie Fowler McCormick*, 191.

TRICKLE DOWN EDITH, 1896–99

1. HFM to AMB, May 15, 1896, WHS, AMB Collection, Box 440, HFM/1896 folder.
2. Will Leonard, "The Long, Silent Death of Villa Turicum," *Chicago Tribune*, August 14, 1966, J26.
3. Benjamin and Cohen, *Great Houses of Chicago*, 80.
4. Eleanor Page, "This Was 1000 Lake Shore Dr.—before High Rises," *Chicago Tribune*, September 19, 1965.
5. Benjamin and Cohen, *Great Houses of Chicago*, 102–9.
6. E. McCormick, "Four Family Divisions."
7. Virginia Gardner, "Servants Recall Grand Manner of Edith McCormick," *Chicago Daily Tribune*, August 28, 1932.
8. Gardner, "Servants Recall Grand Manner of Edith McCormick."
9. Chernow, *Titan*, 416.
10. American Art Association, *Splendid Library of the Late Mrs. Rockefeller McCormick*.
11. American Art Association, *Collection of the Late Edith Rockefeller McCormick*, 158–59.
12. American Art Association, 78–79.
13. American Art Association, *Contents of the Residences of the Late Edith Rockefeller McCormick*, 72.

14. Mary Dougherty, "'Life as It Seemed to Me,' by Mrs. McCormick," *New York Evening Journal*, September 2, 1932.

15. The $50,000 would be equivalent to nearly $1.4 million in 2020. HFM to JDR, May 1, 1908, RAC/OMR/H/B79/F605.

16. American Art Association, *Collection of the Late Edith Rockefeller McCormick*, 116–18.

17. "Society Woman Wears Anklet," *Chicago Daily Tribune*, April 19, 1911.

18. Stasz, *Rockefeller Women*, 169.

19. Harrison, *Timeless Affair*, 188.

20. "Millions in Matrimony," *Chicago Tribune*, October 12, 1895.

21. Ruth De Young, "Mrs. Edith Rockefeller McCormick's Dream of Museum for Her Art Treasures Revealed," *Chicago Daily Tribune*, November 4, 1932, 6; American Art Association, *Collection of the Late Edith Rockefeller McCormick*, 81.

22. "Women: End of a Princess," *Time*, September 5, 1932.

23. De Young, "Mrs. Edith Rockefeller McCormick's Dream of Museum for her Art Treasures Revealed," 6.

24. Dedmon, *Fabulous Chicago*, 304.

25. Chernow, *Titan*, 417.

26. Meeker, *Chicago, with Love*, 150.

27. Darling, *Chicago Metalsmiths*, 114.

28. "Drink Tea in Lincoln Park," *Chicago Daily Tribune*, May 10, 1912, 3.

29. Stasz, *Rockefeller Women*, 137.

30. Stasz, 137.

31. HFM to AMB, March 3, 1897, WHS, AMB Collection, Box 440, HFM/1897 folder.

32. NFM to Cettie Rockefeller, May 5, 1897, RAC/OMR/1SL/B1/F19.

33. Manchester, *Rockefeller Family Portrait*, 122.

THE SHOW MUST GO ON, 1900–1904

1. E. McCormick, "What My Children Mean to Me," 212.

2. Chernow, *Titan*, 418.

3. HFM to NFM, January 7, 1901, WHS, NFM Collection, Box 85.

4. HFM to JDR, RAC/OMR/A/B32/F249.

5. ERM to NFM, January 9, 1901, WHS, NFM Collection, Box 85.

6. "Rockefeller Gift Ready," *Chicago Daily Tribune*, February 5, 1906.

7. Hirsch, "Happy Birthday to Us!!"

8. Roderick, *Nettie Fowler McCormick*, 228.

9. Chernow, *Titan*, 421.

10. Chernow, 420.

11. Stasz, *Rockefeller Women*, 145.

12. Tarbell, "John D. Rockefeller," 229.

13. Manchester, *Rockefeller Family Portrait*, 68.

14. Chernow, *Titan*, 461.
15. Harr and Johnson, *Rockefeller Century*, 85.
16. Chernow, *Titan*, 458.
17. "Scene of Mr. and Mrs. Harold F. M'Cormick's Garden Party," *Chicago Daily Tribune*, June 3, 1904, 7.
18. "McCormick Child Dies," *New York Times*, June 12, 1904.
19. Meeker, *Chicago, with Love*, 147.
20. E. McCormick, "What My Children Mean to Me," 211.

DANGERS, 1905–10

1. Fields, *Katharine Dexter McCormick*, 42.
2. Fields, 64.
3. Harrison, *Timeless Affair*, 160.
4. "Memorandum concerning medical reports," WHS, SRM Papers.
5. Rodkin, "Exceedingly Strange Case of the McCormick Sex Machine."
6. Fields, *Katharine Dexter McCormick*, 44.
7. "Memorandum concerning medical reports," WHS, SRM Papers.
8. Rodkin, "Exceedingly Strange Case of the McCormick Sex Machine."
9. HFM to AMB and SRM, April 19, 1906, WHS, AMB Collection, Box 440, HFM/1906 folder.
10. Rodkin, "Exceedingly Strange Case of the McCormick Sex Machine."
11. Fields, *Katharine Dexter McCormick*, 83.
12. Unidentified newspaper article, "Mrs. C. A. Strong Dead," RAC/OMR/H /B112/F846.
13. Interview with Ramona Pauling Berent and Sabrina Pauling, 2010.
14. Mathilde McCormick to JDR, December 14, 1916, RAC/OMR/A/B33/F252.
15. HFM to SRM, March 9, 1905, WHS, AMB Collection, Box 440, HFM/1905 folder.
16. Stasz, *Rockefeller Women*, 159; HFM to AMB, June 25, 1908, WHS, AMB Collection, Box 440, HFM/1908 folder.
17. HFM to JDR, May 22, 1905, RAC/OMR/H/B79/F605.
18. "Granddaughter of J. D. Rockefeller Recovering from Appendicitis," *Chicago Daily Tribune*, February 10, 1906.
19. Stasz, *Rockefeller Women*, 159.
20. ERM to HFM, April 9, 1906, Chicago History Museum, HFM Papers, Box 272, Folder 7.
21. Chernow, *Titan*, 597.
22. Appointment books, WHS, HFM Collection, Box 82.
23. Souter and Souter, *Chicago Air and Water Show*.
24. HFM to Cyrus McCormick Jr., July 4, 1910, WHS, AMB Collection, Box 441, HFM/1910 folder.
25. Morgan, *Charles A. Platt*, 115.

26. Cohen and Benjamin, *North Shore Chicago*, 124.

27. Pfeiffer, *Frank Lloyd Wright: The Heroic Years*, 208.

28. Manson, *Frank Lloyd Wright to 1910*, 202.

29. Ruth De Young, "Mrs. Edith Rockefeller McCormick's Dream of Museum for Her Art Treasures Revealed," *Chicago Daily Tribune*, November 4, 1932, 6.

30. Will Leonard, "The Long, Silent Death of Villa Turicum," *Chicago Tribune*, August 14, 1966, J26.

31. Morgan, *Charles A. Platt*, 120.

32. F. Smith, "'Villa Turicum,' the Country Estate," 10.

33. ERM to JDR, November 1, 1910, RAC/OMR/A/B32/F248.

34. Coventry, Meyer, and Miller, *Classic Country Estates of Lake Forest*, 145.

35. Shaw, "Garden of No-Delight," 16.

36. Chernow, *Titan*, 422.

37. ERM to Woodrow Wilson, February 20, 1909, in *Papers of Woodrow Wilson*, 65.

38. "J. D. Rockefeller Here to Testify; Visits Daughter," *Chicago Daily Tribune*, July 6, 1907.

39. Chernow, *Titan*, 540–41.

40. "Guard Young McCormick," *New York Times*, September 21, 1906.

GRAND CAUSES, 1909–11

1. Fields, *Katharine Dexter McCormick*, xi.

2. Fields, photo gallery.

3. "Details of Wedding Arranged," *Chicago Tribune*, November 17, 1895.

4. Harrison, *Timeless Affair*, 136.

5. Brubaker, "130 Years of Opera in Chicago," 157.

6. Harold F. M'Cormick, "Grand Opera in Chicago," *Chicago Daily News*, August 5, 1935.

7. ERM speech as reported in *Chicago Commerce*, October 22, 1921.

8. Brubaker, "130 Years of Opera in Chicago," 157.

9. Davis, *Opera in Chicago*, 109.

10. Meeker, *Chicago, with Love*, 150–51.

11. Meeker, 151.

12. Davis, *Opera in Chicago*, 88–89.

13. Garden and Biancolli, *Mary Garden's Story*, 210.

14. "Mrs. McCormick's Career," *New York Times*, August 26, 1932.

15. Margot, "Mrs. McCormick Society's Outstanding Figure for over Thirty-Five Years," *Chicago Daily News*, August 26, 1932, 1.

16. "Paderewski Appears in Mrs. Harold F. McCormick's Musical," *Chicago Daily Tribune*, January 10, 1908.

17. Villella, *Chicago Symphony Orchestra*, 1.

18. Deanna Isaacs, "The Fate of the Three Arts Club," *Chicago Reader*, January 26, 2006.

19. Garland, "New Idea in Theater Management," 21.
20. ERM to JDR, March 22, 1913, RAC/OMR/A/B32/F249.
21. Friedrich August von Kaulbach to ERM, December 28, 1912, RAC/OMR/A/B32/F248.
22. HFM to AMB, April 4, 1896, WHS, AMB Collection, Box 440, HFM/1896 folder.
23. Ackerman, *Three Early Sixteenth Century Tapestries*.
24. Henry Favill to Emil Kraepelin, June 1908, WHS, AMB Collection, Box 440, HFM/1908 folder.
25. HFM to AMB, October 3, 1914, WHS, AMB Collection, Box 441, HFM/1914 folder.
26. HFM to AMB, September 10, 1908, WHS, AMB Collection, Box 440, HFM/1908 folder.
27. Bushnell, "International Aviation Meet," 12.

TRYING TO STAY SANE, 1911–13

1. "Lorimer Car Hits McCormick Auto," *Chicago Daily Tribune*, January 22, 1913, 2.
2. "Ice, Steel, Luck, Save Many," *Chicago Daily Tribune*, March 14, 1912, 2.
3. "Ruins Treasures of H. F. M'Cormick," *Chicago Daily Tribune*, August 14, 1910, 1.
4. Noll, *Aryan Christ*, 202.
5. "Mrs. M'Cormick Ill, Seeks Rest," *Chicago Daily Tribune*, September 6, 1911.
6. "Fort Sheridan Gunfire Damages Lake Forest Estates," *Chicago Daily Tribune*, October 27, 1922, 34.
7. HFM to JDR, September 22, 1911, RAC/OMR/A/B32/F248.
8. "Mrs. Harold McCormick Plans Tiny Venice at Lake Forest," *Chicago Daily Tribune*, June 30, 1911.
9. "Outline a Venice at Lake Forest," *Chicago Daily Tribune*, August 15, 1909.
10. "Will Honor Harold F. McCormick," *Chicago Daily Tribune*, June 25, 1912.
11. HFM to AMB, July 12, 1897, WHS, AMB Collection, Box 440, HFM/1897 folder.
12. "Mrs. Harold F. M'Cormick Ill in Eastern Sanitarium," *Chicago Daily Tribune*, July 24, 1912.
13. HFM to JDR, July 13, 1912, RAC/OMR/A/B32/F248.
14. Noll, *Aryan Christ*, 204.
15. Carl Jung to Smith Ely Jelliffe, October 16, 1932, in Burnham, *Jelliffe*, 247.
16. Rodkin, "Exceedingly Strange Case of the McCormick Sex Machine."
17. Chernow, *Titan*, 599.
18. HFM to AMB, October 14, 1912, WHS, AMB Collection, Box 441, HFM/1912 folder.
19. Noll, *Aryan Christ*, 205.

20. HRM to JDR, December 28, 1913, RAC/OMR/A/B32/F249.

21. Hannah, *Jung*, 109.

22. Mme. X., "Society Learns New Steps of Dances Now All the Rage," *Chicago Daily Tribune*, November 10, 1912, H2.

23. "Society Prepares to Welcome Amundsen," *Chicago Daily Tribune*, January 29, 1913, p9.

24. Marion Walters, "Chicago Suffragists Widen Scope of Activity," *Chicago Daily Tribune*, December 8, 1912, H5.

25. "Mrs. Harold McCormick Joins Woman Suffrage Movement," *Chicago Daily Tribune*, December 13, 1912, 13.

26. E. McCormick, "Four Family Divisions," 259.

27. "McCormick Mansion Provides a Radiant Setting for Affair," *Chicago Examiner*, June 7, 1916.

28. Review of Memorial Institute, October 12, 1909, Chicago History Museum, HFM Papers, Box 272, Folder 4.

29. ERM to HRM, April 9, 1906, Chicago History Museum, HFM Papers, Box 272, Folder 7.

30. Weaver, *Medical Report of the Durand Hospital*.

31. "Durand Hospital Ready," *Chicago Daily Tribune*, February 25, 1913, 13.

32. "Women Triumph in Arab Trousers," *Chicago Daily Tribune*, January 11, 1913, 3.

33. "H. F. McCormicks Give Italian Garden Dance," *Chicago Daily Tribune*, February 1, 1913, 9.

34. Noll, *Aryan Christ*, 207.

A NEW FATHER FIGURE, 1913–14

1. Ammann, *Im Dienste der Reichsten Frau*, 101–2 (my translation).

2. Noll, *Aryan Christ*, 200.

3. Noll, 212.

4. "Little Miss M'Cormick Lake Forest Hostess," *Chicago Daily Tribune*, August 20, 1913, 9.

5. "M'Cormick Flies in New Airboat," *Chicago Daily Tribune*, July 28, 1913, 2.

6. Mme. X., "Over the Lake in an Aeroplane the Supreme Event in One Woman's Life," *Chicago Daily Tribune*, August 31, 1913, E3.

7. "M'Cormick Flies in New Airboat," 2.

8. Whet Moser, "The First Aerial Footage of Chicago," *Chicago Magazine*, September 28, 1912, https://www.chicagomag.com/Chicago-Magazine/The-312/September-2012/The-First-Aerial-Film-of-Chicago/.

9. "Madcap Autoist Spreads Terror," *Chicago Daily Tribune*, July 21, 1913, 1.

10. "Airmen Rescuers Get Duckings," *Chicago Daily Tribune*, August 4, 1913, 2.

11. HFM to JDR, October 3, 1914, RAC/OMR/A/B32/F249.

12. Noll, *Aryan Christ*, 200.

13. Chernow, *Titan*, 603.
14. Noll, *Aryan Christ*, 208.
15. HFM to JDR, December 28, 1913, RAC/OMR/A/B32/F249.
16. Noll, *Aryan Christ*, 208.
17. Ammann, *Im Dienste der Reichsten Frau*, 118 (my translation).
18. Vetro, *Cleofonte Campanini*. Credit goes to Archivio Storico del Teatro Regio di Parma, Settore Casa della Musica—Comune di Parma, Italy.
19. Basini, "Cults of Sacred Memory."
20. Campanini, *Giuseppe Verdi and the Glory*.
21. HFM to Cleofonte Campanini, September 2, 1913, WHS, HFM Collection, Box 29.
22. Ammann, "Driving Miss Edith," 15.
23. Vetro, *Cleofonte Campanini*, 200-201.
24. Vetro, 201.
25. Manchester, *Rockefeller Family Portrait*, 98.
26. ERM to JDR, June 25, 1914, RAC/OMR/A/B32/F249.
27. HFM to JDR, August 1, 1914, RAC/OMR/A/B32/F249.
28. ERM to JDR, August 2, 1914, RAC/OMR/A/B32/F249.
29. Noll, *Aryan Christ*, 211.
30. ERM to JDR, November 26, 1917, RAC/OMR/A/B33/F252.
31. Alta Prentice to ERM, August 24, 1914, RAC/OMR/H/B79/F604.
32. ERM to Alta Prentice, August 26, 1914, RAC/OMR/H/B79/F604.
33. E. McCormick, "Four Family Divisions," 259.
34. HFM to JDR, October 3, 1914, RAC/OMR/A/B32/F249.
35. HFM to AMB, September 18, 1914, WHS, AMB Collection, Box 441, HFM /1914 folder.
36. Noll, *Aryan Christ*, 210.
37. HFM to NFM, October 12, 1914, WHS, NFM Collection, Box 137.
38. Harrison, *Timeless Affair*, 166–67.
39. Benjamin and Cohen, *Great Houses of Chicago*, 79.
40. HFM to NFM, November 28, 1914, WHS, NFM Collection, Box 137.
41. Noll, *Aryan Christ*, 223.

IN FOR THE LONG HAUL, 1915–16

1. ERM to JDR, March 14, 1915, RAC/OMR/A/B32/F250.
2. HFM to AMB, March 14, 1915, WHS, AMB Collection, Box 441, HFM/1915 folder.
3. Cyrus McCormick to JR, November 15, 1915, RAC/OMR/H/B79/F603.
4. HFM to JDR, September 1, 1915, RAC/OMR/A/B32/F250.
5. H. McCormick, *Via Pacis*.
6. Noll, *Aryan Christ*, 226.
7. Luening, *Odyssey of an American Composer*, 137.

8. Luening, 142.

9. Bowker, *James Joyce*, 243.

10. Ellmann, *James Joyce*, 422.

11. Stern, *C. G. Jung*, 150.

12. Bowker, *James Joyce*, 267.

13. Joyce, *Letters of James Joyce*, 454.

14. James Joyce to Frank Budgen (not dated), in Joyce, 130.

15. Ellmann, *James Joyce*, 469.

16. Ellmann, 469.

17. Ammann, *Im Dienste der Reichsten Frau*, 127–28 (my translation here and in subsequent citations of this work).

18. HFM to JDR, September 1, 1915, RAC/OMR/H/B79/F604.

19. Ammann, *Im Dienste der Reichsten Frau*, 154.

20. Ammann, 150.

21. Ammann, "Driving Miss Edith," 18.

22. Noll, *Aryan Christ*, 215.

23. HFM to JDR, October 31, 1915, RAC/OMR/A/B32/F250.

24. HFM to JDR, June 18, 1915, RAC/OMR/A/B32/F250.

25. Cinderella, "Mrs. McCormick Not to Return Soon?," *Chicago Daily Tribune*, June 17, 1915.

26. "Italian Steamship 'Ancona' Victim of Austrian Submarine: Harold M'Cormicks Not on Sunken Steamer," *Chicago Daily Tribune*, November 10, 1915, 1.

27. ERM to JDR, December 5, 1916, RAC/OMR/A/B32/F251.

PSYCHOLOGICAL CLUB, 1916–17

1. Noll, *Aryan Christ*, 223.

2. Stern, *C. G. Jung*, 149.

3. "Mrs. H. F. McCormick to Build a Hospital," *New York Times*, February 1, 1916.

4. ERM to JDR, January 31, 1916, RAC/OMR/A/B33/F251.

5. Alta Rockefeller Prentice to JDR, October 13, 1921, RAC/OMR/A/B31/F243.

6. Manchester, *Rockefeller Family Portrait*, 43.

7. JDR to ERM, March 4, 1916 RAC/OMR/A/B32/F251.

8. ERM to JDR, July 20, 1916, RAC/OMR/A/B32/F251.

9. ERM to JDR, September 26, 1920, RAC/OMR/A/B33/F254.

10. JDR to ERM, July 14, 1917, RAC/OMR/H/B79/F604.

11. Chernow, *Titan*, 624.

12. 1917 Edith Rockefeller Trust Document, RAC/OMR/H/B83/F638.

13. ERM to JDR, January 24, 1918, RAC/OMR/A/B33/F252.

14. HFM to JDR, August 25, 1917, RAC/OMR/A/B33/F252.

15. Jung, *Red Book*, 206.

16. Carl Jung to Alphonse Maeder, as cited in Shamdasani, *Cult Fictions*, 25.

17. ERM to JDR, March 27, 1919, RAC/OMR/A/B33/F253.

18. ERM to JDR, June 22, 1917, RAC/OMR/A/B33/F252.
19. Jehle-Wildberger, *C. G. Jung und Adolf Keller*, 50–51(my translation).
20. Hannah, *Jung*, 130.
21. Ljunggren, *Russian Mephisto*, 142.
22. Ammann, *Im Dienste der Reichsten Frau*, 149.
23. Stasz, *Rockefeller Women*, 222.
24. Noll, *Aryan Christ*, 233.
25. Mary Dougherty, "'Life as It Seemed to Me,' by Mrs. McCormick," *New York Evening Journal*, September 3, 1932.
26. Ammann, *Im Dienste der Reichsten Frau*, 132–34.
27. J. C. McNally to HFM, August 6, 1917, WHS, HFM Collection, Box 29.
28. J. C. McNally to HFM, August 8, 1917, WHS, HFM Collection, Box 29.
29. "$1,000 Sent from Switzerland for Ambulance," *Chicago Daily Tribune*, December 19, 1917.
30. "Yarrowdale Sailors Entertained at 'Tea,'" *New York Times*, March 18, 1917.
31. "Says Mrs. M'Cormick Freed French Ace," *New York Times*, April 12, 1923.

A FAMILY IN TATTERS, 1917–20

1. "Mrs. McCormick Gave Freedom to Children," *New York American*, February 17, 1927.
2. Noll, *Aryan Christ*, 226.
3. Noll, 234.
4. Mathilde McCormick to JDR, December 14, 1916, RAC/OMR/A/B33/F252.
5. Mathilde McCormick to JDR, June 23, 1917, RAC/OMR/A/B33/F252.
6. JDR to Mathilde McCormick, April 12, 1918, RAC/OMR/A/B33/F252.
7. Noll, *Aryan Christ*, 215.
8. HFM to AMB, October 3, 1914, WHS, AMB Collection, Box 441, HFM/1914 folder.
9. ERM to JDR, January 24, 1918, RAC/OMR/A/B33/F252.
10. ERM to JDR, February 8, 1917, RAC/OMR/A/B33/F252.
11. ERM to JDR, May 18, 1920, RAC/OMR/H/B79/F604.
12. Noll, *Aryan Christ*, 226.
13. Shamdasani, *Cult Fictions*, 22.
14. Stern, *C. G. Jung*, 150.
15. Harrison, *Timeless Affair*, 173.
16. Davis, *Opera in Chicago*, 117.
17. Marsh, *150 Years of Opera in Chicago*, 80.
18. Marsh, 80.
19. Mme. X., "What's Doing in Society," *Chicago Daily Tribune*, January 11, 1914, D2.
20. Ammann, *Im Dienste der Reichsten Frau*, 104.
21. "Reveals Secret of $5,000 Wee Dog," *Chicago Daily Tribune*, November 1, 1913, 3.

22. Marsh, *150 Years of Opera in Chicago*, 78–79.
23. Harold F. M'Cormick, "Grand Opera in Chicago," *Chicago Daily News*, August 12, 1935.
24. Garden and Biancolli, *Mary Garden's Story*, 169.
25. HFM to Cleofonte Campanini, October 1, 1919, WHS, HFM Collection, Box 30.
26. HFM to Max Pam, March 10, 1920, WHS, HFM Collection, Box 31.
27. Meeker, *Chicago, with Love*, 245–46.
28. Ammann, *Im Dienste der Reichsten Frau*, 153.
29. HFM to JDR, July 1920, RAC/OMR/A/B33/F254.
30. HFM to AMB, July 16, 1920, WHS, AMB Collection, Box 442, HFM/1920 folder.
31. Meeker, *Chicago, with Love*, 248.
32. "Marriage a Surprise," *Chicago Herald and Examiner*, December 20, 1920, WHS, HFM Collection, Box 84.
33. Stasz, *Rockefeller Women*, 218.
34. Harrison, *Timeless Affair*, 189–90.
35. Walska, *Always Room at the Top*, 197.
36. Walska, 197.
37. Walska, 198.
38. Adams, *Ganna*, 75.
39. HFM to JDR, October 4, 1920, RAC/OMR/A/B33/F254.
40. Nettie McCormick to JDR, October 25, 1920, RAC/OMR/A/B33/F254.
41. Davis, *Opera in Chicago*, 131.
42. "'Richest Singer in World' Flees on Eve of Debut," *Chicago Daily Tribune*, December 20, 1920.
43. Adams, *Ganna*, 56.
44. Davis, *Opera in Chicago*, 131.
45. Davis, 133.
46. HFM to JDR, January 19, 1920, RAC/OMR/A/B33/F254.
47. HFM to JDR, January 19, 1920, RAC/OMR/A/B33/F254.
48. JDR to ERM, January 5, 1920, RAC/OMR/A/B33/F254.
49. JDR to HFM, January 27, 1920, RAC/OMR/A/B33/F254.
50. HFM to JDR, February 9, 1920, RAC/OMR/A/B33/F254.
51. HFM to JDR, January 19, 1920, RAC/OMR/A/B33/F254.
52. Stasz, *Rockefeller Women*, 218.
53. Ammann, *Im Dienste der Reichsten Frau*, 141.
54. HFM to JDR, January 19, 1920, RAC/OMR/A/B33/F254.
55. ERM to JDR, September 24, 1920, RAC/OMR/A/B33/F254.
56. ERM to JDR, March 10, 1921, RAC/OMR/A/B33/F255.
57. JDR to HFM, May 6, 1920, RAC/OMR/A/B33/F254.

TRYING TO FIND A WAY HOME, 1919–21

1. Burnham and Bennett, *Plan of Chicago*.
2. Judson Stone to Ezra Warner, September 3, 1930, CZS.
3. Ross, *Let the Lions Roar!*, 11.
4. Judson Stone to ERM, November 7, 1919, WHS, HFM Collection, Box 30.
5. Judson Stone to Ezra Warner, September 3, 1930, CZS.
6. Quoted in Ross, *Let the Lions Roar!*, 3.
7. Quoted in Ross, 3.
8. "County to Have Great Zoo," *Riverside News*, January 2, 1920, 1.
9. "What Do Animals Think?," *Chicago Daily News*, January 26, 1923, 1.
10. Ross, *Let the Lions Roar!*, 7.
11. "The McCormick Gift," Forest Preserve District of Cook County Yearbook 1927, pp. 101–4, CZS.
12. Memorandum for Mr. Rockefeller, September 1921, RAC/OMR/A/B33/F255.
13. Ammann, *Im Dienste der Reichsten Frau*, 107.
14. Mathilde Oser to HFM, February 14, 1921, WHS, AMB Collection, Box 442, HFM/1921 folder.
15. HFM to JDR, February 9, 1920, RAC/OMR/A/B33/F254.
16. Adams, *Ganna*, 93.
17. HFM to AMB, July 4, 1921, WHS, AMB Collection, Box 442, HFM/1921 folder.
18. Stasz, *Rockefeller Women*, 240.
19. "Denies He Is Engaged to Miss Anne Stillman," *New York Times*, April 6, 1921.
20. JDR to HFM, April 8, 1921, RAC/OMR/A/B33/F255.
21. HFM to JDR, April 14, 1921, RAC/OMR/A/B33/F255.
22. HFM to JDR, February 24, 1922, RAC/OMR/A/B33/F256.
23. Mathilde McCormick to JDR, June 23, 1917, RAC/OMR/A/B33/F252.
24. ERM to JDR, February 17, 1922, RAC/OMR/A/B33/F256.
25. HFM to JDR, February 24, 1922, RAC/OMR/A/B33/F256.
26. JDR to ERM, April 9, 1921, RAC/OMR/A/B33/F255.
27. NFM to HFM, July 18, 1921, WHS, HFM Collection, Box 31.
28. Ljunggren *Russian Mephisto*, 126.
29. ERM to John T. McCutcheon, May 29, 1922, CZS.
30. "Mrs. H. F. M'Cormick Back after 8 Years," *New York Times*, September 28, 1921.
31. HFM to AMB, September 21, 24, 29, 1921, WHS, AMB Collection, Box 442, HFM/1921 folder.
32. HFM to JDR, June 8, 1921, RAC/OMR/A/B33/F255.
33. Cyrus H. McCormick to JDR, September 6, 1921, RAC/OMR/A/B33/F255.
34. JDR to ERM, September 7, 1921, RAC/OMR/A/B33/F255.

35. ERM to JDR, September 9, 1921, RAC/OMR/A/B33/F255.

36. "Mrs. H. F. M'Cormick Back after 8 Years."

37. Paul Cravath to JDR, September 23, 1921, RAC/OMR/A/B33/F255.

ON HER OWN, 1921–22

1. "Mrs. H. F. M'Cormick Back after 8 Years," *New York Times*, September 28, 1921.

2. JR to HFM, June 28, 1921, RAC/OMR/H/B80/F612.

3. "Mrs. H. F. M'Cormick Back after 8 Years."

4. ERM to JDR, September 28, 1921, RAC/OMR/A/B33/F255.

5. JDR to ERM, September 28, 1921, RAC/OMR/A/B33/F255.

6. ERM to JDR, September 29, 1921, RAC/OMR/A/B33/F255.

7. JDR to ERM, September 30, 1921, RAC/OMR/A/B33/F255.

8. ERM to JDR, September 30, 1921, RAC/OMR/A/B33/F255.

9. HFM to JDR, October 6, 1921, RAC/OMR/A/B33/F255.

10. ERM to JDR, March 8, 1922, RAC/OMR/A/B33/F256.

11. Muriel McCormick to ERM, undated cable, WHS, Muriel McCormick Papers.

12. "M'Cormicks Live Apart in Chicago," *New York Times*, October 4, 1921, 1.

13. "M'Cormicks Live Apart in Chicago."

14. Memorandum for Mr. Rockefeller, October 7, 1921, RAC/OMR/A/B33/F255.

15. In 2020, that $1 million would be worth $13 million. Chernow, *Titan*, 265.

16. HFM to NFM, January 1919, WHS, HFM Collection, Box 30.

17. Marsh, *150 Years of Opera in Chicago*, 85.

18. George W. Murray to JDR, October 31, 1921, RAC/OMR/A/B33/F255.

19. ERM to JDR, November 19, 1921, RAC/OMR/A/B33/F255.

20. George Murray to JDR, October 31, 1921, RAC/OMR/A/B33/F255.

21. Alta Prentice to JDR, November 30, 1921, RAC/OMR/A/B33/F255.

22. JDR to ERM, November 2, 1921, RAC/OMR/A/B33/F255.

23. ERM to JDR, November 4, 1921, RAC/OMR/A/B33/F255.

24. Parmalee Prentice to JR, December 6, 1921, RAC/OMR/H/B80/F610.

25. Charles Cutting to Parmalee Prentice, December 16, 1921, RAC/OMR/H/B80/F613.

26. JR to Charles Cutting, December 20, 1921, RAC/OMR/H/B80/F613.

27. Charles Cutting to JR, December 21, 1921, RAC/OMR/H/B80/F613.

28. ERM to JDR, December 15, 1921, RAC/OMR/H/B80/F610.

29. JR to Bertram Cutler, October 5, 1921, RAC/OMR/H/B80/F612.

30. "H. F. McCormicks Divorced; Wife Obtains Decree," *Chicago Daily Tribune*, December 29, 1921.

31. ERM to JDR, December 27, 1921, RAC/OMR/A/B33/F255.

32. JR to ERM, January 3, 1922, RAC/OMR/H/B80/F613.

33. JR to JDR, January 3, 1922, RAC/OMR/H/B80/F613.

34. JR to Muriel McCormick, January 6, 1921, RAC/OMR/H/B89/F670.

35. 1917 Edith Rockefeller Trust Document, RAC/OMR/H/B83/F638.

36. JDR to ERM, cable, December 19, 1921, RAC/OMR/H/B80/F613.

37. Ledger titled "Mrs. Edith Rockefeller McCormick" dated January 17, 1922, RAC/OMR/A/B33/F256.

38. HFM to JDR, December 23, 1921, RAC/OMR/A/B33/F255.

39. JDR to HFM, December 30, 1921, RAC/OMR/A/B33/F255.

40. Roderick, *Nettie Fowler McCormick*, 305.

41. "Gala Audience Drawn to Hear Opera 'Salome,'" *Chicago Daily Tribune*, December 29, 1921, 3.

A YEAR IN THE LIFE, 1922–23

1. ERM to JDR, January 28, 1922, RAC/OMR/A/B33/F256.

2. HFM to JDR, February 24, 1922, RAC/OMR/A/B33/F256.

3. ERM to JDR, February 23, 1922, RAC/OMR/A/B33/F256.

4. ERM to JDR, February 23, 1922, RAC/OMR/A/B33/F256.

5. ERM to JDR, February 23, 1922, RAC/OMR/A/B33/F256.

6. ERM to JDR, February 25, 1922, RAC/OMR/A/B33/F256.

7. HFM to JDR, February 24, 1922, RAC/OMR/A/B33/F256.

8. Fowler McCormick to JDR, February 21, 1922, RAC/OMR/A/B33/F256.

9. Muriel McCormick to JDR, February 21, 1922, RAC/OMR/A/B33/F256.

10. Mathilde McCormick to JDR, February 24, 1922, RAC/OMR/A/B33/F256.

11. JDR to ERM, February 21, 1922, RAC/OMR/A/B33/F256.

12. JR to HFM, February 25, 1922, RAC/OMR/H/B89/F668.

13. "M'Cormick Family Affirms Mathilde's Betrothal to Oser," *New York Times*, February 20, 1922, 1.

14. ERM to JDR, February 23, 1922, RAC/OMR/A/B33/F256.

15. HFM to AMB, July 1918, WHS, AMB Collection, Box 441, HFM/1918 folder.

16. Chernow, *Titan*, 531.

17. ERM to JDR, February 17, 1922, RAC/OMR/A/B33/F256.

18. HFM to Heinrich Stiefel, March 1, 1922, RAC/OMR/A/B33/F256.

19. Harrison, *Timeless Affair*, 190.

20. ERM to JDR, June 6, 1922, RAC/OMR/A/B33/F256.

21. "Stillman Affair Near a Decision: Bribe Is Denied," *Chicago Daily Tribune*, May 14, 1922, 5.

22. Brock, *Charlatan*, 71.

23. Brock, 72.

24. Brock, 72.

25. Statement from *Thornrose Examiner* photographer dated 1922, WHS, HFM Collection, Box 31.

26. "Lost Manhood Restored," *Belleville News Democrat*, June 28, 1922.

27. "New Harvester Head Is Hero of Big Industry," *Chicago Daily Tribune*, June 3, 1922, 4.

28. "Ganna Walska and M'Cormick on Honeymoon," *Chicago Daily Tribune*, August 12, 1922, 5.
29. "M'Cormick Reweds Walska in Chicago," *New York Times*, February 14, 1923, 17.
30. HFM to JDR, August 13, 1922, RAC/OMR/A/B33/F257.
31. "Memorandum concerning medical reports," WHS, SRM Papers.
32. HFM to JDR, October 31, 1922, RAC/OMR/A/B33/F257.
33. "Miss M'Cormick and Oser Married," *New York Times*, April 14, 1923.
34. HFM to JDR, August 29, 1923, RAC/OMR/A/B33/F258.
35. "Mrs. McCormick's Philosophy of Control of Man's Destiny as Revealed in an Interview," *Chicago Daily News*, August 30, 1932.
36. Eliot, "Ulysses, Order and Myth," 175.
37. "Watch for Wedding of Mrs. M'Cormick," *New York Times*, December 13, 1922.

PARTNERSHIP, 1921–25

1. "Dato Reveals Inside Story of Mrs. McCormick's Deals," *Chicago Herald and Examiner*, January 3, 1938, 1.
2. Meeker, *Chicago, with Love*, 152–53.
3. "Dato Reveals Inside Story of Mrs. McCormick's Deals," 1.
4. "Edward Dato, Land Investor in 1920s, Dies," *Chicago Tribune*, February 17, 1964, C10.
5. "Dato Reveals Inside Story of Mrs. McCormick's Deals," 1.
6. Minutes of Special Meeting, October 1, 1923, RAC/OMR/H/B80/F613.
7. "Dato Reveals Inside Story of Mrs. McCormick's Deals," 1.
8. "Dato Reveals Inside Story of Mrs. McCormick's Deals," 1.
9. Announcement of Krenn & Dato School of Salesmanship, undated, Box 5, Krenn & Dato Collection, Skokie Historical Society.
10. Edward A. Dato, *Making Millions in Real Estate* brochure, June 1, 1924, Box 5, Krenn & Dato Collection, Skokie Historical Society.
11. *Krenn & Dato Times*, 1927, Chicago History Museum, Krenn & Dato Papers.
12. Sales brochure for Suffield Terrace, 1928, Box 5, Krenn & Dato Collection, Skokie Historical Society.
13. "Mrs. McCormick in Real Estate," *New York Herald*, December 24, 1923.
14. "Developments Exceeding a Hundred Million Dollars" ad, undated, Box 5, Krenn & Dato Collection, Skokie Historical Society.
15. Photograph of administrative building available online at Illinois Digital Archives: Skokie History Project, http://www.idaillinois.org/cdm/singleitem /collection/skokiep002/id/2412/rec/11.
16. "Pay $540,000 for North Shore Polo Grounds," *Chicago Daily Tribune*, November 2, 1924, G22.
17. "3300 North Lake Shore Drive," FitzGerald, 2018, https://www.fitzgerald associates.net/project/3300-north-lake-shore-drive.

18. *Krenn & Dato Times*, May 1927, Chicago History Museum, Krenn & Dato Papers.

19. Wittelle, *Pioneer to Commuter*, 177.

20. "Dato Reveals Inside Story of Mrs. McCormick's Deals," 1.

21. "Developments Exceeding a Hundred Million Dollars" ad.

22. "Dato Reveals Inside Story of Mrs. McCormick's Deals," 1.

23. Chernow, *Titan*, 265.

24. JDR to ERM, December 27, 1923, RAC/OMR/A/B33/F258.

25. JDR to ERM, January 13, 1925, RAC/OMR/A/B34/F259.

26. JR to JDR, January 16, 1925, RAC/OMR/A/B34/F259.

27. ERM to JDR, July 7, 1922, RAC/OMR/A/B33/F256.

28. Ross, *Let the Lions Roar!*, 10.

29. Ross, 13.

30. "Real Estate and the Zoo," *Chicago Journal*, October 15, 1923.

31. "Not a Good Time for Zoos," *Chicago Journal*, October 16, 1923.

32. "Kids and Animals," *Chicago Daily Tribune*, November 4, 1923, 1.

33. Ross, *Let the Lions Roar!*, 15.

34. "Trustees Accept Zoo Plans; Work Starts in Fall," *Chicago Daily Tribune*, June 3, 1926, 15.

35. Ross, *Let the Lions Roar!*, 4.

36. "Mrs. M'Cormick Shown Unusual Honor by Swiss," *New York American*, October 12, 1921.

37. Virginia Gardner, "Servants Recall Grand Manner of Edith McCormick," *Chicago Daily Tribune*, August 28, 1932.

38. Margot, "Mrs. McCormick Society's Outstanding Figure for over Thirty-Five Years," *Chicago Daily News*, August 26, 1932, 1.

39. "Luncheon for Howard Carter," *Chicago Tribune*, May 20, 1924, 23.

40. "What'll Muriel Say? Mathilde M'Cormick Asks," *Chicago Daily Tribune*, February 18, 1922, 1.

41. "Say Mrs. M'Cormick Will Wed Architect," *New York Times*, August 13, 1922.

42. Assorted cables, WHS, Muriel McCormick Collection.

43. "Actress McCormick," *New York Times*, June 4, 1922.

44. Muriel McCormick to JDR, December 9, 1922, RAC/OMR/A/B33/F256.

45. "Hears of Movie Offer to Muriel M'Cormick," *New York Times*, August 31, 1922.

46. Muriel McCormick to JDR, November 8, 1922, RAC/OMR/A/B33/F257.

47. "Muriel McCormick Loses," *New York Times*, May 30, 1927.

48. "Why John D's Granddaughter Changed Parents," *Helena Daily Independent*, February 6, 1927.

49. "Grandchild of Rockefeller under Knife," *Chicago Daily Tribune*, June 7, 1925, 1.

50. "Grandchild of Rockefeller under Knife," 1.

51. Arthur Sears to Muriel McCormick, April 5, 1926, WHS, Muriel McCormick Collection.

52. Judson Stone to Willard Cave, April 14, 1926, WHS, HFM Collection, Box 32.

53. "Declared Insane after Annoying Mrs. M'Cormick," *Chicago Daily Tribune*, July 27, 1923, 5.

54. "Rich Chicago Society Folk Get $50,000 Death Threats," *Philadelphia Evening Public Ledger*, April 13, 1931.

55. "Watchman for Gold Coast Home Dies of Wound," *Chicago Tribune*, July 2, 1924, 16.

56. "Opera Singer Takes Poison at Congress," *Chicago Daily Tribune*, October 13, 1921, 1.

57. Ammann, *Im Dienste der Reichsten Frau*, 92.

58. "Ex-chauffeur of Mrs. McCormick Declared Sane," *Chicago Daily Tribune*, August 15, 1923, 11.

59. Ammann, *Im Dienste der Reichsten Frau*, 184.

60. Emile Ammann to JR, October 28, 1948, RAC/OMR/H/B80/F608.

ELDER STATESWOMAN, 1925–28

1. "Calls Woman Negative," *New York Times*, January 26, 1922.

2. "Mrs. McCormick's Philosophy of Control of Man's Destiny as Revealed in an Interview," *Chicago Daily News*, August 30, 1932.

3. Samuel Melamed to JR, February 28, 1934, RAC/OMR/H/B80/F609.

4. Ruth De Young, "Mrs. Edith Rockefeller McCormick's Dream of Museum for Her Art Treasures Revealed," *Chicago Daily Tribune*, November 4, 1932, 6.

5. American Art Association, *Splendid Library of the Late Mrs. Rockefeller McCormick*.

6. Samuel Melamed to JR, February 28, 1934, RAC/OMR/H/B80/F609.

7. "Book for Which Mrs. Harold McCormick Paid $21,000," *Chicago Daily Tribune*, May 20, 1911.

8. American Art Association, *Splendid Library of the Late Mrs. Rockefeller McCormick*.

9. Samuel Melamed to JR, February 28, 1934, RAC/OMR/H/B80/F609.

10. Molly Stark, "What Makes a Woman's Life Worth While? As Answered by Mrs. Edith Rockefeller McCormick," p. 1 of an unidentified newspaper article, in WHS/Clippings.

11. "Mrs. M'Cormick Tells When Woman Is Slave," *New York Times*, March 21, 1921, 3.

12. Kathleen McLaughlin, "Woman's Fair Called Guide to Life Work," *Chicago Daily Tribune*, May 17, 1928, 27.

13. "Mrs. McCormick Asks World Love," *Chicago Daily Tribune*, March 21, 1922, 1.

14. ERM to JR, May 1, 1923, RAC/OMR/H/B80/F613.

15. Miller, "Yesterday's City," 62.

16. "Krenn & Dato at the Woman's World's Fair," *Krenn & Dato Times*, May 1927, Chicago History Museum, Krenn & Dato Papers.

17. Miller, "Yesterday's City," 58–72.

18. "National Affairs: Credit," *Time*, April 27, 1925.

19. MacLeod, *Enchanted Lives, Enchanted Objects*, 218.

20. McLaughlin, "Woman's Fair Called Guide to Life Work," 27.

21. E. T. Hertz to Mrs. McKinlock, May 9, 1925, RAC/OMR/H/B81/F619.

22. "Mrs. McCormick Joins Ranks for Double Drive," *Chicago Tribune*, July 2, 1924, 12.

23. "Rockefeller's Daughter to Run N.Y.-Chicago Airships of 200-Passenger Capacity," *San Francisco Chronicle*, April 15, 1922.

24. "Proposed National University Campus," May 4, 1931, RAC/OMR/H/B81/F620.

25. "Mrs. Edith Rockefeller McCormick to Build a New City on the North Shore," *Chicago Tribune*, June 24, 1925, 20.

26. "Hoosier Given $1,500 Prize by Mrs. McCormick," *Chicago Daily Tribune*, September 15, 1925, 31.

27. "Proposed National University Campus."

28. "Proposed National University Campus."

29. Olmsted Brothers to JR, February 11, 1930, RAC/OMR/H/B80/F609.

30. Office of John D. Rockefeller Jr. to Olmsted Brothers, February 17, 1930, RAC/OMR/H/B80/F609.

31. Frank Staley to JDR, February 1925, RAC/OMR/A/B34/F259.

32. JR to JDR, February 26, 1925, RAC/OMR/A/B34/F259.

33. Ross, *Let the Lions Roar!*, 25.

34. Thalia, "Women of Society and Clubs to Have Part in Chicago Fair," *Chicago Daily Tribune*, April 19, 1928, 25.

35. Nancy R———, "Plans to Beautify Home at Bellevue and the Lake Shore," *Chicago Daily Tribune*, March 28, 1925, 21.

36. Morgan, *Charles A. Platt*, 140.

37. First Will and Testament, ERM, RAC/OMR/H/B81/F662.

38. "Daughter of John D. Rockefeller Considers Her Business Is Real Estate, Hobby Collecting, Psychology Profession," *Boston Globe*, June 18, 1931.

39. Willoughby, "New Manuscript Acquisitions for Chicago."

40. Goodspeed, *As I Remember*, 229.

41. ERM to Edgar J. Goodspeed, February 25, 1934, University of Chicago Collection, Edgar J. Goodspeed Papers, Series 1, B6/F6.

42. Goodspeed, *As I Remember*, 230.

43. ERM to Edgar J, Goodspeed, March 5, 1928, Special Collections Research Center, University of Chicago Library, Edgar J. Goodspeed Papers, Series 1, B6/F6.

44. Goodspeed, *As I Remember*, 233.

45. Edgar J. Goodspeed notes, June 7, 1928, University of Chicago collection, Edgar J. Goodspeed Papers, Series 1, B6/F6.

46. Mary Dougherty, "'Life as It Seemed to Me,' Described by Mrs. McCormick," *New York Evening Journal*, August 30, 1932.

47. Chernow, *Titan*, 597.
48. Mrs. Edith Rockefeller McCormick Gifts 1922–1933, RAC/OMR/H/B81 /F621.

FULL STEAM AHEAD, BLINDLY, 1926–28

1. "News of Chicago Society," *Chicago Daily Tribune*, October 23, 1927, 1.
2. Thalia, "Noted British Woman to Be Honor Guest at a Tea Tomorrow," *Chicago Daily Tribune*, October 3, 1928, 37.
3. "National Affairs: Political Entertainments," *Time*, December 17, 1928.
4. "Society Goes to Luncheon with Royal Visitor," *Chicago Daily Tribune*, November 15, 1926, 2.
5. Virginia Gardner, "Servants Recall Grand Manner of Edith McCormick," *Chicago Daily Tribune*, August 28, 1932.
6. Margot, "Mrs. McCormick Society's Outstanding Figure for over Thirty-Five Years," *Chicago Daily News*, August 26, 1932, 1.
7. "Mrs. McCormick Aims to Renovate Brains," *New York American*, October 3, 1921.
8. Margot, "Mrs. McCormick Society's Outstanding Figure for over Thirty-Five Years," 1.
9. Edith Rockefeller McCormick, "The Comparative Value of the Rich Girl and the Poor Girl as a Wife," *Chicago Tribune*, April 16, 1911, 53.
10. "Give $275,000 for School of Industrial Art," *Chicago Tribune*, April 9, 1925, 21.
11. American Art Association, *Collection of the Late Edith Rockefeller McCormick*.
12. "Springtime at French Lick Is Colorful, Gay," *Chicago Daily Tribune*, April 12, 1931, H1.
13. JR to ERM, November 8, 1928, RAC/OMR/H/B80/F609.
14. Meeker, *Chicago, with Love*, 155.
15. Meeker, 151–52.
16. Meeker, 153.
17. Mathilde Oser to JDR, August 14, 1926, RAC/OMR/A/B34/F259.
18. "A Less Known Source for 'Citizen Kane,'" *New York Times*, November 5, 1985, A30.
19. Claudia Cassidy, "Ganna Walska, Diamondiferous Diva," *Chicago Tribune*, October 10, 1971, I10.
20. Harrison, *Timeless Affair*, 192–93.
21. "Divorce Rumor Is All News to H. F. M'Cormick," *Chicago Daily Tribune*, February 11, 1927, 3.
22. Adams, *Ganna*, 141.
23. Walska, *Always Room at the Top*, 405.
24. Herman Devries, "Madame Walska Tells Plans for American Tour," *Chicago Evening American*, September 4, 1929.
25. Walska, *Always Room at the Top*, 200–201.

26. "Mrs. McCormick's Career," *New York Times*, August 26, 1932.
27. "H. F. M'Cormick Silent on Rumor of Plan to Rewed," *Chicago Daily Tribune*, November 25, 1931, 8.
28. "Mrs. Rockefeller M'Cormick Urges Loves as Business Getter," *Chicago Daily Tribune*, December 27, 1925, B1.
29. E. McCormick, *Song Cycle*.

DISASTER, 1928–32

1. Stasz, *Rockefeller Women*, 268.
2. ERM to JR, August 2, 1928, RAC/OMR/H/B80/F609.
3. Stasz, *Rockefeller Women*, 268–69.
4. Nellie Crandall to JR, November 8, 1935, RAC/OMR/H/B80/F608.
5. Lewis McArthur to JDR, June 17, 1932, RAC/OMR/A/B34/F262.
6. Edwin Krenn to Frank Staley, June 3, 1931, RAC/OMR/H/B81/F620.
7. ERM to JDR, June 28, 1930, RAC/OMR/H/B34/F261.
8. "Chicago Opera Abandoned for Coming Season," *Chicago Daily Tribune*, June 23, 1932, 15.
9. Marsh, *150 Years of Opera in Chicago*, 104.
10. "Opera Backers Exceed Quota but Work On," *Chicago Daily Tribune*, April 21, 1932.
11. ERM to JR, December 23, 1931, RAC/OMR/A/B34/F262.
12. Frank Staley to JR, July 8, 1932, RAC/OMR/H/B81/F620.
13. Stasz, *Rockefeller Women*, 81.
14. Bertrand Cutler to JR, March 5, 1932, RAC/OMR/H/B80/F609.
15. ERM to Bertrand Cutler, March 5, 1932, RAC/OMR/H/B80/F609.
16. JR to ERM, May 12, 1932, RAC/OMR/H/B80/F609.
17. Bertrand Cutler to JR, March 5, 1932, RAC/OMR/H/B80/F609.
18. ERM to JDR, April 17, 1931, RAC/OMR/A/B34/F262.
19. JR to JDR, December 24, 1931, RAC/OMR/H/B80/F609.
20. Manchester, *Rockefeller Family Portrait*, 118.
21. Chernow, *Titan*, 646.
22. JR to Thomas Debevoise, September 1, 1932, RAC/OMR/H/B80/F616.
23. Stasz, *Rockefeller Women*, 284.
24. ERM to JR, December 23, 1931, RAC/OMR/H/B80/F609.
25. Bertrand Cutler to JR, March 5, 1932, RAC/OMR/H/B80/F609.
26. Virginia Gardner, "Servants Recall Grand Manner of Edith McCormick," *Chicago Daily Tribune*, August 28, 1932.
27. Edwin Krenn to Frank Staley, June 3, 1931, RAC/OMR/H/B81/F620.
28. Edwin Krenn to Frank Staley, June 3, 1931, RAC/OMR/H/B81/F620.
29. ERM to JR, June 4, 1932, RAC/OMR/H/B80/F609.
30. Chicago Study, RAC/OMR/H/B81/F619.
31. Bertrand Cutler to JR, March 5, 1932, RAC/OMR/H/B80/F609.

32. Frank Staley to JDR, April 23, 1932, RAC/OMR/H/B81/F620.
33. Mary Dougherty, "'Life as It Seemed to Me,' by Mrs. McCormick," *New York Evening Journal*, September 2, 1932.
34. Margot, "It Will Be 68 Years before We See Clearly, Says Mrs. McCormick," *Chicago Daily News*, February 25, 1932.
35. ERM to JR, February 16, 1931, RAC/OMR/H/B80/F609.
36. Lewis L. McArthur to JR, June 17, 1932, RAC/OMR/A/B34/F262.
37. JR to ERM, July 1, 1932, RAC/OMR/A/B81/F620.
38. Judith Cass, "Noted Home on Drive Closed for Summer," *Chicago Tribune*, July 8, 1932, 13.
39. "Fifi Stillman Is Bride Again," *Chicago Daily Tribune*, June 6, 1931, 1.
40. ERM to JDR, October 20, 1922, RAC/OMR/A/B33/F257.
41. Stasz, *Rockefeller Women*, 240.
42. "Find McCormick at Work in His Father's Plant," *Chicago Daily Tribune*, March 26, 1925, 2.
43. "The Press: Names in the News," *Time*, June 15, 1931.
44. ERM to JDR, May 28, 1931, RAC/OMR/A/B34/F262.
45. HFM to SRM, June 6, 1931, WHS, AMB Collection, Box 448, HFM/1931 folder.
46. ERM to JDR, May 28, 1931, RAC/OMR/A/B34/F262.
47. JDR to Fowler McCormick, May 28, 1931, RAC/OMR/A/B34/F262.
48. Muriel McCormick to JDR, July 1, 1929, RAC/OMR/A/B34/F261.
49. Mathilde Oser to JDR, July 3, 1929, RAC/OMR/A/B34/F261.
50. "Threats to Kidnap Oser Children Denied," *New York Times*, July 2, 1929.
51. ERM to JDR, May 27, 1929, RAC/OMR/A/B34/261.
52. "Business: Dowager at the Drake," *Time*, August 1, 1932.

DEATH, 1932

1. JR to JDR, August 9, 1932, RAC/OMR/A/B34/F262.
2. HFM to AMB, August 13, 1932, WHS, AMB Collection, Box 448, HFM/1932 folder.
3. "Sister Arrives for Visit with Edith M'Cormick," *Chicago Daily Tribune*, August 14, 1932, 6.
4. JR to Thomas Debevoise, September 1, 1932, RAC/OMR/H/B80/F616.
5. "Fifi Crashes Flying to Injured Son," *Chicago Daily Tribune*, July 21, 1932, 1.
6. "Miracle of Nursing Revives Mrs. M'Cormick to See Her Daughter," *Chicago Herald and Examiner*, August 19, 1932.
7. "Edith McCormick Rallies after Coma," *Chicago Daily Tribune*, August 19, 1932.
8. "Edith McCormick Rallies after Coma."
9. "Mrs. Edith R. McCormick Sinks; Rallies: Rockefellers Rush to Mrs. Edith McCormick's Bedside," *Chicago Daily Tribune*, August 21, 1932, 1.

10. Kathleen M'Laughlin, "Mrs. Edith M'Cormick Dead," *Chicago Daily Tribune*, August 26, 1932.

AFTERMATH, 1932

1. Kathleen M'Laughlin, "Hold Funeral Rites for Edith R. M'Cormick," *Chicago Daily Tribune*, August 28, 1932, 1.
2. "20,000 at Rites for Mrs. M'Cormick," *Chicago Daily News*, August 27, 1932.
3. M'Laughlin, "Hold Funeral Rites for Edith R. M'Cormick," 1.
4. JR to John Drake, August 25, 1932, RAC/OMR/H/B80/F616.
5. M'Laughlin, "Hold Funeral Rites for Edith R. M'Cormick," 1.
6. Daniel Burnham to JR, November 1, 1932, RAC/OMR/H/B80/F616.
7. Clay, *Labyrinths*, 321–22.
8. Trustees of the John McCormick Memorial Institute, October 15, 1932, RAC/OMR/H/B80/F616.
9. MacLeod, *Enchanted Lives, Enchanted Objects*, 218.
10. Noll, *Aryan Christ*, 235.
11. "Mrs. McCormick's Career," *New York Times*, August 26, 1932.
12. "Women: End of a Princess," *Time*, September 5, 1932.
13. Seymour Korman, "Edith McCormick Estate's Assets Are Told in Full," *Chicago Tribune*, December 31, 1935.
14. First Will and Testament, Edith Rockefeller McCormick, RAC/OMR/H/B81/F662.
15. Stasz, *Rockefeller Women*, 283.
16. "Edith M'Cormick Executors Sue Dato for Bonds," *Chicago Daily Tribune*, June 16, 1933, 6.
17. "Krenn Loses His $24,000 Life Income," *Chicago Daily Tribune*, January 28, 1933, 1.
18. American Art Association, *Collection of the Late Edith Rockefeller McCormick*.
19. "3,500 Attend Edith McCormick Sale," *Chicago Daily Tribune*, January 21, 1934.
20. "14,000 Flock to Preview of Edith McCormick Sale," *Chicago Daily Tribune*, January 19, 1934.
21. "3,500 Attend Edith McCormick Sale."
22. American Art Association, *Collection of the Late Edith Rockefeller McCormick*.
23. "Muriel Keeps Up Buying at M'Cormick Sale," *Chicago Daily Tribune*, January 5, 1934, 15.
24. "Muriel Outbid at Auction of Dinner Service," *Chicago Daily Tribune*, January 6, 1934, 13.
25. "Muriel Outbid at Auction of Dinner Service," 13.
26. "Auction in Edith McCormick Home Brings $47,676," *Chicago Daily Tribune*, January 18, 1934, 8.
27. "Muriel Keeps Up Buying at M'Cormick Sale," 15.
28. Nadelhoffer, *Cartier*, 236.

29. "Auction in Edith McCormick Home Brings $47,676," 8.

30. "List Jewelry Left by Mrs. M'Cormick," *New York Times*, November 4, 1932.

31. ERM to Goodspeed, June 20, 1932, Special Collections Research Center, University of Chicago Library, Edgar J. Goodspeed Papers, Series 1, B6/F6.

32. Memorandum on the Rockefeller McCormick New Testament, September 28, 1932, RAC/OMR/H/B34/F259.

33. Goodspeed, *As I Remember*, 239.

34. "Wind Up Estate of Mrs. Edith R. McCormick," *Chicago Daily Tribune*, November 15, 1951, N9.

35. Stasz, *Rockefeller Women*, 283.

36. Stasz, 283.

37. Meeker, *Chicago, with Love*, 156.

LEGACY

1. Dick and Dick, "Skin Test for Susceptibility to Scarlet Fever."

2. Weaver, *Medical Report of the Durand Hospital*.

3. Hirsch, "Happy Birthday to Us!! JID Reaches 100."

4. "Mrs. McCormick Tells Real Aim Inspiring Zoo," *Chicago Daily Tribune*, January 26, 1923, 5; Ross, *Let the Lions Roar!*

5. Marsh, *150 Years of Opera in Chicago*.

6. *Krenn & Dato Times*, December 1927, Chicago History Museum, Krenn & Dato Papers.

7. Campanini, *Giuseppe Verdi and the Glory*.

8. Interview with Ramona Pauling Berent and Sabrina Pauling, 2010.

9. Stasz, *Rockefeller Women*, 303.

10. Interview with Ramona Pauling Berent and Sabrina Pauling, 2010.

11. Interview with Ramona Pauling Berent and Sabrina Pauling, 2010.

12. Interview with Fowler McCormick Stillman, 2010.

13. Interview with Fowler McCormick Stillman, 2010.

14. Hannah, *Jung*, 158.

15. Stasz, *Rockefeller Women*, 290.

16. Stasz, 304.

17. Stasz, 304.

18. "Shame Suffered by Mrs. Doubleday," *New York Times*, October 26, 1933.

19. "H. F. M'Cormick Sued by Widow; Asks $2,000,000," *Chicago Daily Tribune*, December 4, 1938, 5.

20. "M'Cormick Whistles over Air," *Chicago Daily News*, January 19, 1933.

21. July 1931, WHS, HFM Collection, Box 84.

22. .See https://www.salvador-dali.org/en/artwork/catalogue-raisonne/1940 –1951/555/portrait-of-mrs-harold-mccormick.

23. Walska, *Always Room at the Top*.

24. Stasz, *Rockefeller Women*, 289.

25. "Harold M'Cormick's Widow Sues Second Husband for Trust," *Chicago Daily Tribune*, February 27, 1951, A9.

26. Eleanor Page, "Bulletin Board: Family in Mourning," *Chicago Tribune*, July 29, 1970, B2.

27. Fields, *Katharine Dexter McCormick*.

28. Miriam Kleiman, "Rich, Famous, and Questionably Sane," *U.S. National Archives and Records Administration* 39, no. 2 (Summer 2007), https://www.archives.gov /publications/prologue/2007/summer/mccormick.html.

29. Harrison, *Timeless Affair*, 195.

30. Harrison, *Timeless Affair*.

31. Stasz, *Rockefeller Women*, 284.

32. Chernow, *Titan*, 624.

33. "Krenn Reveals Secret Wedding to Art Student," *Chicago Daily Tribune*, February 12, 1936, 3.

34. "Sues to Divorce Edwin Krenn, Realty Dealer," *Chicago Daily Tribune*, June 7, 1941, 7.

35. "Edwin Krenn Dies; Mass Is Set for Today," *Chicago Tribune*, October 22, 1965, B24.

36. Ammann, *Im Dienste der Reichsten Frau*.

37. Memorandum from Rockefeller Foundation/Paris Office, December 21, 1934, RAC/OMR/H/B80/F608.

38. Stasz, *Rockefeller Women*, 303.

39. Mary Dougherty, "Mrs. McCormick's Views," *New York Evening Journal*, August 29, 1932.

SOURCES

Ackerman, Phyllis. *Three Early Sixteenth Century Tapestries.* New York: Oxford University Press, 1932.

Adams, Brian. *Ganna: Diva of Lotusland.* San Bernardino: CreateSpace Independent Publishing Platform, 2015.

Alofsin, Anthony. *Frank Lloyd Wright—the Lost Years, 1910–1922.* Chicago: University of Chicago Press, 1993.

American Art Association. *Collection of the Late Edith Rockefeller McCormick: Laces, Jewelry, Furs, French and English Silver, French Furniture, Tapestries and Rugs, Chinese Art.* New York: American Art Association and Anderson Galleries, Inc., 1934. Auction catalog.

———. *Contents of the Residences of the Late Edith Rockefeller McCormick.* New York: American Art Association and Anderson Galleries, Inc., 1934. Auction catalog.

———. *The Splendid Library of the Late Mrs. Rockefeller McCormick.* New York: American Art Association and Anderson Galleries, Inc., 1934. Auction catalog.

Ammann, Emile. "Driving Miss Edith." *Spring: A Journal of Archetype and Culture* 52 (1992): 1–19.

———. *Im Dienste der Reichsten Frau.* Leipzig: Montana Verlag, 1933.

Bair, Deirdre. *Jung: A Biography.* New York: Little, Brown, 2003.

Basini, Laura. "Cults of Sacred Memory: Parma and the Verdi Centennial Celebrations of 1913." *Cambridge Opera Journal* 13, no. 2 (July 2001): 141–61.

Benjamin, Susan, and Stuart Cohen. *Great Houses of Chicago, 1871–1921.* New York: Acanthus, 2008.

Birmingham, Stephen. *The Grandes Dames.* New York: Simon and Schuster, 1982.

Bowker, Gordon. *James Joyce: A New Biography.* New York: Farrar, Straus and Giroux, 2011.

Boyle, T. C. *Riven Rock.* New York: Viking, 1998.

Brock, Pope. *Charlatan: America's Most Dangerous Huckster, the Man Who Pursued Him, and the Age of Flimflam.* New York: Crown, 2008.

Brubaker, Robert L. "130 Years of Opera in Chicago." *Chicago History* 8, no. 3 (1979): 156–69.

Bulliet, C. J. *How Grand Opera Came to Chicago.* Chicago: n.p., 1942.

Burgess, Charles. *Nettie Fowler McCormick: Profile of an American Philanthropist.* Madison: State Historical Society of Wisconsin, 1962.

Burnham, Daniel, and Edward Bennett. *The Plan of Chicago*. Princeton: Princeton Architectural Press, 1993.

Burnham, John, ed. *Jelliffe: American Psychoanalyst and Physician and His Correspondence with Sigmund Freud and C. G. Jung*. Chicago: University of Chicago Press, 1983.

Bushnell, George D. "The International Aviation Meet, 1911." *Chicago History*, Spring 1976, 12–18.

Campanini, Francesco, dir. *Giuseppe Verdi and the Glory: The Monument of the Centennial*. Parma: Campanini Films, 2015.

Chernow, Ron. *Titan: The Life of John D. Rockefeller, Sr.* New York: Vintage, 2004.

Clay, Catrine. *Labyrinths: Emma Jung, Her Marriage to Carl, and the Early Years of Psychoanalysis*. New York: Harper, 2016.

Cohen, Stuart Earl, and Susan Benjamin. *North Shore Chicago: Houses of the Lakefront Suburbs, 1890–1940*. New York: Acanthus, 2005.

Coventry, Kim, Daniel Meyer, and Arthur Miller. *Classic Country Estates of Lake Forest*. New York: W. W. Norton and Company, 2003.

Darling, Sharon S. *Chicago Metalsmiths*. Chicago: Chicago Historical Society, 1977.

Davis, Ronald. *Opera in Chicago*. New York: Appleton Century, 1966.

Dedmon, Emmett. *Fabulous Chicago*. New York: Random House, 1953.

Dick, George F., and Gladys H. Dick, "A Skin Test for Susceptibility to Scarlet Fever." *Journal of the American Medical Association* 82, no. 4 (January 1924): 265–66. https://jamanetwork.com/journals/jama/article-abstract/238057.

Eliot, T. S. "Ulysses, Order and Myth." *The Dial* 75 (November 1923): 175.

Ellmann, Richard. *James Joyce*. Rev. ed. London: Oxford University Press, 1982.

Fields, Armond. *Katharine Dexter McCormick: Pioneer for Women's Rights*. Westport, Conn.: Praeger, 2003.

Fosdick, Raymond B. *John D. Rockefeller, Jr.: A Portrait*. New York: Harper and Brothers, 1956.

Garden, Mary, and Louis Leopold Biancolli. *Mary Garden's Story*. New York: Simon and Schuster, 1951.

Garland, Hamlin. "A New Idea in Theater Management." *The Metropolitan*, February 1912, 21–25.

Gimpel, Rene. *Diary of an Art Dealer*. London: Hodder and Stoughton, 1966.

Goodspeed, Edgar J. *As I Remember*. New York: Harper, 1953.

Griswold, Mac, and Eleanor Weller. *Golden Age of American Gardens: Proud Owners, Private Estates, 1890–1940*. New York: Harry Abrams, 1991.

Hannah, Barbara. *Jung: His Life and Work; A Biographical Memoir*. New York: Putnam, 1976.

Harr, John Ensor, and Peter J. Johnson. *The Rockefeller Century: Three Generations of America's Greatest Family*. New York: Charles Scribner, 1988.

Harrison, Gilbert A. *A Timeless Affair: The Life of Anita McCormick Blaine*. Chicago: University of Chicago Press, 1979.

Hirsch, Martin S. "Happy Birthday to Us!! JID Reaches 100." *Journal of Infectious Diseases* 189, no. 1 (January 2004): 1–2. https://doi.org/10.1086/379742.

Jehle-Wildberger, Marianne. *Adolf Keller: Ecumenist, World Citizen, Philanthropist.* Eugene: Cascade Books, 2013.

———. *C. G. Jung und Adolf Keller: Über Theologie und Psychologie, Briefe und Gespräche.* Zurich: Theologischer Verlag, 2013.

Johnson, Curt, and R. Craig Sautter. *Wicked City: Chicago from Kenna to Capone.* New York: Da Capo Press, 1998.

Joyce, James. *Letters of James Joyce.* Vol. 2. Edited by Stuart Gilbert and Richard Ellmann. New York: Viking, 1966.

Jung, Carl G. *The Red Book: Liber Novus.* Edited by Sonu Shamdasani. New York: W. W. Norton, 2009.

Levine, Neil. *The Architecture of Frank Lloyd Wright.* Princeton: Princeton University Press, 1996.

Ljunggren, Magnus. *The Russian Mephisto: A Study of the Life and Work of Emilii Medtner.* Stockholm: Almqvist and Wiksell, 1994.

Luening, Otto. *The Odyssey of an American Composer: The Autobiography of Otto Luening.* New York: Scribner, 1980.

MacLeod, Dianne Sachko. *Enchanted Lives, Enchanted Objects: American Women Collectors and the Making of Culture, 1800–1940.* Berkeley: University of California Press, 2008.

Manchester, William. *A Rockefeller Family Portrait: From John D. to Nelson.* Boston: Little, Brown, 1958.

Manson, Grant Carpenter. *Frank Lloyd Wright to 1910: The First Golden Age.* New York: Reinhold, 1958.

Marsh, Robert C. *150 Years of Opera in Chicago.* DeKalb: Northern Illinois University Press, 2006.

McCormick, Edith Rockefeller. "Four Family Divisions." *The Delineator,* October 1911, 259.

———. *Song Cycle.* Milwaukee: William A. Kaun Music, 1927.

———. "What My Children Mean to Me." *The Delineator,* September 1909, 211.

McCormick, Harold F. *Via Pacis: How Terms of Peace Can Be Automatically Prepared While the War Is Still Going On.* Chicago: A. C. McClurg, 1917.

McGuire, William. "The Wrong McCormicks." *Journal of Analytical Psychology* 40, no. 1 (1995): 99.

McKinney, Megan. *The Magnificent Medills: America's Royal Family of Journalism during a Century of Turbulent Splendor.* New York: Harper, 2011.

McLynn, Frank. *Carl Gustav Jung.* New York: St. Martin's Press, 1997.

Meeker, Arthur, Jr. *Chicago, with Love: A Polite and Personal History.* New York: Knopf, 1955.

Miller, Kristie. "Yesterday's City: Of the Women, for the Women, and by the Women." *Chicago History,* Summer 1995, 58–72.

Morgan, Keith N. *Charles A. Platt: The Artist as Architect*. Boston: MIT Press, 1985.

Nadelhoffer, Hans. *Cartier: Jewelers Extraordinary*. New York: Abrams, 1984.

Noll, Richard. *The Aryan Christ: The Secret Life of Carl Jung*. New York: Random House, 1997.

Pfeiffer, Bruce Brooks, ed. *Frank Lloyd Wright: Complete Works*. Vol. 3. Toyko: Edita, 1988.

———. *Frank Lloyd Wright: The Heroic Years, 1920–1932*. New York: Rizzoli, 2009.

Pollack, Howard. *John Alden Carpenter: A Chicago Composer*. Urbana: University of Illinois Press, 2001.

"The Renaissance Villa of Italy Developed into a Complete Residential Type for Use in America: The House of Harold McCormick, Esq. at Lake Forest, Ill. Charles A. Platt, Architect." *Architectural Record* 31 (March 1912): 201–25.

Roderick, Stella Virginia. *Nettie Fowler McCormick*. Rindge, N.H.: R. R. Smith, 1956.

Rodkin, Dennis. "The Exceedingly Strange Case of the McCormick Sex Machine." *The Reader*, April 2, 1998. https://www.chicagoreader.com/chicago /the-exceedingly-strange-case-of-the-mccormick-sex-machine/Content?oid =895951.

Ross, Andrea Friederici. *Let the Lions Roar! The Evolution of Brookfield Zoo*. Brookfield: Chicago Zoological Society, 1997.

Shamdasani, Sonu. *Cult Fictions: C. G. Jung and the Founding of Analytical Psychology*. London: Routledge, 1998.

Shaw, Frances. "The Garden of No-Delight." *Poetry Magazine* 29, no. 1 (October 1926): 16.

Smith, Amanda. *Newspaper Titan: The Infamous Life and Monumental Times of Cissy Patterson*. New York: Knopf, 2011.

Smith, F. A. Cushing. "'Villa Turicum,' the Country Estate." *American Landscape Architect*, June 1930, 9–14 and 17–18.

Souter, Gerry, and Janet Souter. *The Chicago Air and Water Show: A History of Wings above the Waves*. Charleston, S.C.: History Press, 2010.

Stasz, Clarice. *The Rockefeller Women: Dynasty of Piety, Privacy, and Service*. New York: St. Martin's Press, 1995. Lincoln, Neb.: toExcel, 2000. Page references are to the 2000 edition.

Stern, Paul. *C. G. Jung: The Haunted Prophet*. New York: Dell, 1977.

Tarbell, Ida M. "John D. Rockefeller, A Character Study." *McClure's Magazine*, July 1905, 226–49.

Toub, Micah. *Growing Up Jung: Coming of Age as the Son of Two Shrinks*. New York: W. W. Norton, 2011.

Turnbull, Michael. *Mary Garden*. Portland, Ore: Amadeus Press, 1997.

Vetro, Gaspare Nello. *Cleofonte Campanini: L'altro direttore*. Parma, Italy: Cavaliere azzurro, 2001.

Villella, Frank. *Chicago Symphony Orchestra, 125 Moments.* Chicago: Chicago Symphony Orchestra Association, 2015.

Walska, Ganna. *Always Room at the Top.* New York: R. R. Smith, 1943.

Weaver, George H. *Medical Report of the Durand Hospital of the John McCormick Institute for Infectious Diseases for Twenty Years.* Ann Arbor: Edwards Brothers, 1933.

Willoughby, Harold R. "New Manuscript Acquisitions for Chicago." *University of Chicago Magazine,* January 1929, 128–33.

———. *The Rockefeller McCormick Manuscript and What Came of It: A Bibliographical Record.* Chicago: The New Testament Department, University of Chicago, 1943.

Wilson, Woodrow. *The Papers of Woodrow Wilson.* Edited by Arthur S. Link. Vol. 19. Princeton: Princeton University Press, 1966.

Wittelle, Marvyn. *Pioneer to Commuter: The Story of Highland Park.* Highland Park, Ill.: Rotary Club of Highland Park, 1958.

ARCHIVES AND HISTORICAL SOCIETIES

A. C. Buehler Library, Elmhurst College (Ill.)

Archivio Storico del Teatro Regio (Parma, Italy)

Art Institute of Chicago Archives

Cedar Rapids Historical Society (Iowa)

Chicago History Museum

Chicago Public Library

Chicago Symphony Orchestra Archives

Chicago Zoological Society Library

Donnelley and Lee Library, Lake Forest College (Ill.)

Elmhurst Public Library (Ill.)

Highland Park Historical Society (Ill.)

Highland Park Public Library (Ill.)

History Center of Lake Forest–Lake Bluff (Ill.)

Jung Institute (Zurich)

Kenosha History Center (Wis.)

Lake Forest Library (Ill.)

McCormick Family Archives, Wisconsin Historical Society (Madison)

Newberry Library (Chicago)

Niles Historical Society (Ill.)

Psychology Club Zurich (Switzerland)

Riverside Historical Society (Ill.)

Rockefeller Archive Center (Tarrytown, N.Y.)

Skokie Historical Society (Ill.)

Special Collections Research Center, University of Chicago Library

University of Illinois in Chicago Archives

INTERVIEWS WITH AUTHOR

Linda Barbera-Stein
Ramona Pauling Berent
Sabrina Pauling
Bruce Brooks Pfeiffer
Steven Rockefeller
Alex Stillman
Fowler McCormick Stillman

AN INTERVIEW

WITH AUTHOR ANDREA FRIEDERICI ROSS AND SIU PRESS MARKETING MANAGER CHELSEY HARRIS

CH: Talk about the challenge of finding the pieces of this under-told story, the parts that needed to be uncovered.

AFR: It's the thrill of the hunt! I love gathering pieces together and gradually forming a picture. As I look to my next subject, that's the part I really savor: digging through archives, guessing where other pieces might be found, encountering lots of dead ends but knowing there must be other evidence yet out there. Then, once a personality begins to take shape, I can't wait to put it into words. Since I believe Edith's papers were destroyed after her death, her puzzle was a particular challenge. Frankly, many women's stories have been unfairly erased. The responsibility to tell her story honestly and fully felt daunting at times, but I consider it an honor to be able to serve as her biographer.

CH: How long did it take you to put this story together? Talk about the emotional journey.

AFR: Ten years. Honestly, the process took a serious toll on my self-esteem. I kept trying to write this as historical fiction, but it's hard to fit an entire life story into the story arc necessary in fiction. Balancing the factual accuracy I desired with the fiction character development necessary to maintain interest was really tricky. I wrote draft after draft and faced rejection again and again. I'm sure I had over one hundred rejections for the historical fiction versions. But, in the end, I'm proud that I persevered and am pleased with this biographical format. Payoff is always sweeter after sustained effort, right?

CH: How has Edith's story affected you?

AFR: Her quote "No one is too rich nor too poor, too nobly born, nor too humble to escape responsibility for living to the fullest every hour of his life" haunts me, especially during this prolonged pandemic. These days, it feels like I'm just getting through each day as best as possible—a far cry from living every hour to the fullest! And, given that her life was suddenly cut short, I feel guilty for not eking the most out of each day.

I'm also more aware than ever that wealth does not generate happiness. I wonder what path her life might have taken had she been born poor or middle-class. Had she been forced to make a living, might she have found greater happiness in academia or writing? Her story is evidence that wealth can sometimes be more of a barrier than a blessing.

CH: The book reads like good fiction, though it's nonfiction. Could you talk about your prose style or writing philosophy?

AFR: I had intended to write this book as historical fiction and attended classes and workshops in fiction writing. While my historical fiction treatment never really jelled, many of the techniques commonly used in fiction— tension, story arc, character development—ultimately helped move the biography along at a faster clip. So I suppose I'm grateful for the lessons learned during the earlier failed attempts!

CH: How can we place Edith in women's history? What actions did she make, and how did she exercise her voice?

AFR: While Edith was by no means a leader in the women's suffrage movement, her story is remarkable in that it shows her evolution of thought. As she aged, she abandoned her mother's belief that women were meant to be primarily mothers and wives and began to find her own way in business, in society, and in thought. I find it a wonderful reminder that we do change and grow all throughout life and that it's not only acceptable but beneficial to leave behind beliefs we may have favored in our younger years.

CH: Can you talk a little about how women's stories are treated? Edith's story has been overlooked and muted. Have there been echoes of that in this book's reception? Do you feel like the experience for you has been the same?

AFR: It's exciting to finally see women's stories being told. For so long, their half of history was neglected, and now we are finally realizing that it's an important part of the whole. But many institutions are still adhering to old standards. A longtime writer at one of Chicago's major newspapers wanted to write an article about the book—here's a never-before-told story about one of Chicago's greatest philanthropists—but his editor refused. They'd run an article earlier in the year about Edith's scandals, and he didn't want to cover her again. So, once again, Edith's contributions received short shrift. It's frustrating. But I am comforted by the fact that at least now her full story is out there.

CH: Edith believed she had a duty to spend money and preserve cultural artifacts. Was the pressure Edith felt to spread wealth and culture prevalent in that time? Do you think she would still feel that duty today?

AFR: That's so different these days. In Edith's time, it wasn't readily possible for most people to see many of the world's treasures. But with the incredible powers of the Internet, we can visit museums and cultural sites around the globe virtually. Imagine her delight in exploring King Tut's tomb online! But I do believe collecting was an important hobby for her; she enjoyed both the process of amassing treasures and the pride of sharing them.

CH: As book lovers, we always want to know about collections. Tell us more about Edith's library. What were some notable volumes?

AFR: The most notable thing about Edith's 15,000-volume book collection was that it was a working library. Unlike so many wealthy people who had libraries just for show, Edith utilized her books. She felt answers were to be found under those covers, if only she could compare and contrast, make connections, and push thought in new directions. We know this from the copious notes found, in her hand, in the margins of her books, usually read and written in the original language. As far as gathering valuable editions and important bindings, bibliophiles examining her catalog have commented that she was a truly knowledgeable collector. Unsurprisingly, Edith also had a fondness for editions bearing bookplates from royalty.

CH: Edith thought it was her responsibility to preserve history. Do you think she would see today's culture as failing her mission?

AFR: I believe Edith saw her responsibility as bringing together different cultures and ideas to cultivate new thoughts. Most likely, Edith's greatest complaint about today's culture would be our fleeting attention spans and fast-forward way of life. Edith believed in study, in deep thought and contemplation. How else to move society forward but to examine our own place within the whole? These skills are tenuous these days, with social media encouraging rapid scrolling and skimming. On the other hand, the ability to share ideas and thoughts globally with one keystroke would have excited her, I think.

CH: What movements do you imagine she would support today?

AFR: In the wake of the COVID pandemic, I think her main concerns would be supporting cultural organizations and mental health. Edith saw culture as a defining metric of a society. Many of the organizations she sponsored—opera, theater, art, classical music—are struggling economically, and I like to think she would have helped bail them out. In addition, her passion for helping people overcome their psychological imbalances would have made her keenly aware of the isolation and depression many people are facing today. Perhaps she would have underwritten some sort of local humanitarian organization addressing these very real concerns.

BOOK CLUB DISCUSSION GUIDE

1. As a woman in the late 1800s, Edith had limited choices and chose the traditional route of marriage and children. Do you think she would have managed well had she gone to university? Can you imagine a career for which she would have been well suited as a young woman?

2. Do you think her childhood and the way she was raised had significant impacts on her outlook and actions as an adult? If so, how?

3. The role of a parent among the upper class in the early 1900s was quite different from today's standards. What do you think about her hands-off parenting philosophy?

4. Was her marriage to Harold good for her in the long run, or did it hold her back?

5. Edith's intellectual curiosity seemed to have no bounds. She continued her studies—languages, philosophy, religion, psychology—up until her final days. How do you think this affected her relationships with her family and others?

6. Do you believe Edith and Edwin were lovers or merely friends? The fact that they managed to keep the nature of their relationship private despite all the scrutiny and speculation is impressive.

7. Consider the impact that Carl Jung and James Joyce have had on others. Without Edith, they might never have achieved such success. Besides lending financial support, how can you help support young artists and dreamers in your community?

8. Do you think Edith's father and brother were justified in withholding financial assistance to her toward the end of her life?

9. Had Edith's life gone according to plan and her financial outcome had been different, both Chicago and Lake Forest might now have Rockefeller McCormick museums showcasing her collections. Do you think this would change your opinions about her spending habits?

10. Though Edith seemed to invest scarce emotional energy in the zoo project beyond her initial donation of land, Brookfield Zoo ended up being one of her greatest lasting legacies. Consider the ripple effect you have on other people. What minor project of yours might end up being most worthwhile?

11. If it is true that her male family members burned her correspondence after she died, why do you think they did so?

12. How did Edith both adhere to and reject societal expectations for women at the turn of the twentieth century?

INDEX

Andrea Friederici Ross is the author of *Let the Lions Roar! The Evolution of Brookfield Zoo*. She is a native of the Chicago area and a graduate of Northwestern University. Formerly working in management of the Chicago Symphony Orchestra and Brookfield Zoo, Ross now works in a grade school library, where she encourages young readers to develop a lasting love of books. In her free time, she writes bios for rescue dogs and researches forgotten women of history. To contact Ross, visit www.friedericiross.com.